Edmund duke of
4th son of EDWAR
m. Isabel of Castile

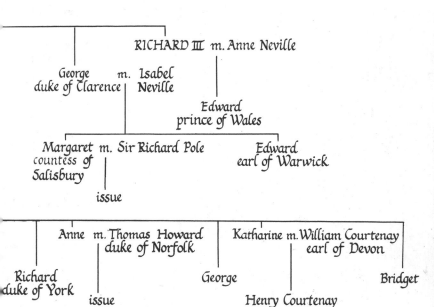

Anne   m.   Richard
Mortimer   earl of Cambridge

RICHARD III m. Anne Neville

George   m. Isabel
duke of Clarence | Neville

Edward
prince of Wales

Margaret m. Sir Richard Pole   Edward
countess of   earl of Warwick
Salisbury

issue

Anne m. Thomas Howard   Katharine m. William Courtenay
       duke of Norfolk   earl of Devon

Richard   George   Bridget
duke of York
       issue   Henry Courtenay

Select Pedigree of the
HOUSE OF YORK

THE MAKING OF
HENRY VIII

By the same author

ANNE BOLEYN

THE MAKING OF HENRY VIII

Marie Louise Bruce

COLLINS
St James's Place, London
1977

William Collins Sons & Co. Ltd
London · Glasgow · Sydney · Auckland
Toronto · Johannesburg

First published 1977
© Marie Louise Bruce 1977
ISBN 0 00 211541 7
Set in Monotype Fontana
Made and printed in Great Britain by
William Collins Sons & Co. Ltd, Glasgow

Contents

Illustrations

Acknowledgements

I should particularly like to thank Professor Chrimes for reading the book in galley and offering many valuable suggestions, Dr Roy Strong for his advice on portraits of Henry VIII as a child, Mr Alan Barrett for translating long passages of medieval Latin, Miss Alex Stone for access to books on historical costume, and Miss Elizabeth M. Walter for her skilled and patient editing. I should also like to thank my husband, George Bruce, for his professional advice and Miss Alison Plowden for uncovering for me a previously hidden source. No acknowledgement of help would be complete without mention of that given by the staffs of the London Library, the British Library, the Bodleian Library, the Ashmolean Museum and the Reading Public Library.

Prologue

When Henry VIII came to the throne contemporaries greeted the event as the dawn of a new and glorious age. The seventeen-year-old king was marvellously handsome, sweet-tempered, idealistic, religious, a patron of learning, a lover of peace, 'our divine prince'. 'Oh, my Erasmus,' Lord Mountjoy wrote in Latin to the famous scholar, 'if you could see how all the world here is rejoicing in the possession of so great a prince, how his life is all their desire, you could not contain your tears for joy. The heavens laugh, the earth exults, all things are full of milk, of honey and of nectar! Avarice is expelled the country. Liberality scatters wealth with bounteous hand. Our king does not desire gold or gems or precious metals, but virtue, glory, immortality. I will give you an example. The other day he wished he was more learned. I said, "That is not what we expect of your Grace, but that you will foster and encourage learned men." "Yea surely," said he, "for indeed without them we should scarcely exist at all." '

On his death thirty-seven years later, Henry left behind a sharply contrasting record, one of selfishness, greed and brutality unrivalled by any other English monarch. And at the beginning of the seventeenth century Sir Walter Ralegh wrote: 'If all the pictures and patterns of a merciless prince were lost in the world, they might all again be painted to the life out of the story of this king.' Posterity's view of his character has not altered much since. Five of the men and women who had been closest to Henry he had sent to their deaths; he had promised clemency to the leaders of rebellion, only to have one of them die in the most lingering and humiliating way conceivable even by sixteenth-century man.

The images that the name Henry VIII conjures up in the modern mind are mostly horrific, if picturesque. In place of the angelic youth one sees the small, hard, suspicious eyes, hears the oddly high voice quoting Machiavelli, 'If my cap knew my counsel I would throw it in the fire.' One sees him galloping with a great sword incognito through the night to watch a farce of himself decapitating monks right and left, a spectacle that made him laugh so heartily that he was discovered. One sees the megalomaniac who broke with Rome to make himself Caesar-Pope of England, a severance which, though generally popular in the kingdom, came at the time it did for an extraordinary reason: so that the king could rid himself of one wife and marry another in the hope of thus obtaining a male heir to the throne. It was an act that put England at serious risk of invasion, which would eventually come in 1588 in the shape of the Armada.

One sees the man who dissolved the monasteries on such a vast scale that he changed the face of England – a man who had at the same time the temerity to rewrite the Lord's Prayer, and who convinced himself that he was the special favourite of God. But, above all, the name Henry VIII brings to mind the victims of his cruelty: Catherine of Aragon, divorced from bed and board and threatened with execution; Anne Boleyn, executed as the result of a far-fetched plot; Katherine Howard, beheaded for adulterous intention; Cromwell and Wolsey dying on the block and on the way to the block, Sir Thomas More cracking jokes on the scaffold steps, Cardinal Fisher's head turning miraculously ruddy on London Bridge, Robert Aske suspended in chains above the city until he died; and the old countess of Salisbury who survived to experience a second stroke of the axe. These are his best-known victims, but there were many more.

What caused this incredible transformation from angelic youth to middle-aged monster? The blow on the head at a joust at the age of forty-five, which caused him to lie unconscious for two hours? Or the reputed onset of syphilis, whose symptom was an ulcerated leg? The most recent medical view is that the head injury did no lasting damage, and that Henry never contracted syphilis. As Sir Arthur MacNalty points out in *Henry VIII – A Difficult Patient*, had he caught this disease, then new to England, and been treated for it, ambassadors at his court could not have failed to notice, since a course of treatment was both drastic and unpleasant. It lasted for six weeks and 'consisted of sweating and the administration of mercury, until the gums became sore and there was a copious flow of saliva. Furthermore Henry throughout his life showed no other sign of syphilis. There is no mention of swellings on the bones, syphilitic inflammation of the arteries or general paralysis or locomotor ataxia, or defects of vision.'

MacNalty estimated that the disease from which Henry began to suffer in 1528 could have been either a varicose ulcer or osteomyelitis, which complaint could only exacerbate characteristics that were already present, unlike syphilis which affects the brain. So there was no radical change at all; characteristics prominent in middle age were latent in the golden youth.

Most biographies of Henry VIII begin, to all intents and purposes, with the start of his reign, but the real story begins earlier. At seventeen his character was no blank page. The invisible writing was already there, the habits of thought and behaviour imprinted by the experiences of childhood. And, I believe, it is into the last seventeen years of the father's reign that we must look for the hidden springs of the son's actions – not merely the inhumanities, but his political insights and skills, his talents and fears and failings, his personal relationships. All these things, I believe, can only be wholly explained by an examination of his childhood, the domestic details of his life in his father's palaces and the people who shared it, the lessons of his times and surroundings. But before examining the influences that were to mould the growing boy, it is necessary to look at the clay they had to work on: Henry's heredity.

CHAPTER I

'The Sovereign Seed'

'Beholde the soveren sede of this rosis twayn,
Renewde of God for owre consolacion.'   *Fayrfax MS*

HENRY TUDOR – the future Henry VIII – was born on 28 June 1491 in the palace of Placentia at Greenwich in a room where tapestry muffled the windows to exclude even the smallest breath of fresh air. Soon after the midwife had bathed him, anointed him with olive oil and sprinkled him with rose-water, he was swaddled in blue velvet and cloth-of-gold and laid in the great cradle of estate. In this impressive piece of nursery furniture, five-and-a-half feet long and two-and-a-half feet wide, decorated with the royal coat of arms, he was proudly put on display to courtiers and ambassadors. But although thus made into a splendid spectacle, little of the person that he really was could be seen, apart from his fair skin and perhaps a down of auburn hair; like all babies, he was a mystery. The latent Roman nose had as yet not even a bridge, the long chin was still hidden in the indefinite contours of infancy, and with it, all the other physical, mental and emotional characteristics that he had inherited.

Henry's ancestors were an international and remarkable collection. They had intermarried with French and Spanish royal families, and they included, as well as the Welsh Tudors – descended from a first cousin of the notorious rebel Owen Glendower – such exceptionally capable and determined kings as William the Conqueror himself, Henry II, Edward I and Edward III. But of all his forebears he had inherited most from his maternal grandfather, Edward IV.

At the age of only nineteen, Edward had marched on London,

attacked and beaten the armies of Henry VI and his queen, Margaret of Anjou, and claimed the crown of England. He had retained it for the rest of his life, except for a period of six months when Henry VI was briefly restored to the throne by the rebel earl of Warwick, and Edward's younger brother, the duke of Clarence. Edward had not only put down the rebellion, he had also succeeded in solving the problem that had bedevilled his predecessors: how to reorganize the royal finances so that the king could 'live of his own' instead of depending on extra taxes demanded from his unwilling subjects. The baby Henry in the great cradle of estate was not only to inherit Edward IV's drive and ability, but also his extrovert charm and impressive physique. Like his grandfather, he would appear to contemporaries 'of visage lovely, of body mighty, strong and clean made', and like his grandfather, he would be greedy and grow eventually 'very fat' in middle age.

He was also to inherit his grandfather's vanity, his sensuousness and his amorousness. Edward IV 'would readily cast an eye upon young ladies and love them inordinately', although he tired of most of them soon after. And it may well have been true that in order to seduce Lady Eleanor Butler he contracted to marry her, a story which, told after his death, was to cause his sons to be declared illegitimate and so to lose their inheritance and consequently their lives. He also offended against the unwritten code for kings by choosing a wife for love instead of political reasons, the beautiful, widowed Elizabeth Woodville, five years older than himself.

But such acts ran in Henry's family. His paternal great-grandmother was Catherine, daughter of the mad French king, Charles VI. Married to King Henry V and widowed at the age of only twenty-one, she also had caused a scandal by marrying for love, choosing as her husband the Welsh Owen Tudor, her wardrobe clerk, Henry's great-grandfather. Henry's own father, Henry VII, derived his hereditary claim to the throne (through his mother Margaret Beaufort) from the issue of yet another scandalous love match, that of John of Gaunt with Katherine

16

Swynford, who had been his mistress for many years before he married her.

The Plantagenet characteristics were to loom large in young Henry, which is not surprising since he was descended from no less than three of Edward III's sons: Lionel, duke of Clarence; John of Gaunt, duke of Lancaster; and Edmund, duke of York. He was to inherit the creative flair of the Plantagenets, their impetuousness and wild bad temper, worsened by the strain of instability from his French great-great-grandfather, King Charles VI. He was also to inherit their tendency to cruelty and fatal family quarrels. Some of Henry VIII's behaviour to his wives and children seems more explicable when one remembers the quarrels of Henry II and his sons, of Richard II and his cousin Henry IV, and of Edward IV and the duke of Clarence.

Plantagenet characteristics, however, would be tempered in Henry by a child's natural instinct to copy his parents, particularly his father, and his father's character was very different: Henry VII was cool, clever, devious and careful, with an almost prudish fastidiousness, although in 1491 this did not yet show in his face. Far from resembling Sittow's portrait, which shows him in later life with greying hair and claw-like hands, eaten by anxiety and suspicion, Henry VII was only thirty-four when his second son was born, and good-looking, tall by contemporary standards, slight but wiry, with blue-grey eyes and hair that was still reddish-brown. Pietro Torrigiano's bust of the king, now in the Victoria and Albert Museum, has an ageless quality which makes it more revealing than the Sittow portrait for this early date. The Italian sculpted a thin aquiline nose, high cheekbones and prominent brows shading the very deep-set eyes in an autocratic, introverted face that one can nevertheless picture relaxing its rigidity in a quiet smile. According to the contemporary historian Polydore Vergil, the king's appearance was 'remarkably attractive and his face cheerful, especially when speaking'. Spanish observers remarked on the 'vivacity of his expression' and the 'liveliness of his eyes'.

Henry was not the dry stick of popular legend. He was fond of his wife and children, and in these early years he knew how to forget the cares of state in outdoor sports, hawking, hunting, tennis and shooting at the butts; he enjoyed gambling at cards, listening to music and watching the antics of fools and tumblers. He was given, we know, to speeches too flowery even for the fashion of the day, and could be an effusively welcoming host. But his face in repose, as portrayed by Torrigiano, still has a formidable look. He was sometimes so sharp with those who annoyed him that 'his words were vipers'. And his jokes were gratingly sardonic.

Henry VII was a hard man; he had been made so by repeated blows of fortune from his earliest years. His father, Edmund Tudor – earl of Richmond and step-brother to King Henry VI – had died before his birth, which took place when his mother Margaret Beaufort was only thirteen, but his uncle Jasper Tudor, earl of Pembroke, gave him and his mother refuge. Born earl of Richmond and step-nephew to the reigning king, he had lost his privileged position and title at the age of five, when Edward IV seized the crown and gave Henry's birthplace and home, Pembroke Castle, as well as his wardship, to Lord Herbert. The child can have seen little from this date of his young mother. But Herbert was surprisingly kind to him, until he too was wrenched from Henry's life: when Henry was twelve his guardian was executed for treason. Henry VI's restoration to the throne in October of the following year seemed to offer the boy a chance of recovering his earldom and high status. His uncle, Jasper Tudor, returned to England from exile in France and is said to have taken his nephew to court. But the hope of restoring his fortunes was short-lived. Edward IV was triumphant, Henry VI was imprisoned again in the Tower, and Jasper fled back across the Channel.

This time, fourteen-year-old Henry fled too; but ill fortune had not finished buffeting him. By accident they landed, not in friendly France, but in the independent duchy of Brittany. And here Henry spent the next thirteen years, much of them in semi-imprisonment in danger of being handed over at the request of the English king. In 1475 Duke Francis agreed to send him to Edward IV and Henry was actually brought as far as St Malo by the English ambassadors before the duke changed his mind and Henry was allowed to escape. But the ruler of Brittany might easily change his mind again; Henry remained a potential bargaining counter with England and his future was terrifyingly uncertain. When in 1483 the young earl learned of a conspiracy to set him on the throne in place of Richard III, it must have offered a prospect of almost magical deliverance.

But at first everything went wrong with his plans. The little fleet with which Henry set sail for England in October was scattered by fierce winds. Arriving with only two ships near the south coast to find the shore guarded by Richard's men, Henry could do nothing but return hastily to Brittany. The risings organized to coincide with his invasion were easily put down, and the leader of the rebellion in England, the duke of Buckingham, was beheaded. A few months later Henry again narrowly escaped being handed over. The ruler of Brittany had secretly agreed to deliver him up to Richard III in exchange for a thousand English archers, a plot of which Henry was fortunately warned just in time to escape across the border into France.

When in August 1485 Henry once more set sail in an attempt to wrest the crown from Richard III it was a desperate adventure by a desperate man. But even after he had landed in Milford Haven, marched through Wales, won the battle of Bosworth and been recognized by parliament as king, Henry VII would face repeated challenges to his rule. In the six years before his son Henry's birth he had had to put down two rebellions.

Henry VII would hold England successfully for nearly twenty-four years, but he would never be wholly convinced that she might not still elude him. He would never lose his fear of treachery and sudden death, although he hid this one weakness behind a mask of all-seeing wisdom.

Similarly dramatic changes of fortune had patterned the

life of the baby Henry's mother. The look of serenity in her
best-known portrait was an artistic convention of the times
and yields no suggestion of her past troubles. Born eldest
daughter of Edward IV, she had been compelled at the age of
five, when Henry VI was restored to the throne, to flee with her
mother (Elizabeth Woodville) into sanctuary at Westminster
Abbey. Six months later she had ridden out of the gates on the
saddle of her triumphant father, but when she was eighteen
she had again been forced to seek sanctuary. Edward IV had
died suddenly. She and her sisters and surviving brothers,
Edward aged twelve and Richard aged nine, had been declared
illegitimate, her half-brother, Sir Richard Grey (Elizabeth
Woodville's son by her first husband) and her uncle, Earl
Rivers (Elizabeth Woodville's brother and governor to young
Edward), had been beheaded. And her father's youngest brother
had been crowned King Richard III. The situation seemed full
of danger, but she could not live in sanctuary for ever. She was
tempted out in March 1484 when Richard III promised '*verbo
reggio*', on the word of a king, that: 'if the daughters of
Elizabeth . . . late calling herself queen of England . . . will
come to me out of the sanctuary of Westminster and be guided,
ruled and demeaned after me . . . I shall see that they shall be
in surety of their lives and also not suffer any manner hurt . . .
in their body or persons to be done, by way of ravishing or
defiling contrary to their wills, nor . . . any of them imprison
in the Tower of London.' The new king further promised that
he would marry the older princesses to gentlemen, providing
each on her marriage with an annual income of two hundred
marks.

But how far could Richard be trusted? Elizabeth's brothers
had disappeared from view in the Tower and rumour pronounced them dead. Nervously, she did her best to please the
king, dancing at his court at Christmas 1484 'dressed in clothes
of the same form and colour as those of Queen Anne, his
consort'. There is even a story that she fell in love with her
thirty-one-year-old uncle. But since it appears first in an
eighteenth-century life of Richard III by the unreliable George

Buck, who based his allegation on a letter which no other historian has ever claimed to have seen, the story is unlikely to be true. According to *The Song of the Lady Bessy*, a ballad written shortly after 1485, Elizabeth played a major part in the plot to help Henry VII seize the throne.

In 1484 this plot seemed unlikely to succeed. And when eventually, in the summer of the following year, Henry set sail for Wales, he took with him no more than about two thousand men. Luck and the treachery of three powerful magnates had given Henry the victory and restored to Elizabeth of York the pleasures of her original high status.

Elizabeth lost no time in pleasing this new king too, for her son Arthur was born eight months after she married Henry VII in January 1486.

As queen of England, Elizabeth was to play a purely supportive role in public, portrayed in ambassadors' reports as no more than a kind and gracious presence. Her best known portrait shows a woman beautiful in the style of the day, with long yellow hair, a plump oval face, high brow, even features, large bosom and soft white hands, but it reveals little of her character. Although she is glowingly described by contemporaries as, 'a very handsome woman and of great ability'; as 'very noble' and 'much beloved', and as 'a woman of the greatest charity and humanity', a more sombre note creeps into two despatches from the Spanish envoys. One described her as 'kept in subjection by the mother of the king' and in need of 'a little love', and the other, reporting that the king was much influenced by his mother, added: 'The queen, as is generally the case, does not like it.' But we need not take these reports too seriously. Elizabeth would have been unnatural indeed if she did not occasionally resent her dominating mother-in-law, Margaret Beaufort, but otherwise she seems to have been content.

Of her own free will she had chosen to have the motto 'humble and reverence' embroidered on the blue and purple doublets of her servants. In a world that Elizabeth had hitherto found as shifting as a kaleidoscope, her husband meant stability. He was often autocratic in his personal relations, but he was also a shield against the terrors she had known. Another report by a Spanish envoy opens a window on her relationship with the king; it shows her quarrelling playfully with Henry and refusing to give him a newly arrived letter from Catherine of Aragon, her prospective daughter-in-law, which Henry swore he wished to carry continually around with him. Despite the Spanish envoys' hints, there is little doubt that she lived with her husband, in the words of Thomas More's elegy, 'in peaceable concord'.

But Elizabeth's very passiveness would make Henry VII's influence on his son all the stronger. It would also leave a gap for that exceptionally clever and able woman, Henry VII's mother. For no picture of Henry's parents is complete without adding the image of the tiny, intense Margaret Beaufort, countess of Richmond and Derby, who seems to have shared in every major decision affecting the royal children.

In her life, too, Margaret Beaufort had seen many vicissitudes, although her personal fortunes had never sunk as low as those of her son and daughter-in-law and she had lived continuously at court during the reigns of three previous kings, Henry VI, Edward IV and Richard III. Heiress to great wealth, she had been sought in marriage by both the son of the duke of Suffolk and by Edmund Tudor. Apparently allowed by Henry VI to choose between them at the age of nine, she had done so after a dream in which St Nicholas, patron of maidens, had appeared to her, and bidden her take Edmund. If this was a rationalization of her desires, these were soon pathetically blighted by Edmund's early death, and within three years she had been married again, this time to Lord Henry Stafford, a younger son of the duke of Buckingham – whether willingly or not history does not record. He died also, in 1482, and within a few months she was married to yet a third husband, Thomas, Lord Stanley, later earl of Derby. But the great love of her life was now her only son Henry, whom she had hardly seen since he was five years old. She was one of the chief instigators of the plot that was to set him on the throne. Polydore Vergil records that soon after Richard III's coronation she exchanged messages with Elizabeth Woodville in sanctuary, letters hidden in the black gown of her physician, Dr Lewis, that proposed a pact between the Woodvilles and the House of Lancaster, cemented by the marriage between Henry and Elizabeth of York. In 1483 Lady Margaret also secretly sent money both to her son in Brittany and to the rebels in England. She was fortunate that after the rebellion failed Richard III did no worse than deprive her of her title, give her estates to her husband, and order him to keep her under house arrest.

Undeterred, Margaret Beaufort spent this seclusion persuading her husband and his brother, Sir William Stanley, to join her son's cause. The Stanleys not only possessed great wealth, but also vast estates in Wales and on its borders, where Henry's cause had already captured popular imagination; and as a result of Lady Margaret's machinations, these two powerful men, with the earl of Northumberland, had openly turned traitor on the very field of battle, giving Henry the victory against Richard III's much larger army.

But she never forgot how easily the battle could have gone the other way; how easily her cherished son might have ended the day in Richard's place, a dishonoured corpse, stripped and flung over the back of a horse. She never afterwards lost her fear that fortune's wheel would turn again. And at her son's coronation, according to her confessor (Cardinal Fisher), she 'wept marvellously', for 'she never yet was in that prosperity but the greater it was, the more always she dreaded the adversity'.

It was these three people – the cool autocratic Henry VII, the kind but passive Elizabeth, and the intense intellectual schemer, Margaret Beaufort – all of them emotionally battered, all of them haunted by past insecurities, who were to shape the childhood of the future Henry VIII.

CHAPTER 2

The Royal Nursery

'The child sucketh the vice of his nurse with the milk
of her pap.'   *Thomas Elyot*

HENRY's birth was a far less important event than that of his
elder brother. Five-year-old Arthur was heir to the crown, the
new baby merely his understudy. Immediately after Arthur was
born on 19 September 1486 at Winchester, the exultant King
Henry VII sent messengers galloping through the summer
countryside to all the cities of the realm commanding church
bells to be rung and choristers to sing the *Te Deum Laudamus*,
then used to celebrate victories. It was a memorable time. In
the streets men lit huge bonfires 'in the praising of God and the
rejoicing of every true Englishman'. Queen Elizabeth gave
thanks by founding a chapel in Winchester Cathedral decorated
with her arms and surrounded by the legend '*in gloriam Dei*'.
While the continental poets at court, the blind Augustine
friar from Toulouse, Bernard André, and the Italians, Pietro
Carmeliano and Giovanni Gigli, burst into torrents of
enthusiastic Latin verse praising the baby prince.

No such special celebrations attended the birth of the second
son; if bonfires were lit for Henry no chronicler bothers to
mention them. Bernard André, who was royal historiographer
as well as poet, devoted only fifty words to the event in his *Vita
Henrici VII*, including in the same complimentary passage an
announcement of the birth of a mere female, Henry's elder
sister Margaret. And in choosing his second son's birthplace
Henry VII seems to have adopted the same off-hand attitude.
He selected, not the pre-Norman Conquest seat of government,
Winchester, nor the medieval chief seat of government,

Westminster, where Margaret had been born, but the palace named Placentia by a previous owner, Margaret of Anjou, queen of King Henry VI, because of its pleasant river aspect and graceful pillared halls. It is better known to us by its later name of Greenwich.

Young Henry's small blue-grey eyes first opened here, where breezes came cool from the water and there was less danger than in London from the sweating sickness, that virulent and too often fatal disease which had recently arrived in England, and which attacked in warm weather. In retrospect the king's choice seems fitting enough, for this palace, with its semi-octagonal towers, newly faced in dark red brick, its terracotta floor tiles adorned with the white daisy emblem of Queen Margaret, and its tall mullioned windows overlooking the Thames, was to be the little prince's favourite residence when he grew up, and the birthplace of his own children, Mary and Elizabeth.

But although Henry was only the second son, his infancy was still wrapped in the propaganda with which Henry VII sought to protect himself and his dynasty from being over-thrown, as he had overthrown Richard III. Henry VII claimed the throne partly by right of his descent from John of Gaunt, duke of Lancaster – whose son by his third wife, Katherine Swynford, was John Beaufort, Henry VII's great-grandfather – and partly by right of conquest.

But to make his image more compelling, Henry presented himself also as the divine instrument of an end to a century of conflict, choosing as his main emblem in an age of visual signs the white rose of York superimposed on the red rose of Lancaster, and encouraging his French and Italian court poets to versify a convenient view of history. In reality, the battles of the past hundred years had been caused by the opposing interests of over-mighty subjects brought into the open by the minorities of Richard II and Edward V and by Henry VI's intermittent madness, but such causes were unsuited to Henry VII's purpose. He did not wish to complicate the picture with too many names. So, according to his propaganda, the conflict was the result simply of rivalry between junior and senior branches of the royal family; between the descendants of Edward III's third son, John of Gaunt, duke of Lancaster, and the descendants of Edward III's fourth son, Edmund of Langley, duke of York. Henry IV of Lancaster, supplanter of Richard II, had been succeeded on the throne by his son Henry V and his grandson Henry VI. Then Henry VI of Lancaster had been in his turn supplanted by Edward IV, descended from the duke of York. Now – so ran this simplified royal version of the facts – behold a miracle: Henry, the red rose, had married and made his queen Elizabeth, the white rose, and thus put an end to strife. The poets prophesied an era of peace and unity when God would smile again on England, and their words, recited aloud or set to music, came in time to be heeded by a population many of whom could not read.

Edward IV and Richard III had failed to establish their dynasties; Henry VII was determined to succeed. According to his poets, his children had been conceived with God's special help.

> Beholde the soveren sede of this rosis twayn,
> Renewde of God for owre consolacion
> By dropys of grace that on them down doth rayn;
> Through whose swete showris now sprong ther is ayen
> A rose most riall with levis fressh of hew,
> All myrthis to maynten, all sorous to subdewe.

So wrote one of Henry's propagandists, and ambitious men hastened to give voice to their loyalty. Music was part of the background of fifteenth-century life, and both the king and the queen, as well as the richest lords and gentlemen, kept their own colourfully dressed companies of minstrels who played for dances and on all ceremonial occasions. Courtiers dined either to the instrumental music of the royal minstrels, or to vocal melodies of the king's Gentlemen and Children of the Chapel, while after dinner it was the amateurs' turn; the courtiers themselves often rounded off the meal with the latest popular part song. To judge by a song-book once owned by Dr Robert Fayrfax, Gentleman of the Chapel Royal and a famous composer at Henry VII's court, *Behold the Sovereign Seed* was a favourite choice.

Poets were not the only creators of the new king's propaganda; other artists and craftsmen followed suit. From the moment of his birth, Henry was surrounded by red and white roses. There were roses in the necklaces and chains worn by his mother and father, roses on the bosses of the carved and painted wooden ceilings of his father's palaces, roses on stained-glass windows, on tiled floors and in stonework; roses welded into the gilded harness of royal horses and embroidered on the green-and-white striped tunics of the guard. And, round the margins of printed books and handwritten manuscripts in the royal library, roses rambled too. Like his contemporaries, Henry would grow up a victim of his father's propaganda, believing that the Tudor children had a unique relationship with God and were the offspring of a miracle.

Not content with the effect of all these roses, songs and poems, the king utilized court ceremonial to drive home the message that he and his family were beings apart. The Yorkist court, modelled by Edward IV on Burgundian lines, had been splendid: but the Tudor court was magnificent, using ritual and a display of great wealth to lift the royal family far above the nobility, and make it inconceivable that anyone should try to topple this king from the throne. Henry VII gave his mother the task of improving on Edward IV's court ordinances and for her grandchildren, Margaret Beaufort turned the already impressive ritual of baptism according to the Sarum rite into a glittering drama.

The baby Henry was baptized within a few days of his birth by Bishop Fox at Greenwich, the Church of the Observants being hung with tapestries and luxuriously floored, not just with the usual patterned tiles or green rushes, but with carpets, those new costly treasures from the East reserved normally for walls and tables. Set high on a railed platform, so that all could see, the silver font, brought specially from Canterbury Cathedral, glimmered in the dim light under a fringed canopy of state.

At the appointed time, from the neighbouring palace, the procession advanced: gentlemen two by two, bearing tall unlit white tapers, then a peer or peeress bearing the salt, from which large golden container a few grains, first tasted for poison, would be placed on the child's tongue to symbolize wisdom. Then a second peeress bearing pinned to her shoulder the chrisom (a white linen cloth to wrap round the child's head to protect the consecrated oil after baptism), followed by another high-ranking lady holding the baby, who was nearly hidden by a cloth-of-gold mantle, lined with fur and so long that two people were needed to carry it.

Around the royal babe's procession came more gentlemen with unlit white tapers, while another four supported a canopy of state over the baby and his bearers until they reached the richly hung porch where Bishop Fox intoned the Latin words admitting him into the Catholic Church. Undressed behind a screen, where a large pan of coals prevented him from catching cold, the baby was then carried to the font where total immersion, apart from its religious significance, meant that the public would be left in no doubt that this was a whole, perfectly formed child.

Drops of wax from the bishop's taper, drops of oil and of chrism oil ritualistically mixed with the water. Then . . . 'I name you Henry,' Fox pronounced loudly, and slowly dipped the child three times, 'in the name of the Father . . . the Son . . . and the Holy Ghost.' Two hundred tapers flared into brilliance. Fox made the sign of the cross with the chrism oil on the crown of Henry's head. He was wrapped in the white linen cloth while the heralds put on their coats of many colours and trumpeters blew from the leads, then in the sudden sparkling light, carried to the altar for communion, his tiny fist closed round a miniature white taper.

Cleansed of the evil spirit and baptized with a name carefully chosen for its link with the Lancastrian monarchs, Henries IV, V, and VI, the little prince was borne back to the palace, preceded by the jubilant sound of drums, trumpets and pipes, and by his godparents' gifts, weighty pieces of plate in gold or

silver gilt and the lovely, long-necked Tudor designs. Henry
was then taken up to the queen's presence chamber, where his
parents, who had not deigned to attend a ceremony intended
for public rather than private consumption, waited to give him
their blessing.

Compared with many other princes of his time, young Henry
was fortunate in his parents whose union, made five years
earlier for political reasons, had been secured by affection, and
who formed a picture of harmony and fruitfulness that their
little son would seek in vain to repeat himself in later years.

But he was not to enjoy this happy family atmosphere for
long. In common with most women of high rank of her day,
Elizabeth would not feed her own child; he would not even
live near her, for royal parents and children in the fifteenth
century rarely shared the same roof. The court, which was the
seat of government and diplomacy as well as of upper-class
society, was not a suitable place for small children, since it was
constantly moving from one palace to another, from Greenwich to Westminster to Sheen to Windsor to Woodstock, and
to a host of lesser manors.

Henry VII liked to show himself to the people in the hope of
winning their respect; his was not a large enough personality
to win their love. Moreover, the royal residences must be vacated
to be cleaned, for only when they were empty could rushes
which had become foul with 'leakages of men, cats and dogs'
be wholly renewed down to the wooden floors, instead of just
tidied up with a new layer of rushes on top. All this moving
was disrupting for children, and besides, there was the problem
of security. Too many strangers visited the court, bringing
presents or petitions or information – bringing too, perhaps,
disease or some would-be assassin masquerading as one of the
king's loyal subjects.

A few weeks after the christening the infant Henry left his
mother's abode for Eltham Palace in Kent, about five miles
from Greenwich, and an easy journey for a carefully cushioned
baby, even in one of the unsprung royal carriages, called 'chars',

which, beneath their painted and gilded coats of arms, were no more than very long, very heavy wagons drawn by a single file of horses. Eltham, where Henry was to join his five-year-old brother Arthur and his sister Margaret, aged a year and seven months, was arranged in two almost separate parts, the whole enclosed in a large deer park. As the wooden wheels rattled over the cobbles, Henry's carriage passed through an outer courtyard and under the arch of an imposing gatehouse into a forecourt known as the Green Court, surrounded by new brick and old stone buildings: there were lodgings for courtiers; kitchens and various rooms associated with the preparation of foods, the Pastry, Spicery, Buttery and Slaughter House.

Once through the Green Court, his carriage crossed the bridge over a very wide moat, then under another gatehouse and into another huge courtyard known as the Great Court, with the royal apartments on the left, whose west front Henry VII had ordered to be newly faced, like Greenwich, in brick. The grating of saws, staccato notes of hammers and the cheerful voices of builders would often have sounded in the infant Henry's ears while he lived here, for his father made many alterations to the palace, adding new tiled floors, new glass windows and a new bridge across the moat. Behind the Great Court, five much smaller courtyards divided the rest of this exclusive part of the palace, several stories high, which crowded on this little island like a tall thin cake on a small plate.

But Henry's world in these early weeks was an even smaller one, centring on his nurse, Anne Oxenbrigge. Anne, wife of Godfrey Oxenbrigge, later bailiff of Winchelsea, had been chosen for physical and mental qualities that matched the exacting standards of the pediatricians of the day. These learned gentlemen dictated that the wet nurse must be not only healthy, but also of a 'sanguine complexion', blood predominating among the four humours that medieval man believed governed human character and appearance. This meant in modern idiom that the woman should have rosy cheeks, a white skin, thick reddish hair, a fleshy body and a hopeful, brave, amorous disposition; since this type was supposed to produce milk that 'excelleth all other both in sweetness and substance'. She must have besides a thick neck, broad breasts and be aged about twenty-five, be of a respectable status if not actually a gentle-woman, and without vice, since 'the child sucketh the vice of his nurse with the milk of her pap'.

But while the pediatricians thus made certain that Henry was properly nourished, they could not ensure that he had from Anne the constant loving security that is considered by most modern psychologists to be essential if a baby is to develop into a normal adult able in his turn to give love. Anne's feelings towards her charge were bound to be anomalous. For while the post was rewarding in the material sense – and Anne would receive for the rest of her life annuities from the royal family, work for her husband Godfrey, and, after his death, for his successor Walter Luke – she must also suffer considerable personal deprivation. A wet nurse had to abstain from sex. In addition, if any ill should come to the baby, it was considered to be chiefly the wet nurse's fault. Should he have colic or be slow in teething she was bled or purged, and should her supply of milk decrease, she could be ordered to eat stewed udders of goats or sheep, and even powdered earthworm. No nurse in such circumstances, however sweet and generous her nature, could give unmixed love to the babe in her charge; Anne Oxenbrigge, poor creature, could be no true mother substi-tute.

And to make matters worse, Henry's real mother was absent from Eltham in spirit as well as flesh. Henry's grandmother Margaret Beaufort had laid down the nursery regulations; although she lived mainly either at court or in her house of Colyweston in Northamptonshire, her influence was stronger than Elizabeth's at Eltham. Perhaps to make up for her dis-appointment in not being allowed to interfere in the govern-ment of the kingdom – for which the king preferred to rely on such able advisers as John Morton, archbishop of Canterbury, and Richard Fox, bishop of Exeter – he allowed his mother to exercise her talent for organization on his domestic life, and

Lady Margaret's ideas and ambitions were to set an indelible mark on her second grandson.

In June 1491, aged only forty-eight, this formidable great lady was as obsessed by family ambition as later she was to be by religion, two passions that burned behind the deep-set eyes in her narrow face. For three generations the Beaufort family had stood tantalizingly close to the throne, and at last it was theirs: no one should take it from them. Not without significance was the signature Margaret R on her correspondence. The letter R stood for Richmond, but it could just as well have stood for Regina. She bustled about her son's palaces clad in garments as rich as the queen's, with a retinue of servants clad in her livery of blue and white. Not that Lady Margaret was not fond of her daughter-in-law, who as King Edward IV's eldest daughter gave her son a sort of second claim to the throne, and who was necessary for the procreation of the royal race, but she knew it was her own judgement that must triumph. She was far more competent to protect 'our sweet children', as she referred to her grandchildren, from ill.

Her royal ordinances laid down that Henry's mealtimes be supervised by a physician, and for as long as Anne continued to feed the child, she shared with the king and queen the privilege and essential precaution of having her food and drink tasted for poison. No vengeful Yorkist should rob the children of Margaret Beaufort's blood of their heritage.

Apart from protecting the royal babe from danger, Margaret Beaufort made sure that no one should doubt his exalted rank. The Beaufort line had been shadowed by illegitimacy, for John Beaufort had not been legitimized until he was grown up, and in the act of legitimation Henry IV had later inserted a clause 'excepta dignitate royale', disqualifying the Beauforts from inheriting the royal dignity – an addition that was probably illegal, but which nevertheless left doubt. Lady Margaret's ordinances would blot out this shadow in the golden sunshine of riches and glory. When Henry was not on view in the great cradle of estate, he still lay in considerable splendour in 'a little cradle of tree' a yard and a quarter long, painted 'with fine gold and devices', with four pommels of silver and gold, and silver buckles for the swaddling bands.

Nursery furnishings included two cushions in crimson damask, a cushion of leather for the nurse, and no less than eight large carpets for the floor of the chamber. There were four chamberers or rockers to rock Henry to sleep to the sound of a lullaby or soft minstrelsy, sewers (servers) who set the dishes on the table, panters who bore in the bread and the great salt, yeomen and grooms who picked over and renewed the rushes on the floors each morning and built the fires in winter, 'officers for the mouth' including various types of cooks, and a lady governor (perhaps Lady Guildford) in over-all control.

As soon as Henry's eyes could focus, they saw the leopards and fleur-de-lis of the royal arms. And his first solid meals of humble gruel and mash were served on trestle tables ceremonially laid with white napery by servants wearing his father's livery.

Other aspects of Henry's infancy were, of necessity, no more exalted than the treatment of any ordinary baby today; Lady Margaret's furnishings also included practical items, twenty-four yards of 'fine blanket', forty-four yards of 'fine linen' and two great basins for the nursery laundry. And contemporary medical writings make it clear that fifteenth-century babies were kept surprisingly clean, although one treatise nervously suggests that the daily bath should be stopped as soon as possible. But in some other ways Henry was much less well off than a modern baby. When he was not in the bath in early infancy, he was rolled from head to foot in cloth until he looked 'like a pack of wares'. Henry, however, may not have been too uncomfortably constricted; for even then some physicians believed that the swaddling bands should be wound tight only on a child with a crooked limb. Henry's infant ailments were cosseted according to the best tenets of the day, which advised rubbing chicken fat mixed with dog's milk or hare's brains into the gums for teething troubles, giving camphor water mixed with the juice of beans and peonies for a runny nose, anointing the head with honey for a cold, and clapping a plaster of oil and wax 'hot on the belly' for wind – remedies that were probably at least as effective as those used today for such conditions, although his feeding arrangements were less congenial. Most contemporary physicians agreed that a baby should be kept perpetually a little hungry, a sure recipe in modern medical opinion for a frustrated infancy and possibly for insecurity in later life.

Sometimes the royal children and their household were piled into carts and on to horses and, taking most of their beds, stools, cupboards and chairs of estate with them – for furniture was scarce even in royal households – set off for another abode. Preceded by the important fanfares of their trumpeters, they journeyed to reside a few weeks at Hatfield House in Hertfordshire, or in one of the other royal palaces. But mostly it was at Eltham that young Henry grew from baby to toddler, encouraged to walk as soon as possible with the aid of a tiny wooden pen on wheels, since crawling was considered animal-like and un-Christian. And it was probably at Eltham, too, that one day he tasted bitter wormwood on his nurse's breast and discovered that henceforth he was expected to drink from the unyielding spout of a jug or the pointed end of a cow's horn. Although this was the usual way of weaning a child at that time, when he was between a year and two years old, it was an experience that some modern psychologists would consider most damaging.

When he could walk outside the pen Henry was watched carefully by attendants lest he should fall, damage his spine and develop a humped back. And his steps were encouraged by a popular toy – a little bronze horse on wheels bearing an armoured knight with shield and couched lance; a toy with more than one purpose, since it could be pulled along by a toddler or sent in hurtling noisy combat against a replica propelled by another child. Kneeling on a tiled floor, Henry could send his knight racing towards a rival knight held by his tempestuous elder sister Margaret, or his elder brother Arthur, while the new baby, Elizabeth, born in July 1492, slept in the 'little cradle of tree'.

But this useful toy had still another purpose: to begin Henry's initiation into the military skills which were an essential part of the education of a gentleman and could not be taught too early. They were introduced in the guise of games and sports, one of the most important of which was tilting, and Henry's toy taught him the first principles: if the lance of his knight touched the right spot on shield or helmet an adversary went toppling.

Toys given to fifteenth-century children of Henry's rank were even more bloodthirsty than they are today, as we can see from a contemporary woodcut by Hans Burgkmair which depicts the Holy Roman emperor, Maximilian I, playing with his children, their friends and tutors. All the playthings are connected with slaughter. There is a miniature cannon with real lead and powder, a crossbow with which one child is shooting a songbird out of a tree, a baited trap into which another bird is being lured, and a bow and arrow. We can be sure that Henry's toys would have followed the same pattern. And while he would have had other toys too – wooden tops to whip into a marvellous spin of fuzzy colour, bone skittles to knock down with a wooden ball, and a nearly life-size wooden horse on wheels – he probably preferred his weapons, in common with modern children. But while for normal children games of killing are merely games, for Henry who had been deprived of his mother's love, they could have been a much more serious vent for frustration and hate.

Henry's emotional lacks were not his parents' fault. They were themselves the victims of convention. And although they rarely shared the same roof as their children, they gave constant thought to their welfare. King Henry VII's privy purse expenses bear witness to a number of small items he himself ordered especially for the children during his second son's earliest years: a bow for five-year-old Arthur, price 6s. 8d., 'hoses . . . for my lord Harry', price 14s., 'for a hat for my lord Harry', price 5s., and 'divers yards of silk' bought for young Henry and Margaret. There was also constant coming and going between the brilliant ambulatory court and Eltham.

35

Messengers brought presents. In 1493 the king paid 10s. to one of Arthur's attendants for bringing 'two bream', caught presumably by this prince on one of his first attempts to fish (fishing being then, as now, a hobby favoured by all classes); and in November of the following year he paid his eldest son's lute-player £1 in reward for some unspecified service. Periodically, a prince or princess went to stay at court, or the royal parents would come to visit at Eltham Palace for a few days, riding over surrounded by the silks and velvets of their courtiers, the serene queen, the king whose face was already lined by the cares of his brief but densely troubled and demanding reign. Then suddenly, through leaded windows adorned with coats of arms, the children saw the Great Court full of jingling horses and attendants scurrying to attend their lord and lady, the king's men in green and white, the queen's in blue and purple. Later in the evening there might be the unwonted treat for the older children of sharing their father's favourite relaxations: staring at the antics of tumblers (acrobats) and at human freaks, like 'Joan, the Flemish giant' and 'a fellow' that ate 'coals', and listening to the wit or lunacy of the king's many fools, including 'Dick the fool', 'Patch the fool', 'the foolish duke of Lancaster', 'the Scottish fool' and 'Diego the Spanish fool' who, saddled and bridled, cavorted about as a horse.

But the excitement and laughter of these occasions, even the caresses of his parents, could not make up to Henry for the lack of permanent maternal love. So while Henry in his first two years was surrounded by extreme luxury and made to feel that he was the offspring of a miracle, he was also being emotionally damaged.

CHAPTER 3

Rival Dukes of York

'It began to be rumoured that Richard, King Edward's
son, was alive.'   *Polydore Vergil*

THOUGH men longed to believe the propaganda that the Tudor
had brought peace and order at last to their land, it would
take many years to convince them. And while Lord Henry in
shirt and hose toddled after his brother and sister and played
with his toy weapons in the care of Anne Oxenbrigge, the
moated nursery palace in its green park seemed an island in a
sea of menace. Few believed yet that the wars between York and
Lancaster were really over, for King Henry VII was a new-
comer who might be deposed at any moment. Henry's future
tutor, the poet John Skelton, expressed the general view in his
Latin treatise *Speculum Principis* (Mirror of a Prince), written in
1501 for the boy Henry, when he described him as surrounded
by 'grievous wounds and deaths, days of suspicion and fear,
incalculable secret hates, loyal words and deeds the opposite, the
frightening curse of war, rare friendship, a thousand nuisances,
a pretence at love, cowardly hearts...'

Skelton went on to predict an even blacker future for Henry
the man: 'And tomorrow perhaps more unexpected perils and
many inevitable dangers will be common. Fate has decreed no
stability, only short-lived prosperity, unendurable adversity,
now success, now failure – everything under the sun is subject
to change.'

By 1492 the government of England had been subject to
change for so many years that rebellion had become almost an
expected event; and although few of the ordinary people had
been killed, the royal family tree had been lopped repeatedly,

with seven royal princes killed in battle or murdered in the twenty-five years preceding King Henry VII's accession.

To be a son of the reigning monarch was to invite sudden violent death. This was early brought home to Henry by the fate of two other princes whose story he absorbed piecemeal in much the same way as he learned first to chuckle at, then repeat, the words of his nurse's rhymes. Only a few years before the births of Henry VII's sons, and as recently as 1483, two other small boys, aged twelve and nine, had played and hunted in the royal deer parks. Henry, as he learned to understand the speech around him, may have heard their names spoken by attendants in voices hushed by fear: Edward, prince of Wales, and his younger brother, Richard, duke of York – boys who, had they lived, would have been young Henry's uncles. A short while ago nine-year-old Richard had cantered in carefree splendour through the park, his harness and saddle decked in crimson velvet and green cloth-of-gold. He had run laughing through the great palace rooms in the grandest of robes: black satin lined with purple velvet, green with black sarsenet, and a mantle of blue velvet lined with white damask fastened with gold buttons. The gaudy details of Richard's garments, noted in his father's lists of expenses, throw a lurid light on the small boy so soon and so tragically to vanish from the pages of history.

A realistic and ruthless king, Edward IV had been aware of danger to his sons and tried his best to ordain against it: the gates of the palace were to be shut at nine in the evening, not opened again until morning, between six and seven; no one bearing a weapon might enter; round the princely chamber at night 'a sure and good watch' was to be set. But these royal ordinances, almost certainly used for the Tudor princes as well, were not enough to ensure safety. King Edward IV, who had thus provided against so many contingencies, could not ordain against the danger of his own premature death, which overtook him on 9 April 1483, aged only forty, as the result of a mysterious illness that caused him suddenly to collapse during a fishing trip.

Within three months his younger brother had been crowned as King Richard III and had put his nephews in the Tower. At first their lives did not seem threatened; for the children were not in prison, they were in the royal palace there – for a few weeks, that is. Beyond the thick walls, in the palace gardens, prying Londoners saw them for a while playing with their bows and arrows; then mysteriously they disappeared for ever, although the discovery that they had gone was gradual, since the Tower contained, besides the palace, so many other buildings with hidden apartments and cells. Today most historians agree that the princes were dead by October 1483, probably murdered, but one of the many rumours of the time maintained that the younger, Richard, duke of York, had escaped, and this possibility was seized upon by rebel elements which had been plotting to overthrow King Henry VII ever since his accession.

Within eight or nine months of Henry's birth in June 1491, disturbing reports came from Ireland of a youth with long blond hair, his looks only slightly flawed by a peculiarity of the left eye which lacked 'lustre', who had landed, dressed in silk, off a ship in Cork, and claimed he was King Edward IV's younger son. The story that he told – it survives in a letter to Queen Isabella of Castile – was as marvellous as any adventure in Sir Thomas Malory's recently published *Morte D'Arthur*, and it cast a similar enchantment.

After the assassination of his brother, this elegant youth claimed, he had been delivered to a gentleman who had been ordered to kill the younger prince too; instead he had secretly sent the prince away, having made him promise that he would not divulge his identity for a certain period of time. For nearly eight years he had wandered around in peril and misery and in the care of two governors, until one of them died and the other returned to his own country. Then he had decided to claim his rightful throne.

It was a strange, vague tale, conveniently without names or places. Nevertheless, already he had the support of a leading Irish noble, the earl of Desmond. The reason why throughout Henry VII's reign leading Irish lords were to support the

Yorkists had its roots in the past when a duke of York, lord lieutenant of Ireland from 1447 to 1457, had given the Irish to understand that he was in favour of home rule, and despite the killing of a previous earl of Desmond by order of Edward IV or his queen, this hope had persisted, so that now even a Yorkist imposter was preferred to a Lancastrian king. Already the Irish had supported the carpenter's ten-year-old son Lambert Simnel who, pretending to be the earl of Warwick, had figure-headed a rebellion against Henry VII in 1487. By March 1492, while young Henry still crawled over the luxurious carpets on the nursery floor, King James IV of Scotland was receiving letters signed jointly by Desmond and 'Richard Plantagenet'. And as the Lord Henry grew, the new pretender's influence, incredibly, grew as well, casting a lengthening shadow of trouble to come.

Taking advantage of his enemy's problem, King Charles VIII, officially at war with Henry VII, invited 'Richard Plantagenet' to the French court, there receiving him with all the honour due to a king's son, granting him a guard of honour and other courtesies. Soon the pretender would be writing to yet another powerful monarch, Queen Isabella of Spain, loftily demanding her support by right of kinship and signing himself, 'Second son of the late King Edward and duke of York. Richard.'

This ambitious youth played his part with such assurance in this perilous adventure that some writers still claim today that he was telling the truth. Did he convince most of his supporters, and was it only the knowledgeable few who used him as a stalking horse to catch their own game? Whatever the answer to this fascinating but insoluble question, the little boys at Eltham, Arthur and Henry, remained at risk.

If the pretender did land in England, their danger would be great, for as Vergil wrote pedantically, plots now began to multiply, 'just as in spring the trees always clothe themselves in a multitude of flowers'. An invader did not need a vast force to usurp the throne from an unpopular king, as the worried Henry VII knew from his own experience in 1485.

Fortunately for the infant Henry, one of his father's favourite mottoes, 'Cleave to the crown though it hang on a bush', was written not only in heraldic manuscripts, but also deep in the king's own heart. Henry VII attacked his enemy with the sharp weapons of propaganda and diplomacy. In little more than a year he claimed to have discovered the blond imposter's secret true identity: he was Peter Warbeck – originally spelt Werbeque – not even of gentle birth but son of a mere citizen of Tournai, in Flanders. This was a fortunate discovery, for if once they could be convinced of his 'low' origin, Englishmen, who mostly still believed in a divinely appointed hierarchy, would never crown Perkin, as King Henry VII contemptuously referred to his young rival, using the common diminutive of the more dignified Peter.

At the same time as they thus successfully ferreted out his identity, King Henry VII and his council focused their considerable collective mental power on dividing Warbeck from his allies. As part of a peace deal with France, spelt out in the Treaty of Etaples of 3 November 1492, Henry VII extracted from King Charles VIII a promise that he would not aid pretenders to the English throne. The 'duke of York' had to abandon his guard of honour, pack his baggage and find another refuge.

But irritatingly – from the English point of view – Warbeck did this all too easily. In his native Flanders, then part of the scattered territories of the independent duchy of Burgundy, the dowager duchess, King Edward IV's forty-six-year-old sister Margaret, welcomed him to her court, claimed him as her long-lost nephew and coached him in the part. Determined to do all she could to replace the Lancastrian king with a Yorkist, out of loyalty to her family, and out of greed – she hoped to regain the fine house of Hunsdon and the large income from grants that she had lost when Edward IV died – Margaret had already helped that earlier pretender, Lambert Simnel. And she had the tacit support of fifteen-year-old Philip, archduke of Austria and duke of Burgundy, and of his council, who were aware that this claimant of the English throne could be a useful political tool. When in July 1493 Henry sent an embassy to protest at Margaret's action, Philip replied with polite evasiveness that the dowager was free to do as she wished in her own lands. Henry VII's next drastic step shows the intense concern with which he viewed the Warbeck threat: he halted trade with the low countries, England's chief market for her main export, wool and cloth.

By November 1493 Warbeck had gained another more powerful ally, Philip's father. News came back to England that, at the funeral of his own father, the Holy Roman emperor Frederick III, in Vienna, Maximilian had given Warbeck a place of honour. Afterwards Maximilian who was now himself emperor (although he still used his former title, King of the Romans) escorted the burgess's son back to the dowager duchess's palace in Mechelen and presented him with a bodyguard of twenty archers bearing the Yorkist badge of the white rose on their blue-and-purple doublets. The King of the Romans had thus publicly acknowledged him as the rightful King Richard IV of England.

On hearing this unwelcome news, the best Henry VII could do was to send over to Mechelen an embassy of tabards and trumpets. A band of English heralds and other officers-of-arms, impressively sprinkled with the fleurs-de-lis and leopards of England, remonstrated face to face with Maximilian and the dowager duchess, then marched into the town to make a proclamation: that the youth calling himself Richard Plantagenet was an imposter. Furiously, Maximilian threatened to imprison them, but somehow the officers-of-arms and their trumpeters scuttled safely back to England. It had been a colourful, but ineffectual, protest.

In the grand residence, called suitably enough the *Hôtel des Anglais*, which Maximilian had given him, Warbeck defiantly hung out his own leopards and fleurs-de-lis on a banner with the legend: '*Arma Richardi Principis Walliae et Ducis Eboraci filii et haeredis Eduardi Quarti, nuper Dei gratia Regit Angliae et Franciae, Domini Yberniae*' (Arms of Richard, Prince of Wales and Duke of York, son and heir of Edward IV, lately Ruler by the grace of God of England and France and Lord of Ireland).

Meanwhile, so he claimed in his letter to Queen Isabella, the kings of Denmark and Scotland had sent to offer him friendship and brotherhood; many of the chief men in England, he added, had done the same in secret.

By the autumn of 1494 King Henry had discovered the alarming truth of Warbeck's boast. That Warbeck had supporters in England he had known for some time, ever since March 1493, when from small ports and coves on the south coast, a trickle of Yorkist sympathizers had secretly pushed off their boats and set sail, bound for the court of Margaret of Burgundy. Henry knew that messengers went to and fro between this small group and a Yorkist party in England, which had been much encouraged when one of the Englishmen in Flanders, Robert Clifford, wrote to say he was convinced that the graceful blond youth was truly King Edward IV's son. And in an attempt to stop this flow of dangerous people and treasonable conspiracy, he had posted guards on the numerous footpaths leading down to all the beaches of southern England. At the same time he had sent his own informers in the guise of Yorkist supporters to Margaret's court, and these spies gave him a disturbingly impressive list of conspirators still in England who were plotting to put Warbeck on the throne. They included Lord Fitzwalter, Sir Thomas Thwaites, Sir Simon Mountford and the dean of St Paul's. But as the king sent out orders to arrest and try these men for treason he could not be sure there were not others. How deep did the roots of this conspiracy go? It was clear to him that he must do all he could to gain popular support; if he could win the hearts of the people for his children, for instance, he need fear no rivalry from the ghosts of a dead dynasty.

It was not Arthur this time who was to be the subject of his father's propaganda, but Henry. The three-year-old boy had already received a number of imposing titles: constable of Dover Castle and warden of the Cinque Ports, earl marshal of England and, on 12 September 1494, lieutenant of Ireland. Now, however, he was about to be given a title of far greater significance, one that would make him a small but important pawn in his father's life and death game of politics: the king had decided that he would create a new real duke of York out of his own flesh and blood to make Warbeck appear the counterfeit he was. The new duke would be seen by as many people as possible, and the ceremony of his creation would be surrounded by unforgettable weeks of pageantry, the whole elaborate affair to take place at Westminster Palace at the approaching feast of All Hallows (1 November).

The announcement was made when the king was staying at Woodstock Palace, whose site is now marked in Blenheim Park. Trumpet notes suddenly hushed the bustle of Woodstock village fair, and craftsmen and farmers looked up to see the brilliant tabards of the king's heralds, the trumpeters behind them. Light flashed as the trumpets, hung with banners, were lowered. 'Oyez, oyez, oyez.' One of the heralds took a very deep breath, for fifteenth-century heraldic announcements needed a great lung capacity.

For as much as it is come to the notice and knowledge of four gentlemen of the king our sovereign lord's most loyal and honourable court, that his highness entendeth and purposeth by God's grace and sufferance in brief time to give creation of duke unto the right high and excellent prince my lord Henry, second son to our sovereign lord King Henry VII, and at like times it hath been used always and accustomed of auncynnyte [old] within this his most noble realm of England, for the laud and honour of such feasts, to have justis [joust] and tourney [tournament] according to their articles, the king our sovereign lord, considering the noble and courageous desires of the said four noble men, hath thankfully granted their petitions in this behalf, and licensed them, and all other gentlemen of his said realm or other nations, to accomplish the articles following, and whosoever jousteth best in the justis royal shall have a ring of gold, with a ruby . . . and whosoever tourney the best, and fairest accomplishes his

44

strokes, shall have a ring of gold, with a diamond of like value . . .

This impressively long-winded announcement set the ball rolling. Tourneying was one sure way that a courtier could attract the sovereign's attention, and there was no lack of gentlemen to answer the challenge. Far from it; six more gentlemen issued a new challenge to another six 'to make them disport' on 12 November.

Meanwhile, the royal summons had gone out to those who were to officiate at the banquets and to partake in a preliminary ceremony: the lord Henry, and twenty-two others, were to be created Knights of the Bath. On the morning of 28 October the king sent an escort of lords and gentlemen to fetch from Eltham Palace his second son who was about to enjoy his first important public occasion, playing a part which would be impossible for most children of his age today. To understand how he accomplished it one must look at his education to date, an early training very different from that which a modern child receives.

A boy of Henry's high rank had no need to be able to wash or dress himself, for all these things were done for him by a bevy of servants. But his manners from an early age must be shiningly polished. From the time he could walk his attendants had been drilling him in that mixture of manners and etiquette known as 'courtesy', which was so admired in the fifteenth century that it was even supposed to be of divine origin. Courtesy included a few common rules of behaviour that are still sometimes taught to children today: don't eat or drink with your mouth full, sit up straight at meals, keep your elbows off the table, don't interrupt your elders; but Henry also had to learn rules peculiar to his own times, with their veneration for degree and ceremony. He learned how to behave with those above and below him in rank, how to remove his cap and fall on one knee when his father spoke to him; then how to present a gift with one hand while holding his hat in the other, difficult feats of balancing for a small boy.

When meeting someone of his own rank, or to whom he wished to be especially polite, he must know how to sweep off his hat at the same time as clasping right hands, while on entering a house, he must remember to take off his hood, if wearing one, but replace his hat. Most important of all, he learned how to behave at the court ritual of dinner, with its trumpet-heralded courses and processions of dishes led by the steward bearing his white staff of office. For in later life at public banquets he would eat on a dais, alone except for especially high-ranking guests on either side of him, before a closely watching audience of his subjects. Henry's early training in table manners was doubtless made more memorable by the boxed ears and birching then used to imprint knowledge in boys of all classes.

He was taught how to eat with knife, spoon and the first two fingers and thumb of his left hand (for forks were not yet in general use). He was taught never to drink behind the back of anyone important, and how to wash his hands before and after a meal – which was a little ceremony in itself. Before the almoner said grace, the carver took two basins from the servant known as the ewerer; one of the basins having a spout and containing scented water. The carver then advanced to Henry's seat, knelt on one knee and poured this water over Henry's hands into the lower basin, while another attendant waited with the towel. The ceremony was repeated after grace at the end of the meal, the double basin being reserved for those of the highest rank only. Everyone else had his hands washed by just one esquire who held the humbler ewer, basin and towel.

Henry also learned how to drink with style from a heavy gold cup with a lid which was presented by yet another patient attendant on one knee. But when the king was present the boy had to perform these same services for his father and, as he grew older, he would learn how to carve for him too, a complicated art in the late fifteenth century since he would have to tackle a very much wider variety of meats than is eaten today – including venison, rabbit, leverets, swan, peacock, heron, boar's head, plovers, osprey, larks and quails, as well as many different

kinds of fish. The carver must not only know how to dis-
member each creature and which bits were delicacies to serve
first, but also how to mix the carved meat with the heavily
spiced sauce that almost always accompanied it.

At the same time as he learned this patchwork of ritual named
courtesy, Lord Henry also practised that most essential accom-
plishment of his day: riding. The little prince had graduated
from wooden horse to real horse almost as soon as he could sit
upright in the high cantled saddle, and he learned to ride with
elegance and dash, for this again marked the all important
difference between those of gentle birth and those below them
in the accepted social hierarchy.

On the afternoon of 28 October 1494 the lord Henry's
knowledge of courtesy and horsemanship was put to the test; at
about three o'clock he entered the city of London, riding not
pillion but 'sitting alone upon a courser'. Lined up to receive
him were the mayor, alderman and city companies, their robes
and liveries a blaze of colour against gabled houses of grey
stone and brown-and-white timbering. Surrounded by an
escort of nobles and gentlemen, massive gold chain over his
shoulders and velvet cap pulled low over his long auburn hair,
the little boy on the huge, richly caparisoned horse trotted
briskly through the city and down the Strand – that ribbon of
great houses and glittering goldsmiths' shops between river and
green fields – until he rode through the gates of Westminster
Palace where his father the king waited.

What did Henry look like then? The assumed portraits of
Henry as a child, including the best known in the Bibliothèque
de Méjanes, Aix-en-Provence, show him dressed in the fashion
of a much later date and so are of doubtful authenticity. But we
do know that Henry was advanced both physically and mentally
for his age. The chronicler who saw him ride through the city
took him to be four years old, although he would not attain
that age until the following June; and to ride that long way
bespeaks rare self-confidence in so young a child. His cherubic
face, with its renowned English-rose complexion, alive with
quick interest and high spirits, called forth the affection of the

citizens' wives, merchants, craftsmen, farmers, carters, students and apprentices who crowded along the route. In the little boy who rode into the ancient palace courtyard that autumn afternoon of 1494 Henry VII had chosen the best possible person for his political purpose.

The ceremonies began on 30 October with a banquet, when the prospective Knights of the Bath had the honour of serving the king. To the diminutive Henry was given the task of helping to wash the king's hands. Lord Clifford held the empty basin, Lord Fitzwarren bore the water and Lord Henry, a child balancing unsteadily on one knee, managed successfully to offer the towel. Afterwards, to the sound of flutes, viols and drums, and surrounded by a troupe of dancers and acrobats, Henry was led to his ceremonial bath to be made clean in spirit as well as body – for though more frequently taken than sometimes thought today, baths in the fifteenth century were still rare enough to be used as a symbol of purification.

No less than twenty of these herb-scented symbols in sponge-lined tubs had been prepared in the Parliament Chamber, Lord Harrington's and Lord Clifford's in the Queen's Closet, Lord Henry's in the King's Closet. Henry naturally took precedence. And the fact that it would have been something of an ordeal for him would have made the occasion unforgettable. It cannot have been easy at his age to behave with dignity while his counsellors, who had been chosen to teach him the laws of knighthood, removed his clothes and reverently placed him in the scented warm water. And he was obliged to listen in silence as Lord Oxford read the ritualistic words with their idealistic call to chivalry:

> Right dear brother, great worship be this order unto you and almighty God give you the praising of all knighthood. Be ye strong in the faith of holy Church and in the protection of all widows and oppressed maidens. And above all earthly things love the king thy sovereign lord and his right defend unto thy power.

Then the king dipped his hand in the water, made the sign of

48

the cross on his small son's shoulder and kissed it. The counsellors lifted young Henry from the bath, into the canopied, curtained bed prepared nearby, dried him and dressed him in 'hermit's weeds', a gown of coarse cloth. Meanwhile, the king had ceremoniously visited all the other knights in their baths, ritualistically making the sign of the cross on their shoulders, too. Gaily dressed minstrels struck up again, the knights were led by their counsellors to the chapel, where they would keep vigil until dawn, one part of the arduous ceremony that Henry was presumably spared, although he was spared no other.

The next day he woke to be once more approached by his counsellors, each of whom, beginning with Lord Oxford, great chamberlain of England, clothed him in a new garment, a fine shirt, silken hose, a blue robe, white girdle and white gloves. At last when fully dressed, the by now bewildered child foregathered with the other prospective knights in St Stephen's Chapel, whence advancing towards the foot of the stairs by the Star Chamber each of them mounted a horse and rode into the King's Hall, where Sir William Sandes carried Lord Henry up to the king.

At the royal command the duke of Buckingham and the marquis of Dorset fixed the right and left spur respectively to the boy's feet. The king himself girded on the white sword, lifted his right hand, touched young Henry lightly on the neck, said simply: 'Be a good knight,' and kissed him; then – an appealing touch of grandeur – set the new knight, still only a very little boy, upon the table for all to admire.

Perhaps the lord Henry was becoming tired of the long ritual, because for the next stage he needed assistance too. When all the knights had been dubbed and the time arrived for going into the chapel, Sir William Sandes had to carry him up to the altar and there offer his white sword for him, and afterwards Henry dined in his own room instead of with his fellow knights in the Parliament Chamber. But there was still another ceremony to come.

The following day, All Hallows, Lord Sandes carried him again into the presence of the king, crowned this time in his crimson robes of state, and surrounded by Morton, now a cardinal, an impressive assortment of peers, and officers-of-arms in their heraldic tabards; Henry VII invested his son with the long crimson velvet cloak lined and edged with miniver, with a miniver hood, the coronet, sword and gold verge of a duke; at the same time the king made a gift to him of a thousand pounds a year, for nobles were expected to spend lavishly on big houses, elaborate clothes and entertainments. At the banquet that followed, when the king's largesse had been cried, the new duke of York's largesse was cried also in French, the language of chivalry.

> *Largesse . . . de très haut, puissant, et excellent prince, second fils du roi notre seigneur, duc de Yorc, lieutenant-général d'Irlond, comte marishall d'Angleterre, et guardien de Cinque Ports, largesse par trois fois.* (Largesse of the very high, powerful and excellent prince, second son of our lord king, duke of York, lieutenant of Ireland, earl marshal of England and guardian of the Cinque Ports, largesse three times.)

If much of the meaning of the previous ritual failed to get through to Henry, this final touch was one he could understand. The herald rattled the large gold cup full of coins donated to the heralds in the new duke's name and the little boy knew then that he was indeed rich and important. So, in the name of God and the ideal of knighthood, began the making of one of the most cruel and egotistical of English kings.

The duke of York's star part in the proceedings was now finished. At the tournament that followed over a period of several days, he was a mere glorious spectator, sitting on a cloth-of-gold cushion in the king's box, hung with blue cloth of Arras powdered with gold fleurs-de-lis.

An intelligent three-year-old absorbs a lot of what goes on around him, even though he may not consciously remember it afterwards. This was his first experience of a form of entertainment without which no major court celebration was complete, and although for sophisticated courtiers the tournament may already have seemed an empty shell of the original knightly ideal, it would henceforth always be full of excitement for Henry, who revelled in the different styles of combat with swords and spears, as well as in the more spectacular joust when, divided by a central barrier, two armoured knights rode furiously against each other.

It was a game that called for a combination of skills: fine horsemanship, a good eye, courage and strength. A jouster scored a total victory if he unhorsed his opponent, and won points for breaking his spear on his opponent's armour or striking the crest of his opponent's helm. All over England in country and in town, boys and youths played at jousting with long wooden poles, for only gentlemen might joust properly with real spears and lances. The sport that had captured ordinary people's imagination captured the three-year-old duke's too, close as he always was to the feelings and enthusiasms of his time. As well as the skill of the sport, he loved the tournament's colour and flamboyant display, the martial music played by trumpeters, the heraldic announcements as challengers and defenders rode on to the field, the symbols of romantic chivalry. And in November 1494 there was the extra personal delight of a very special compliment to the new duke of York.

The first day's challengers rode horses trapped in the king's colours of green and white, a-jingle with gilt bells; but next day when the challengers rode out from Westminster Hall into the tiltyard, they wore short coats, known as journates, over their armour in the duke of York's own colours, blue and tawny, and gleaming against the black velvet harness of their horses, gold 'lozenges', every one containing a tiny red rose and a white, symbolic of young Henry's Lancastrian-Yorkist parentage.

Each challenger rode under a brilliantly plumed and crested pavilion, one tawny, one light tawny, one black and one scarlet. The day ended in a banquet with dancing and the romantic presentation of the prizes by a high-born lady, Henry's sister, Princess Margaret. The winning knight knelt on one knee while this important little girl held out to him the 'ring with a ruby' or the 'ring with a diamond'.

The festivities – the king's clever move to widen the basis of his support – went on until 13 November. Long after he had returned to the more monotonous regime of Eltham, their brilliance glowed in Henry's memory, reminding him of a setting in which he had won love and approval; and from both his father and his grandmother, Lady Margaret, Henry had inherited an exceptional memory.

But, along with delightful thoughts of the tournament and of adulation, went a growing and disturbing knowledge: his father had created him duke of York. But incredibly, infuriatingly, he was not the only duke of York. There was another, a rival, who strutted just across the sea in Burgundy with his own royal bodyguard, clad challengingly in the Yorkist colours of blue and purple. A name is a very personal, prized possession to a small child, and another person had seized Henry's, an enemy who, if he were victorious, would imprison the little boy and perhaps have him murdered.

CHAPTER 4

Traitors and Pretenders

'Fate has decreed no stability, only short-lived prosperity,
unendurable adversity, now success, now failure.'
John Skelton

———————

By now Henry, Margaret and Arthur were eating the usual vast quantities of meat, largely mutton and chicken, which were served in aristocratic nurseries of the period for breakfast as well as dinner and supper, except on Fridays and other fast days when they ate salt fish, herrings, sprats or buttered eggs instead. The meat was roasted on a spit or minced and heavily spiced, because meat was often not fresh. And since water was rarely safe, already despite his tender age, Henry's horn or pewter cup was filled with small beer. He ate fruit (cooked apples, pears and plums, raw cherries and strawberries), but consumed many fewer vegetables than children do today, bread and pastry being the usual accompaniment to meat. Herbal remedies, purging and bleeding were used to correct any resulting ills. It was a diet that, for a boy like Henry, healthy enough to survive it, encouraged his natural vigour, aggression and confidence, as well as his rapid physical and mental development, as we can see from John Skelton's poem written in November to celebrate the boy's creation as duke of York. Skelton had named him 'the Hector of the north' and 'a brilliant pupil', which suggests that he was not only unusually strong for his age, but also knew his alphabet and was beginning the difficult process of learning to form his letters. The Tudors were a precocious family.

As the cold weather drew in, grooms of the chamber lit huge fires in his rooms and pulled thick hangings over the ill-fitting

windows and oak doors that made most people's lives in winter
a misery. In the light of beeswax candles on great tapestries,
classical and biblical heroes battled and celebrated noble
victories, stimulating the little boy to dream of himself per-
forming heroic deeds. Further to keep him cosy, there were fur-
lined gowns and fur bedspreads for the canopied and curtained
bed which, greatly privileged, he would sleep in alone.

But despite this comfort in his immediate surroundings, in
the background of Henry's life in the forthcoming year there
was to be threat and uncertainty, and this disturbing atmosphere was mainly created by Warbeck. During Henry's recent
stay at court in October and November 1494, the several
conspirators who had been secretly communicating with
Warbeck in Flanders were marched through the cobbled streets
by the yeomen of the Tower and thrown into cells to await
trial, and during the same visit Henry had doubtless often
heard his father refer to the pretender in his usual reassuringly
scornful vein, as though he knew of all the pretender's plots
and was confident of forestalling them.

Then came an event that, even to a small boy, made his father
appear much less in control. Suddenly on his visits to court a
familiar trusted presence was no longer there. One splendidly
dressed court official, Sir William Stanley, had vanished from
the king's apartments, leaving in his place a story of treachery
and extreme danger.

It happened soon after Christmas, which the king kept that
year of 1494 at Greenwich Palace, near enough for the royal
children, dressed in their richest gowns and warned to remember all the rules of courtesy, to ride over to from Eltham. (For
Lord Henry there was first the formality of his appointment as
warden of the Scottish Marches, but the Christmas festivities
that followed had far greater importance for a three-year-old
boy.) There can have been no shadow of premonition over the
child's pleasure as, feeling proudly grown-up, he sat on a
cushion beside his parents' chairs of estate on the royal dais,
watching the plays and disguisings while the courtiers in their
turn admired his auburn curls and compared his sturdy good

looks with the frailer beauty of his elder brother Arthur. Even more than the entertainment, the food would have fascinated the boy, each course consisting of eight or more different dishes, and between the courses subtleties – fantastic sculptures of jelly, paste and sugar – all served in the great hall with the king presiding in one of the red or purple gowns that he wore on feast days; afterwards, in the evening, yeomen of the guard stood behind the king's chair holding aloft a row of flaming torches while the assembled company were dicing or dancing to the music of fife and drum. Throughout, Sir William Stanley, brother to the king's own step-father, supervised the proceedings with his white staff of office.

As lord chamberlain, he was personally responsible for the king's safety, for he ruled over the king's apartments – the bedchamber, privy chamber and presence chamber – and he appointed all the king's most intimate servants – his carvers, cup-bearers, physicians, surgeons, barbers, ushers, knights and esquires of the body. Henry saw him at banquets standing close to his father, supervising the ceremonial serving of the food and tasting wine from the gold cup before the king himself drank from it. The lord chamberlain was an image of security almost as accepted and reliable as his own father, a pillar of young Henry's world.

Had not Stanley rescued his father at Bosworth Field? It was the kind of exciting tale that a precocious little boy could not hear too often from the people around him – how Richard III had sought out Henry Tudor in a wild rush. Tudor and Plantagenet were locked for minutes in personal combat with the long heavy swords then in use, while Henry's own followers, hard pressed themselves, expected what seemed the inevitable end. Had Stanley's retainers not suddenly galloped across the field and cut down and killed King Richard, the Tudor dynasty might never have begun. It was an act that must have made him a hero to the small boy.

According to Polydore Vergil, Stanley had been a pillar of the king's world too, until shortly before Christmas. Then

Robert Clifford had left Warbeck's little band in Burgundy, sailed to England and claimed the pardon that secretly had been offered to him if he would return and inform on his fellow conspirators.

When on the morning after Twelfth Night, the king suddenly went with a small section of the court, including Sir William Stanley, to the Tower of London, the move did not seem ominous; the old palace in the south-east corner of this double-walled and moated fortress beside the wide river Thames had been used for centuries by the reigning monarch as one of his regular residences. The little duke of York would be brought to the Tower often to admire the menagerie of wild animals kept there. Now, however, its walled and moated fastness and its proximity to prison cells and instruments of torture would serve the Tudor king's purpose as it had served King Richard III's.

In his gorgeously hung rooms in the Tower, with their view over the river and the scattering of houses beyond, Henry VII had the informer Clifford brought before him. Later rumours would whisper that the king had known of Stanley's contact with the rebels all the time; but Polydore Vergil had no doubt about the element of surprise. 'At first,' says Vergil, 'the king could not be persuaded to believe Robert's statement.' It is a peculiarity of Henry VII's that he always trusted his most important ministers – perhaps because he had himself selected them with great care – although he was quick to suspect treason among his subjects as a whole and even more suspicious of those who alleged treason in others. He is known to have given one informant such a tough interrogation that years later he swore, 'If ye knew King Harry our master as I do, ye would beware how that ye break to him in any such matters, for he would take it to be said but of envy, ill will and malice.' The king believed in sifting the evidence personally and well, but on this occasion he was clearly convinced that Clifford told the truth, because as the informer finally left the Tower he collected £500, an enormous reward by contemporary standards.

The king then ordered Stanley's arrest. It was the moment when the removal to the Tower proved worth while. The guard simply marched the shocked lord chamberlain the few yards across a cobbled courtyard from comfortable palace apartments to the frightening prison tower of the king's choice – perhaps the Beauchamp Tower, whose secure upper rooms were frequently used as prison cells; for in the circle of these ancient walls a short walk could translate a man from the proud heights of wealth and importance to the uttermost depth of misfortune. With good reason would young Henry grow up, like his contemporaries, to see fortune as a fickle woman or an ever revolving wheel.

The deputy constable of the Tower brought Stanley to trial before his peers at Westminster Hall. There he was accused that he did 'falsely and treacherously plot the death and destruction of the present lord king himself and the overthrow of his kingdom of England'; also, that he had agreed that when Clifford returned from Burgundy and 'should indicate . . . someone from those foreign parts by means of some secret sign arranged between them for the . . . assistance of . . . the said Peter Warbeck . . . William Stanley himself was willing to assist and support them with all his followers' – an interesting detail that suggests a sudden palace coup was planned.

Vehemently, but vainly, Stanley protested his innocence. Under the high, gilded wagon roof in the great hall where, as an important royal officer, he had arranged and partaken of feasts and revels, he was condemned to a traitor's dreadful death.

At Eltham, Henry would hear the actions of his father's lord chamberlain discussed for years to come. The treachery of such a trusted and intimate servant was a shattering and alarming blow for the whole royal family, and as in all families, the elder children, Arthur and Margaret, would have explained the alarm in terms their younger brother could understand. No guards, no assay, no weapons were proof against a false lord chamberlain. When Henry in later years reflected on the incident it brought home to him the oppressive truth that a king

57

must suspect everyone, even those closest to him. And, unlike his father, when he grew up he would always be ready to see treason in his most trusted ministers. For this unattractive development in his character the Stanley affair must bear much of the blame.

The final scene was to be played out according to medieval expectation. As young Henry was to learn, a traitor's punishment must be deterrent and at the same time reassure the citizens in general that their king would uphold and administer the law; that was his most important function. Admittedly, the ideal king tempered justice with mercy, but even the greatest thinkers of the time, like Thomas More and Erasmus, held that there were crimes for which mercy was unsuitable. A convicted traitor must pay the penalty, although if he were fortunate enough to be a gentleman he might be spared some of the more agonizing refinements.

Stanley's condemnation in Westminster Hall was followed by twelve days of execution whose savagery, in fifteenth-century eyes, was wholly deserved and justly meted out; sad, but necessary if order was to be maintained. The occasional appalling death, with hackings and quarterings, was another symbol in an age of visual symbols; the executions would be described in detail in the city chronicles and talked of for months and years to come – at Eltham Palace as well as everywhere else.

Of the conspirators who had been in communication with Warbeck, Stanley, the most important, was to die last. On Wednesday, 4 February 1495, five of the gentlemen traitors – some imprisoned since November and some only since January – were tied to hurdles, harnessed to horses and dragged over London's rough streets from Newgate to Tower Hill. There, bruised, bleeding and shocked, they were marched up the steps of the scaffold and across to the straw-circled block, where the masked executioner awaited them, impassively grasping the axe. Three were beheaded, and two were reprieved as they bared their necks for the blow, the last-minute reprieve being a device of King Henry's to draw large crowds, adding to the popular spectacle of execution yet another grisly attraction, another element of dramatic suspense. Coolly efficient, Henry VII knew how to gain wide respect for the royal justice. His son would be less cerebral, more impulsive.

On Thursday, 5 February 1495, two other conspirators who were not of gentle birth, an English sailor and a Dutchman, were dragged from Newgate to Tyburn, hanged, cut down while still alive and then beheaded. And on the Friday 'Petit Jean', a man from Brittany, suffered similar awesome punishment.

The climax to this gruesome programme came on Monday, 16 February, at about eleven o'clock, when Sir William Stanley was led out of the Tower between two armed guards. On the high scaffold in the middle of the crowds pressed into the wide open space that was then Tower Hill, the lord chamberlain was beheaded.

Although members of the court sometimes witnessed such legal butchery and London citizens brought their children to view the scene, it is unlikely that the king allowed his second son to watch. However, the boy could not fail to see and callously grow used to grim evidence of the royal justice, for it was all around. On every journey by river to his father's palaces at Westminster and Sheen, Baynard's Castle and Windsor, as the sweating green-and-white-liveried watermen rowed the royal barge towards London Bridge, the small child noticed with a thrill of horror the heads of the traitors high above. All except Stanley's, which perhaps in gratitude for his rescue at Bosworth Field, the king had had buried with the lord chamberlain's body in the Thames-side village of Sion. Raised on poles on top of the stone tower at the north end of the wonderful bridge, the heads were to become a sight as familiar to the little boy as the blue skies and blossom of spring.

Other lesser experiences, too, inured Henry to cruelty, which was at the core of many contemporary games and entertainments. Part of the fun of Blind Man's Buff lay in the buffeting you could inflict with your hood or bonnet before the blind man caught you. The point of watching youths 'joust' at the movable quintain was to see if they could be quick enough to escape a blow on the back with the heavy bag of sand on the other end of the quintain as it swung round. Henry watched 'throwing at cocks' at Shrove Tuesday fairs, cock-fights and bear-baiting, and in May he himself probably indulged in the children's sport of spinning the chafer, attaching a thread through a May bug's tail for the fun of seeing it try to whir away. And the entry in the king's chamber expenses mentioning a payment for spurs for one of his court fools, as well as many references to the bridles, saddles and hoofs that these unfortunates wore, strongly suggests that they were roughly ridden for laughs.

That spring of 1495, following the executions of the conspirators, Henry saw more than usual of his father, for the king visited Eltham and shortly afterwards summoned his second son to Windsor. Here on 19 May 1495, the little duke walked in procession to St George's Chapel for another ritualistic ceremony that would endow him with still greater status, and help to imprint the image of the new royal family on King Henry VII's apathetic subjects. Attired in his own miniature blue mantle over a surcoat embroidered with tiny golden garters, he was conducted to a stall beneath a banner bearing his own coat of arms and there duly initiated as Knight of the Order of the Garter, the highest honour in the land. It was yet more food for the boy's growing sense of importance.

The thought of his newly acknowledged worth would have increased his own sense of outrage when he heard people speak of that other duke of York, his rival Peter Warbeck. Warbeck, the child knew, was a threat to all he owned. Not only his dukedom and the lands and castles that his great-uncle Jasper, duke of Bedford, had promised to leave him in his will, but also, and more important to Henry at this age, his toys. For Warbeck had promised to give away everything that Henry's family owned.

To tempt Maximilian into giving further help, Warbeck had drawn up a deed which, in the event of his having no sons of his own to succeed him, made Maximilian and Maximilian's son, Philip, his heirs. He had also promised Margaret of Burgundy all the property and grants that she had lost at Edward IV's death; Warbeck was always to be generous with possessions he had not got. The critical question for the king was: in exchange for these bribes, with how big a force would Maximilian and Margaret support the pretender? And if he invaded, how many Englishmen would rally to his cause? Stanley's betrayal was disturbing evidence that people still believed that the Tudor dynasty could be supplanted.

It was a tense time for those living at court, as well as around England's coasts, and tension communicates itself to children. The king's guards could not be at every possible landing spot, but Henry VII had reinforced them with propaganda. On doors of churches near the sea royal officials had nailed proclamations contemptuously describing Warbeck's true origins, and these notices had done their work.

Henry was four when the invasion came. Warbeck's choice fell on Deal in Kent, a perfect lonely anchorage which he sailed for on Friday, 3 July 1495.

Suddenly, over the calm water appeared a line of strange vessels, fourteen small ships. They loomed nearer, put out row-boats, and laden with soldiers, swords, halberds, harquebuses, lances, pikes, crossbows and banners bearing the emblems of the duke of York, these approached. 'Who are you? What is your purpose?' the lone guard found the courage to hail them. 'We are followers of the duke of York,' the men replied. 'We ask for no other lord,' the resourceful guard shouted back. 'We will live and die with him. Let him and his company land.'

The men jumped ashore, planted their banners on the beach, began to unload their weapons. 'I will fetch ale to refresh you,' the guard offered welcomingly and galloped off to the town of Sandwich where the mayor hastily summoned a meeting. Should they join the rebels or support the Tudor? Some Kentishmen were for joining Warbeck; others reminded them how little good had come of Kentish rebellions in the past. On this cynical note, according to Polydore Vergil, they seized weapons and made for the bay.

Meanwhile, Peter Warbeck, who had remained with part of his force out at sea, growing suspicious at the long wait for a few casks of ale, had commanded his men to withdraw, but too late. Before they could scramble into the row-boats a mob of armed villagers behind the brave mayor of Sandwich rushed down on them, encouraging each other with shouts of 'The king is coming', and 'This fellow can go back to his father and mother who live in France and are well known there'.

So vigorously did the mob lay about them that, according to the report of a Spanish ambassador to the English court, they slaughtered no less than a hundred and fifty men, then threw some of the survivors into carts and roped the unlucky rest between the traces, forcing them to pull their fellows like horses. Seeing what was happening, Warbeck withdrew his ships in panic and left his followers to their fate. When the footsore, exhausted procession arrived in London, forty-two prisoners were clapped in Newgate prison, the rest in the Tower to await trial and execution, which was to be more than usually symbolic. As a warning to future invaders, many of them were to be hanged at sites carefully chosen round the coast and at Wapping on the Thames, 'so that at every full sea' the tide 'flowed over them and their gibbet'.

With this defeat for Warbeck the threat had, for the moment, moved away from the king and his growing family at Eltham. Safe in the green deer park and instructed by a skilled teacher, Henry could soon begin to learn the art of shooting with a longbow, not only with accuracy but also, and just as important in the fifteenth century, with gentlemanly elegance, the left foot placed gracefully in front of the right. His elder brother Arthur was already exceptionally good at archery; it was exciting to try and beat him, to bend the curved yew and see his arrow, plumed with goose or peacock feathers, hurtle towards the bright target.

But Maximilian and Margaret were not Warbeck's only supporters. The really ominous support came from inside the kingdom, as Henry would discover in a few years' time when he began to read England's recent history. The danger to the Tudor dynasty did not originate in enthusiasm for the young Perkin. Warbeck was a mere symptom: the disease lay deeper. And since the rebellions of his childhood with their attendant suspicion and anxiety were to contribute to Henry's sense of insecurity in later life, it is necessary to diagnose it.

Though recognized, like Henry IV, as *de facto* king by parliament, Henry VII's hereditary claim was tenuous in the extreme. When Henry came to the throne there were at least five males alive with a better hereditary claim than his: Edward, earl of Warwick, son of George, duke of Clarence, brother of Edward IV; and the sons of Edward IV's sister Elizabeth – including John, Edmund, Richard and William de la Pole. Not surprisingly, therefore, King Henry VII's rule was to be challenged throughout his reign by a nightmare succession of pretenders. The claim of the ten-year-old earl of Warwick was so obviously and dangerously superior to Henry's own that, before he even reached London after the battle of Bosworth, Henry sent an order that the boy was to be imprisoned in the Tower.

Before Warbeck arrived in Cork in 1491 there had been two separate plots, both using the earl of Warwick as a figurehead. One of these plots, to release Warwick from the Tower, had been discovered nearly two years before young Henry's birth and quickly dealt with. For his part in the scheme the abbot of Abingdon had been hanged in December 1489. The earlier plot, however, had given the king much more trouble, and the little duke of York came to know a great deal about the resulting rebellion, because its central figure still lived, a man with a job which any little boy of the day would envy and admire.

By the age of four Henry was beginning to be fascinated by the many popular outdoor sports of the day: tennis and shooting with a crossbow at the butts; fishing and chasing hares, and fowling, either with net and lights at night or with a stuffed canvas stalking horse, from behind which a boy could shoot his arrows unseen. But the most fashionable and therefore the most magical sports of all were hawking and hunting. Every summer the king left the cares of state for weeks at a time while he rode from deer park to deer park with his hawks and his hounds. To own his own hawk was one of the ambitions of a boy of high birth. And while young Henry does not seem to have achieved this until he was nine – when the king's privy purse expenses listed 'hawk bells given at Hatfield for my lord the duke of York, 8s.' – he would have watched his father's hawks much earlier. We can picture my lord of York, aged four, standing with his short sturdy legs apart, his small blue eyes fixed on the bird that gripped the king's embroidered leather glove. In a moment, the bird's hood removed, the jesses on its legs loosed, it would soar into the sky. It was the excitement of killing clothed in elegant luxury; not only were the summer woods and meadows and thickets beautiful all round, but the hawk was beautiful too, its jesses often of crimson silk, its legs hung with two silver bells giving each a different musical note as the bird rose to its prey.

Hawks had a special mystique and were highly valued. Henry VII had passed a law protecting most of the species that bred in England, forbidding their use in sport and making anyone taking an egg from a nest liable to imprisonment for a year and a day, with a fine as well. So hawks at this date were imported expensively from abroad. The type of hawk a man could fly depended on his rank, a valuable bird being a badge of high status, often perching behind his master at mealtimes.

The king's hawks were cared for in the royal Charing Cross mews, near the river Thames. Training and looking after them was a skilled job and, to a little boy, the young man who performed it was a special and privileged person; but there was something else special about him too. For this son of a carpenter, who dressed neatly according to his rank and doffed his cap to the king, was Lambert Simnel who had himself years ago claimed the crown, the boy who at the age of ten had been trained to impersonate the child earl of Warwick by an ambitious priest, Richard Simons. Knowing Simnel would have made the incredible story come alive for young Henry.

On 24 March 1487, the Yorkist Irish lords and a number of Irish bishops conducted the ten-year-old carpenter's boy to Christ Church, Dublin, where he was anointed, crowned with a gold circlet sacrilegiously lifted from a statue of the Virgin Mary, and proclaimed King Edward VI. The pathetic Simnel's forces, which consisted of about six thousand ill-armed Irish and two thousand German mercenaries sent over by Margaret of Burgundy – a substantial army by fifteenth-century standards – then advanced into England to challenge the king. They were commanded by John de la Pole, earl of Lincoln, whom King Richard III had nominated as his heir.

The rival forces met at Stoke, where the rebels' ambitions were speedily thrown in the dust. The king won the battle, the earl of Lincoln was killed and Simnel captured alive.

In deciding Simnel's fate, Henry VII had acted out one of his characteristic jokes. Instead of executing or imprisoning him, he had made the crowned and consecrated 'King Edward VI' tend greasy haunches of mutton and venison over the huge hot open fires in the royal kitchens, later mercifully promoting him from turnspit to keeper of the hawks.

The sight of the keeper of the hawks was a reminder for the little prince of the recurring rebellions against his father. Before Warbeck, Simnel. After Warbeck, who? In the teeth of such repeated challenges, for how long could the Tudor dynasty survive? For the nursery attendants in the palace of Eltham it was an alarming question too, for their future also might be at stake. And as young Henry's comprehension rapidly expanded, their uncertainty cannot have failed to increase his own.

The boy learned quickly. In November 1495, his father's privy purse expenses record, 'For a book bought for my lord of York, £1.' Probably he was already learning some words in Latin and French, although serious lessons, by Tudor standards, would not start for another couple of years.

But as he ran and played about the palace an altogether different type of knowledge was seeping into him without the help of any teacher – the blood-stained history of his own ancestors. Each king had set his stamp on Eltham, his emblem in carved wood, sculptured stone or the deep rich colours of stained glass; each king had built his identity into the fabric of the palace. The outer courtyard had been built by King Richard II whose favourite emblem, the white hart, was symbolic of this victim king, first deposed, then promised his life, and finally murdered in Pontefract Castle by order of Henry IV. This strong plain pragmatic usurper, who survived to die a natural death, had also left his mark on Eltham. His new two-storied royal apartments had carried the Lancastrian motto '*Soueignez de moy* – remember me' – in the windows. As though to placate God, angry at the murder of a consecrated king, the seven windows of Henry IV's study depicted religious subjects, and the ceiling's sixty-eight wooden bosses were carved with angels bearing scutcheons and scrolls.

Henry IV's grandson, the gentle weak-minded King Henry VI, had built new lodgings at Eltham for his wife, Margaret of Anjou, the queen whose uncompromising and martial temperament led eventually to his own murder in the Tower of London, and the butchery of his eighteen-year-old only son after the battle of Tewkesbury. King Edward IV, another usurper king, who had survived to reign for twenty-two years, had rebuilt the great hall, with his badge, the *rose-en-soleil*, the Yorkist white rose superimposed on one of Richard II's emblems, the gold rising sun, shining out from the spandrels of the north doorway, as Edward's own brilliance shone over his kingdom. Although King Henry VII added his own embellishments to Eltham, inevitably some of his Plantagenet predecessors' adornments remained to tell their startling story to an observant small boy.

It was a story of extreme contrast, black chasms of failure and golden pinnacles of success, a story with a simple moral: weakness and gentleness mean defeat and death, only the most ruthless and cunning kings survive. Such was the heritage that would colour Henry's view of kingship, and of his father as king, and particularly of his father's treatment of rebellion.

CHAPTER 5

In the Tower

'In the latter end of May the commons of Cornwall
assembled them in great numbers of the which was captain a blacksmith.'   *Vitellius MS*

———

REBELLION was not the only grim recurring threat in Henry's
childhood; in the autumn of 1495 he experienced the first of no
less than five family tragedies.

Before ordering his court to move from one palace to another,
King Henry VII despatched searchers to make sure that there
was no sickness in the area. As a result of this measure there is
no record of bubonic plague attacking the royal households
during young Henry's childhood, though there were unfortunately other illnesses just as lethal that the king could do
little to prevent. Typhoid and smallpox were endemic, as was
malaria, which was generally referred to at the time as the
ague or tertian fever; there was no cure at all for appendicitis,
and no reliable cure for the sweating sickness – thought to have
been a type of 'flu – though many amateur leeches boasted they
had found one. As usual with fifteenth-century deaths, we do
not know which of the many possible ailments killed three-
year-old Elizabeth, the child exactly a year younger than
Henry and nearest in age to him; all we know is that she died on
4 September 1495 at Eltham. Elizabeth seems to have been
particularly dear to her family, for her father had her body
conveyed to Westminster Abbey with great pomp and buried
on the right of the altar in the blessed aura of St Edward's
shrine. There Elizabeth lies still in her own small marble
tomb among the array of dead kings and queens, although her
effigy of copper gilt has been stolen.

67

Henry was too young to grieve long for his little sister's death; nevertheless it would have sent a chill shiver through his world. Henceforth to Henry's fear of rebellion would be added the fear of death from illness, bringing into his life at this early age another element of insecurity.

As winter approached, Peter Warbeck again appeared dangerous for he had persuaded King James IV of Scotland to help him. James had received him at Stirling Castle in a chamber newly decorated with arras for the occasion, had styled him 'the prince of England, Richard, duke of York', and allotted him splendid lodgings in the town. He had also kitted him out in princely garments: purple-striped black hose, a purple gown, a white damask 'spousing' gown, plain black hose, and a velvet 'greatcoat of the new fashion . . . with sleeves'.

A retinue of six servants and two trumpeters in red hose had been clothed at the Scottish king's expense and a tournament had been staged in Warbeck's honour. King James had even married him – presumably in the white 'spousing' gown – to his wife's relative, Katherine Gordon, daughter of the earl of Huntly. And to show that he meant to support the 'English prince' in every way possible, he had summoned his subjects for military service.

The summer of 1496 was yet another anxious season for England as Henry reached the age of five, his child's body strengthening with constant riding, archery, wrestling and playing with toy lances.

On 17 September Peter Warbeck crossed the border, gold-fringed banners on newly gilded poles, the king of Scots by his side, and proclaimed himself King Richard IV of England. However, although Yorkist discontent still smouldered in North Country breasts, not one single Englishman rallied to Warbeck's cause. The poor pretender lost heart, and on hearing that Lord Neville was approaching with an army of four thousand men, he fled in the middle of the night, bundling his forces back over the river Tweed in half the time it had taken them to make the original crossing.

Warbeck's second defeat preceded a major new event in Henry's life. His family was again to be depleted. The title, the Prince of Wales, was more meaningful in the fifteenth century than it is today, and even as a child the prince was expected to live at Ludlow Castle on the borders of his principality and eventually to become president of the council which enforced law and order there. The date when Arthur began to live at Ludlow is not known, but to judge from a letter of Margaret Beaufort's in which she wrote, 'all our sweet children be in good health', he was still part of the children's ménage in April 1496. According to Henry VII's privy purse expenses, he was at court in September, but by the following May he had left the south of England, so it was probably in the winter of 1496 or the spring of 1497 that, heralded by trumpeters, he rode for Ludlow with his seal, his retainers, his minstrels and his fool. Henceforth he continued to pay periodic visits to court, but he was no longer brought up at Eltham.

Henry's feelings at his brother's departure are not difficult to guess. Arthur was his father's best-loved son, for he was heir to the king's great achievement; and a child is always quick to sense which member of the family is his parent's favourite. Henry followed the classic example of the child who, feeling himself less loved, becomes intensely jealous and competitive; but Henry's situation was especially frustrating. He knew that, no matter how he tried to excel, he could never be on equal terms with the heir to the throne, for Arthur was addressed as 'my lord prince', Henry merely as 'my lord of York'. And as the brothers grew older and Arthur became king, their difference in rank would become marked by court etiquette. According to their grandmother's ordinances, on entering Arthur's presence chamber Henry would be obliged to remove his hat and remain bare-headed until Arthur graciously told him to 'be covered'. If he deputized for Arthur on state occasions he would sit under a royal canopy of state, but to emphasize his inferior rank, the front would be firmly and humiliatingly rolled up so that it did not cover more than the back half of his head.

In the circumstances Henry would have been abnormal if the

fading trumpet notes of Arthur's departure had not filled him with subconscious relief. At least now he was the most important person in Eltham Palace. Because although each royal child had his or her own minstrels and other servants, from this time on the Eltham ménage was known under Henry's name, as we can see from still surviving royal commissions which license a butcher and fishmonger to purvey for 'the household of Henry duke of York' 'oxen, calves, lambs, sheep, coneys, pullets, capons, hens, geese, and fresh water fish'. Margaret was older than he, but as second in line to the throne Henry took precedence – a satisfying situation. And as a further sign of his new delightful superiority, in May 1497 he was invited to court by himself.

Presumably he had joined his parents for the May Day festivities at Greenwich and then accompanied them to Sheen when they moved there on 13 May. For it is at Sheen that we next catch a glimpse of the duke in a London chronicle. Apart from the pleasing attention that young Henry received from ambitious courtiers at the palace, Sheen itself had its own magic for an imaginative and aggressive small boy. Burnt down by Richard II in anguish at the death of his wife, it had been rebuilt by England's hero king, Henry V who, before his death at only thirty-five, had won the French crown for his heir. And it was by order of this all-conquering monarch that carved antelopes and swans skipped and sailed beguilingly over the painted wooden ceilings of the king's parlour and chamber, adorned on the cornices with lions and fleurs-de-lis.

The warrior king's son, Henry VI, who had lost not only France, but also through his madness the crown of England for the House of Lancaster, had added glass windows painted with figures, flowers and his own royal arms and beasts – as well as a high brick wall round the king's private garden, and a stone cloister with an octagonal lead cistern on which could still be seen his own motto '*Dieu et moun droyt*'; and that of his wife, Margaret of Anjou, '*Humble et loyall*', ironically meek words for this termagant queen. Here too, nostalgically, were carved his and her initials, H and M, surmounted by a crown.

Affection for Sheen was enough to fan the hatred that, in common with most Englishmen, he had been taught to feel, at the name of France.

But as the little boy wandered round the formal palace garden another threat to the Tudor line was gathering force. This time it came from the West Country and the trouble sprang directly from the aftermath of Warbeck's attempted invasion the previous September. Fear of the Scots appeared then to have borne golden fruit for the thrifty Henry VII: in January 1497 parliament had voted him a large sum of money for the defence of the kingdom, £120,000 in taxation and a loan of a further £40,000, to be raised by a commissioner in each county. Some of this money went to pay for an army of eight thousand men, between the ages of sixteen and sixty, which were mustered in the spring for the purpose of teaching the Scots a lesson, but some of the money could not be raised.

Cornwall, then as now, was poor. The inhabitants scratched a living mining tin, farming tiny unprofitable farms and fishing. The money required by Henry VII made them nothing less than desperate. The day after Lord Daubeny left Sheen Palace to lead the royal army against the Scots, the king heard of a new rebellion: a vast mob of Cornishmen, led by Michael Joseph, a blacksmith, and Thomas Flammock, a lawyer, rose suddenly in May. When the news reached Sheen, they had already reached Exeter and were marching towards London.

So far the Cornishmen had not used the bows and arrows and farm implements that most of them carried as weapons: they only wished, they declared, to protest against too heavy taxation. But what other aims lay behind this declaration? Seen from a twentieth century point of view the Cornish rebellion is a mere incident in Henry VII's reign, all over in about a fortnight, but at the time the movement was mysterious and worrying, for like the Peasants' Revolt in 1381 it could become a direct challenge to the government of the country.

This new rebellion found the king totally unprepared. He

sent word to Lord Daubeny to come south again with his army, and hastily mustering a second force as he went, he himself rode to Woodstock to attempt to block the rebels' path to the capital. For the moment there was a hiatus in the royal defences.

Meanwhile Queen Elizabeth rode for the safety of walled London, taking the duke of York with her. Further to protect her and the boy who was second in line to the throne, the king sent a strong escort of lords and gentlemen, including William Blount, Lord Mountjoy, aged nineteen, who was to play such a large part in young Henry's education.

For a week she and the little duke of York stayed in Margaret Beaufort's mansion in Thames Street, the Cold Harbour built by a previous mayor in 1349, while messengers brought increasingly disturbing news. The rebels' army was snowballing, gathering discontented people from all the counties it traversed, from Devon, Somerset, Wiltshire and Gloucestershire, including a number of gentlemen. An important noble, James Touchet, Lord Audley, son of King Richard III's lord treasurer, had joined the blacksmith and the lawyer at its head, for reasons that still remain unfathomable.

On Monday, 12 June, reports came that the mob, eighteen thousand strong now, was closing in; they had reached Farnham. With her second son, the queen promptly rode out through the arched gateway of the Cold Harbour and hurried towards the safest available stronghold, the Tower of London. The lives of her own two young brothers had been sacrificed to ambition only a few years ago. She was determined to keep this third little prince safe.

The Tower had plenty to interest Henry. He could peer with childish sadism through barred windows of wretched cells where prisoners lay in irons, or try to guess in what rooms – kept secret so that no one could again attempt to rescue him – his second cousin, young Edward, earl of Warwick, wasted his life. He could watch the high-sided sailing ships passing up and down with the tide, importing silks from Italy, carpets from Turkey, spices, monkeys and parrots from the Far East;

Henry VIII as a child

Henry VII,
sculpted from life
by Pietro Torrigiano

Prince Arthur,
from a stained
glass window at
Malvern Priory

Margaret Beaufort,
mother of Henry VII

ELIZABETHA · VXOR
HENRICI · VII ·

Elizabeth of York,
mother of Arthur
and Henry VIII

Toy jousters
made of bronze

Henry VIII's
foot combat armour,
ca. 1515-20

exporting good English wool and cloth. But his steps would almost certainly have wandered most frequently towards the armoury.

In that June week of 1497, over all the busy life of this group of grey-and-white buildings, called collectively the Tower, lay an abnormal sense of sudden urgency. The men of Cornwall were marching on London in a fury and no one, it seemed, would stop them. The armourers, polishing and sharpening the gleaming dangerous weapons, can have had little time for the questions of a small boy, though he was the king's son; behind the extra speed of the work, the rough quick humour of the workers lay excitement and fear. The perceptive child in doublet and hose with velvet cap set straight on his long auburn hair, cannot have mistaken the feeling. The Tower was strong with its huge bronze cannon, its moat and double walls and strategic position on the river, but it was not impregnable. Twice before mobs had descended on London. In 1450 Jack Cade's rabble of peasants had been repulsed at London Bridge. But Wat Tyler's rebels in 1381 had been horrifyingly successful. They had burst into the Tower, molested the queen who had sought safety there, dragged out and executed a number of victims, including an archbishop and the royal treasurer. In the city they had burned, murdered and opened the prisons, inspired by the slogan of one of their leaders, the priest John Ball.

> *When Adam delved and Eve span,*
> *Who was then the gentleman?*

When Henry climbed determinedly to one of the turrets of the White Tower, a brightly clothed little figure, his blue eyes sharp beneath his velvet cap, he could look back towards London and see men grimly preparing to defend themselves against this new enemy. So far, the tough Cornish had still not been violent, and their leaders had promised that they would not hurt the king. But given the promises they had made to the people, that in future no one need pay taxes and that, on reaching London, they would drag to execution the king's evil councillors who were plotting the extermination of the poor, this restraint could only be temporary. Everyone knew what happened when a mob felt its own power. Now London's citizens piled up great heaps of timber against the gates and the sun struck gleams from the weapons of guards posted round the walls. For even a naturally brave small boy it was a sight to make him seek comfort from his mother.

Comfort was not easy for her to give; for her situation in 1497 was reminiscent of a nightmarish moment in her early life, a moment that had been the prelude to one of those unexpected reversals of fortune that had cast deep frightening shadows over her childhood. In the summer of 1470, at the same age as Henry was now, Elizabeth of York herself had been in the Tower, with her sister Mary (who had died in childhood) and her own mother, Queen Elizabeth Woodville. From these same royal apartments she too had gazed anxiously at river and green hills and city walls, waiting for news of her father, King Edward IV. And here, too, she had heard the shattering news that his army had deserted him and joined the rebels, thus forcing him to flee across the sea to Burgundy.

Five-year-old Elizabeth had been hastily conveyed to Westminster with none of the customary advertisements of a royal journey, no gilded barge decked with coats of arms, no banner and streamers, no cheering crowds on the banks, none of the accustomed glory. She was hustled secretly up the water steps, through the gates to the side of Westminster Abbey and into sanctuary. Here in one of the small houses in the shadow of the great Gothic building, she could live safely: anywhere else she would be in danger.

Had Elizabeth of York's husband now made the same mistake of being in the wrong place at the wrong time? It was a frightening thought for Elizabeth and probably for her little son too. In later life Henry was to show all the signs of an Oedipus complex, but other evidence too suggests that Elizabeth was particularly fond of Henry, the child whose brightness was eclipsed by the heir to the throne, and that Henry returned her special affection; so now to balance their anxiety, there was

some compensation. The week that he was to spend in the Tower
was one of the few occasions when Henry had a chance to be
alone with his gentle, modest mother, although at this age
his affection was based on scant knowledge, for he knew her
mainly through his father's propaganda, as a goddess figure,
the white rose of the song he heard often at court.

> In a glorius garden grene
> Sawe I syttyng a comly quene
> Among the flouris that fressh byn.
> She gaderd a floure and set betwene;
> The lyly-whighte rose methought I sawe,
> The lyly-whighte rose methought I sawe,
> And ever she sang:
> This day day dawes, [dawns]
> This gentill day day dawes,
> This gentill day dawes,
> And I must home gone.

At not quite six, Henry was too young to perceive behind
these verses the few flaws that made the goddess a real woman,
but he was old enough to listen already to the tales that
Elizabeth had to tell of her past, and to realize that his own and
his mother's fate in this year of 1497 hung again on the success
of the king. Most children have firm faith in their parents'
ability to protect them, but Henry's faith can hardly have
survived his mother's related experiences. Did Henry VII
command greater loyalty than Edward IV? Only events could
tell. And at the moment of the boy's arrival in the Tower on 12
June his father was nearly eighty miles away at Woodstock,
almost helpless, since Daubeny's army had not yet come south.
If the king were deposed, what then? Henry was aware that for
the family of a deposed king there was at best disgrace, as his
mother Queen Elizabeth had found.

No standing army paraded ready to protect the king should
powerful magnates prove disloyal. Who knew what Yorkist
nobles might not take advantage of the Cornish revolt? And a
figurehead for the rebels still existed, a puppet potentially

almost as useful as Henry VI: the earl of Warwick, Yorkist heir to the throne.

Should fortune's wheel turn against the Tudor, Henry, like his mother, might all too easily find himself a sanctuary child, mixing with thieves, murderers or women who had run off with their husbands' plate. Edward the Confessor's charter protected them all. 'Any person in these precincts,' this canonized king had ordered, 'of what condition or estate soever he be, from whencesoever he come, or for what offence or cause it be . . . be assured of his life, liberty and limbs.' Anyone interfering with this right of sanctuary, St Edward condemned with Judas to 'the everlasting fire of hell'.

For a little boy born in the purple, it was horrifying to think that his mother at the age of five had had to live in sanctuary for six months without setting foot beyond the precincts of abbey and close, that here his grandmother, Queen Elizabeth Woodville, had been forced to give birth to the ill-fated Prince Edward.

As mother and son, bound by their common danger, watched the far hills in June 1497, for sight of the approaching mob, Henry could not fail to be affected by the light and shade of her memories, the second shadow darker and even more frightening than the first. In 1483 she, who had been betrothed to the dauphin of France, was pronounced illegitimate and worse: not even a royal bastard, for her father had been pronounced illegitimate too, and her mother had been accused of marrying him by sorcery.

Proof that this dark moment in his mother's life story lodged deep in Henry's mind can be found in his later use of two of the charges levelled against Elizabeth Woodville. Years afterwards, when he wanted to be rid of his second wife, he would accuse Anne Boleyn of pre-contract and sorcery.

Meanwhile in those summer days of 1497 the Cornish mob continued to move menacingly on London. On the afternoon of 13 June, the day after they had arrived in the Tower, Henry and his mother heard news at last of Daubeny: his army was encamped at nearby Hounslow Heath. The thankful mayor of

London immediately sent off to them wagons loaded with food, ale and wine and the promise of more to come. Everything pointed to the king's victory. The royal army was better equipped than the mob. The king's foot soldiers wore each a helmet and leather tunic and carried a sword as well as bow and arrows. His officers, on horseback, were encased in armour, gentlemen trained in the arts of war. The Cornish, with only a few such skilled and protected gentlemen, appeared no match for the royal forces. But Elizabeth of York's experience had taught her that such appearances could mislead, new leaders could materialize, royal armies could desert, he who reigned today could be prisoner, exile, or naked bloody corpse tomorrow.

The most worrying part of this vigil that the queen kept with her son in the Tower was that nothing seemed to happen for so long. On Wednesday 14 June there was a skirmish between some of Daubeny's spearmen and the Cornish near Guildford, and two of the rebels were taken prisoner. But for the best part of a week there was no proper engagement; the Cornish moved unmolested through Kent and Surrey in a threatening semi-circle round the city, shadowed by the royal armies. Why did the king not act?

The king did nothing but move along the banks of the Thames: Abingdon, Wallingford, Henley, Reading, Kingston . . . Daubeny's army shifted ineffectually from St George's Field on the south bank of the Thames to Croydon, and back again. On Friday night the queen and the duke of York heard that the rebels had advanced to Blackheath, the very place from which the peasant mobs of 1381 and 1450 had descended on London. There, in the furze and rough grass of the heath, they camped. Across the river, young Henry could see their fires lighting up the distant sky, while glowing more cheeringly and closer to him, on the south bank of the river he could see the fires of the royal armies. The king had joined Daubeny in St George's Field. Fortunately a child can sleep through the most fateful night.

But Henry would have woken soon after dawn to general

77

excitement in the Tower and the far-off boom of cannon, and faintly through the still summer air the screams of wounded, the cries of officers trying to rally their followers, and the excited neighing of horses. The royal forces had attacked. For several hours the rebels fought bravely, but by noon the heath was thickly scattered with their bodies, two thousand dead. The rebellion had been crushed. Once again, the king and the royal family were safe.

At two o'clock in the afternoon his father rode over London Bridge, greeted by jubilant, scarlet-clad civic dignitaries. He was followed by prisoners marching chained together, or flung like rubbish into carts. For two centuries the grave mounds of the dead would remain visible on Blackheath.

To the humanitarian Thomas More, writing after the turn of the century, the uprising would seem a pitiful affair: 'that disastrous civil war which began with a revolution in the West Country and ended with a ghastly massacre of the rebels.' But young Henry was taught to feel no pity. From his father he learnt to despise the 'base Cornishmen'. For a rebellion of the mob represented lack of order, a return to the lawlessness that most fifteenth- and sixteenth-century citizens so dreaded. The boy's vigil was over but its fear lingered on, the fear of sudden violent dispossession. Printed too on his mind, never to be eradicated, was his hatred of the rebel mob.

Having offered at St Paul's to thank God for being on his side, Henry VII joined his wife in the Tower, where during the next few days his second son witnessed with interest and awe his father's very individual methods of putting down rebellion.

Though still not quite six, an intelligent child like Henry could not but consider such things when he had a front row seat, when his whole future had been involved in the rebellion and the results were presented before his eyes and ears with all the visual drama of the age. First the trumpets and the loud proclamation: 'All men who took prisoners at the battle shall bring them to the Tower. For each prisoner the lord king will pay a reward.' Then the procession of downcast prisoners, and captors greedily seizing their blood money: twelve pence a peasant, more for those of higher degree.

As usual, King Henry trusted no one but himself to get to the root of treason. Sunday was a day of rest, but on Monday young Henry knew that his father was personally interrogating the three leaders of the rebellion.

A week later Lord Audley, Thomas Flammock and Michael Joseph were marched by the guard through the city, down the Strand to Westminster Hall, and there condemned to die. The king was unexpectedly lenient. The next day the two commoners were dragged on a hurdle from the Tower to Tyburn and hanged, but Henry VII allowed his victims the unusual mercy of dying first before being cut down and hacked into quarters. Although Audley's punishment was more drawn out, this was only because he could be used to teach a grim lesson. Taken to Newgate prison the night before his execution, he was then tied to a hurdle and drawn by horses through the city of London to the Tower, wearing a paper tabard painted with his coat of arms, torn to show that he was no longer worthy of knighthood. But on Tower Hill he was given a quick death under the axe, followed by burial of everything except his head, which was set with the heads of Flammock and Joseph on London Bridge. The quarters of Flammock's body were set on the four gates of London – Ludgate, Newgate, Cripplegate and Aldersgate – obscene reminders to anyone entering or leaving the city of the penalties of rebellion. These poor relics the little duke of York also cannot have failed to see, a sight much closer, and so more ghastly, than the heads above London Bridge. The quarters of Joseph, King Henry ordered to be carried into Devonshire and Cornwall, intending to expose them there, but at the last moment he changed his mind.

Apart from these three leaders, the king had no one executed. The rest of the Cornishmen were sent home unharmed, except for massive fines. Henry VII sought his enemies' money before their blood; he wanted to be rich and popular more than to be feared, to appease rather than to exacerbate, and taking the long-range view of Henry VII's reign, his policy proved very successful. But from the shorter viewpoint of what happened later in the year 1497 it appeared to be a failure, and it was this short view which, because of his own personal involvement, was to present itself in vivid colours to the boy Henry.

In the autumn of 1497 when Henry was six, the Cornishmen rebelled again, this time in favour of that other duke of York, Peter Warbeck.

By July 1497 King James IV of Scotland had decided that his guest was an unprofitable embarrassment. He provisioned a ship with wine, beer, ale, beef, mutton, oatmeal and bread, provided the 'duchess' with a new set of clothes and the 'duke of York' with his monthly pension of £112, and at the beginning of July sent him to try his luck down south.

Warbeck landed near Land's End in Cornwall on 7 September with three ships, a hundred men, and two standards that recalled with startling symbolism Warbeck's tale of his childhood escape from his brother's murderers. The first bore the image of a little boy coming out of a tomb, the second that of a boy coming out of a wolf's mouth. These were carried before Warbeck's tiny army with a third which bore the red dragon of Arthurian legend. The Cornish were angry at the massacre at Blackheath, the royal fines and taxation, and by the time the pretender reached Bodmin, they had swollen his force to three or four thousand men. Ordering Lord Daubeny to lead an army into the West Country, Henry VII arranged to follow it in person, doubtless delighted that he at last had the chance to capture this nuisance of a pretender, this thorn in the Tudor flesh. But in fact the royal army did not even have to fight; fear of its coming was enough to make the rebellion collapse. The king arrived in Taunton to find that most of the Cornish had deserted, while Warbeck himself had fled from his own camp in the middle of the night. When his hiding place, the sanctuary at Beaulieu in Hampshire, was revealed, the king sent soldiers to surround the monastery, then offered Warbeck a pardon if he would give himself up. With his escape to the sea cut off, Perkin had no choice but to agree.

With a last attempt to assume the dignity of a prince, the 'duke of York' discarded the coarse habit in which he had tried to conceal his identity for a gown of cloth-of-gold. But his attempt to impress was in vain, for Henry Tudor had shown his usual cool attention to evidence. Arriving at the lodgings of the king in Taunton and received by an assembly of nobles who had known Edward IV's second son, Warbeck was asked by the king in their presence if he had ever seen any of them before. Surrounded by hostile faces, trembling for his safety, Perkin was forced ignominiously to say no, then to write out and sign a confession giving details of his bourgeois origins in Tournai, the humble names of his parents, grandparents and schoolmasters, and a complete account of his unaristocratic upbringing. Henry VII ordered the document to be printed and nailed up on church doors throughout the kingdom. Young Henry cannot have failed to see copies of his rival's very pleasing confession near Eltham Palace, while drinking in at the same time all the reports he could of Perkin's humiliation in the West Country.

The king was determined to destroy the myth that Edward IV's second son was still alive. Continuing westward to Exeter, he exhibited Perkin, suitably labelled and described by criers, to the people who lined the route. To the Cornish the king showed his usual mixture of mercy and greed. He executed a few leaders as an example, then spared the lives but not the purses of most of the rest, who suffered the usual punishment of heavy fines.

We do not know when the little duke of York first set his blue eyes on the flesh and blood 'duke' who for so many years had menaced his safety, but it was probably when his father returned triumphantly to London. The royal children would almost certainly have been allowed to watch from the gabled window of some convenient house when on 28 November Perkin was led on horseback through Cheapside and Cornhill to the Tower, followed by a trussed-up figure in the hooded gown of a hermit; before joining Warbeck, this man had been one of the king's servants, and he had tried to disguise himself.

The gates of the Tower opened and closed on the 'hermit'. Warbeck was led slowly back along Cheapside to Westminster Palace, through crowds who stared as though he were a monster and threw curses at this low-born foreigner who had dared to invade their kingdom. The 'hermit' and a man called Edwards, one-time servant to the queen and another of Warbeck's followers, were hanged for having been untrue to the oath of loyalty they had sworn on entering royal service.

But the king allowed their leader to live; it was not necessary to commit the distastefully violent act of actually killing him. For King Richard IV was dead. Only a foolish youth called **Perkin** lived on at court at the king's expense, one of the court freaks, a curiosity to be wondered at like Joan the Flemish giant and the foolish duke of Lancaster, and that earlier pretender Lambert Simnel, keeper of the king's hawks. Although he was not allowed to sleep with his wife, and was accompanied whereever he went by two guards, in other ways Perkin led a comfortable life. At night he had a bed in the royal wardrobe, the great store room where close stools, tapestries, linen and other furnishings were kept, and during the day young Henry saw him, accompanied by his two guards, wander more or less as he chose in the precincts of the palace, a final example of the king's scorn for the pretender whom he had always dismissed as 'the boy' or 'Perkin'. Warbeck, a threat for so long, was suddenly a ridiculous object to six-year-old Henry, who at last had the comfort of knowing there was only one duke of York: himself.

The two Cornish risings so close together, however, had left my lord of York with more than an unchallenged title; they had left him with the firm conviction that to be lenient is dangerous.

CHAPTER 6

'Merry Skelton'

'The honor of Englond I lernyd to spelle.'
John Skelton

———————

So the six-year-old boy destined to rule emerged safely from the shadows of rebellion and death that had threatened his father and mother, his brother and sisters and himself. But he did not emerge unscathed. The events of his early years had left him emotionally unbalanced, egotistical, with a deep sense of insecurity, a tendency to suspicion and paranoia and an intensely jealous, competitive streak, characteristics that were still masked by the appeal of early childhood, enhanced by Henry's own intelligence, vitality and good looks. This was the boy whose life and education now came to be dominated by a most extraordinary and exceptional person.

A tutor with high moral standards, who understood his charge and set him a good example, might have corrected some of the worst developments in Henry. But although he had high ideals and was in many ways a jolly, likeable personality, the eccentric priest and poet appointed to the job was an unfortunate choice. John Skelton could be delightfully kind and complimentary to those who pleased him, especially children, but he was also vain and quarrelsome, quick to sense a slight and to revenge it with all the vituperation in his poetic vocabulary. For us today it is hard to see how the royal family could have appointed as tutor a poet who is best known for his ribald satires, his libellous attacks on Cardinal Wolsey in *Colin Clout, Why Come Ye Not to Court?* and *Speak Parrot*; for his bawdy denunciation of drunken women in *The Tunning of Elinour Rumming*; and for his delicately beautiful *Philip Sparrow*, a

83

THE MAKING OF HENRY VIII

poem of great charm and sweetness written for a young girl
whose tame sparrow had been killed by the cat, but a poem
which is nevertheless also sprinkled with salacious innuendoes.
This shocking, fascinating humour gave birth to a number of
apocryphal stories which, published as *The Merry Tales of
Skelton*, turned him into a burlesque figure and alleged that
among other disreputable actions he had kept a wife illegally.

The Skelton who gave rise to these scandalous tales, however,
had not yet emerged when the royal family first considered him
as tutor for the duke of York; at the time none of the more
outspoken satires had yet been written, and he seemed exceptionally suitable, particularly to Margaret Beaufort whose
opinion was paramount with the king and whose protégé
Skelton seems to have been. He was a little pompous, a little
prickly, that was all. Everything they knew of his past was
acceptable. Born about 1460, Skelton had risen in the world
through his outstanding poetic gifts and his mastery of the
newly fashionable classical Latin. He had been crowned with
laurels by no less than three universities – Oxford, Cambridge
and Louvain – and he was an internationally famous poet.
Invited to court by 1489 – probably through Margaret Beaufort,
for whom he had translated *La Pèlerinage de la Vie Humaine* –
he had joined Pietro Carmeliano, the Gigli brothers and Bernard
André in the group of poets who burst into songs in praise of
the Tudor king, his family and policies at politically apposite
moments. He had penned an elegy on the death of the earl of
Northumberland, murdered by rebels on 28 April 1489. And
he had translated numerous Latin works into elegant English.
By 1498 he had also become a priest.

Skelton's piety would have appealed to Margaret Beaufort
who by this date had become extremely religious too. With the
permission of her husband, she had taken a vow of chastity and
exchanged her richly-coloured robes for the nunlike attire of a
vowess, a simple black gown relieved only by the pleated white
lawn of her gable head-dress. A scholar herself, fond of translating French writings and often lamenting the fact that she had
never studied Latin as a child and so could understand little

more difficult than church Latin, Skelton's scholarship would have appealed to her. Skelton was not only a brilliant Latinist, he was also the best of the court poets, far better than Bernard André who was Prince Arthur's tutor. And only the best would do for Margaret Beaufort's second grandson, to whom she once referred in a letter to the king as 'my lord of York, your fair sweet son'.

Major decisions affecting the children were not made by Margaret Beaufort alone, but after consultation between her, the king and Elizabeth – although Elizabeth's opinion seems usually to have been ignored; not unkindly – she was simply less forceful and able than her husband and mother-in-law. Unlike Margaret Beaufort, Henry VII was not interested in scholarship for its own sake, and his reasons for favouring Skelton were bound to be more political. In those days of high child mortality he had to face the possibility that Arthur might die prematurely and that, should this unhappy event occur, Henry must be ready to fill his place. There is no evidence at all for Lord Herbert of Cherbury's statement in his biography of Henry VIII, published in 1649, that Henry was educated for the Church: quite the contrary. When he was still very young arrangements were made in case he should become heir to the throne, as we can see from his great-uncle Jasper Tudor's will signed on 14 October 1496. Jasper left his possessions to Henry with the proviso that, if he became prince of Wales, everything should be transferred to the king. A boy second in line to the throne could not be allowed to take a vow of celibacy; and the suggestion that Henry was intended for the Church is puzzling. It may perhaps have resulted from Dr William Parron's astrological prophecy in 1502 that Henry would become a 'bonus ecclesiasticus'; although in the context this word can mean little more than churchman. Or it may have resulted from a belief that the intensive education Henry received was at that time given only to clerks. But at the turn of the fifteenth century attitudes to education were changing, and Henry VII may well have been influenced by the humanist theory that learning could create the ideal prince. More important, he also knew from personal experience that learning could be most useful, for Latin was the *lingua franca* of educated people from all countries and increasingly the language of diplomacy. He himself often had to rely on his Latin secretary to translate what was going on around him; he intended his sons to be more independent. But practicalities apart, learning was becoming fashionable for young noblemen at European courts, and like many successful fathers who themselves have grown up lacking educational advantages, the king wanted to see his sons have them all.

John Skelton had seemingly been promised the post of tutor to the king's second son by the time of his creation as duke of York, for rushing into Latin verse to celebrate the occasion, the poet already referred to the child as 'a brilliant pupil'. Translated below, the fulsome words of this court panegyric show that at this date Skelton was still a conventional and altogether acceptable royal servant. The three-year-old Henry was not only a 'delightful small new Rose' but also 'half-god, born of kingly stock', Skelton wrote, elaborating in words that flattered to the skies:

My muse, if you have any of the art of the laurel-decked god who plays the sweet-sounding lyre, pray pluck the string and, beloved of the sisters, tune the lyre's notes in songs about the fragrant Rose. There grows from the red rose-bush a fair-flowering shoot, a delightful small new Rose, worthy of its stock, a noble Henry born of famous line, a boy noble in the nobility of his father: and furthermore a brilliant pupil, worthy to be sung as such, whom his mother's rank has ennobled too. See, a new Ebrancus,* crowned with deserved honour, in whom the north believes it has its Hector. Though he be young he is a glorious son. In his tender years his noble nature flowers: neither Narcissus nor Hyperion's son can, if I am judge, outdo him in his rosiness.

Greetings, half-god, born of kingly stock, whom I must

* Legendary founder of the city of York.

celebrate with muses' song; while the spindles of destiny spin out my threads, my muse will sing your greatness.

Skelton's enthusiasm sprang partly from loyalty to the royal House and partly from excitement at the dizzy station in life that his talent had enabled him to reach, but he was also to develop a possessive fondness for the little boy in his charge, a feeling that would turn to jealousy when the 'brilliant pupil' became king and Wolsey took over the post of chief counsellor. It seems that Skelton's affection was to be returned by his pupil, for as a grown man Henry would rescue his discarded old tutor from obscurity and bring him to court, flatter his vanity by giving him the title of *Orator Regius* (Orator Royal) and a green-and-white gown embroidered across in gold silk with the name of the chief muse, Calliope, in recognition of his service to poetry.

In his priest's black gown and round black cap, Skelton probably moved into the duke of York's household in the year 1498, when Henry reached the age of seven; for this was the age when contemporary educationalists believed that a high-born boy should be taken 'from all company of women' and given a tutor, to live with him and be in charge of both his moral and his intellectual education. It was the time too when Henry would be forced to say goodbye to his nurse, kind, resigned Anne Oxenbrigge. Although she had never been a perfect substitute for his mother, parting with her must still have been a wrench.

A boy of Henry's age and ability at this date could by now read and write on parchment, using a swan's pinion feather or, for finer writing, a crow's; he knew some French and some Latin, and had been taught obedience to his teacher, since a bundle of birch twigs was as much part of a schoolmaster's basic equipment as were his rare and precious books; there is no mention of royal whipping boys in the fifteenth century.

Skelton, however, seems to have been a gentle enough tutor, determined to instil his own delight in literature into his pupil, and determined to prove the humanist theory that learning was the path to virtue. By educating a potential ruler, he saw himself as blazing a new trail in the history of mankind: later he would take pleasure in boasting that he had been Henry's 'master . . . in his learning primordial'. The subjects Skelton taught were the conventional ones, consisting of the seven liberal arts, beginning with the trivium – Latin grammar, Latin rhetoric and logic – and continuing with the quadrivium – arithmetic, geometry, astronomy and music – and finally culminating in the study of theology, but his teaching methods had more to do with humanism than with medieval custom. Skelton taught Henry his lessons in English, himself writing a special grammar book for the purpose. Incredible as it seems to us today, the use of the vernacular for all teaching purposes was a revolutionary new idea. Until the close of the fourteenth century children had learned their Latin in French, and now at the end of the fifteenth century Latin was still the medium of all but the most elementary education. But Skelton had a special affection for English. Alone among the court poets he was to write most of his poems in the vernacular rather than in Latin or French, and he generally used, not the conventional Latinate constructions, but colloquial words and phrases that the poorest English labourer could understand. Henry's future pithy use of English owed much to John Skelton.

In yet another teaching method Skelton was revolutionary. Unlike most able pupils of his age, Henry did not have to slog hour after unrelieved hour at his Latin grammar. Skelton also read to him the Latin poets, as his own verse tells us:

> *The honor of Englond I lernyd to spelle,*
> *In dygnyte roialle that doth excelle . . .*
> *I yaue hym drynke of the sugryd welle*
> *Of Eliconys waters crystallyne,*
> *Aqueintyng hym with the Musys nyne.*

Skelton did not wish to create a mere pedant; he wished to fashion a man of refined taste, imagination and feeling, and in the two former, if not the latter, he was successful. After the Latin poets, Skelton read with his pupil the famous Latin historians, for the humanists believed that the lessons of history were essential for the making of the perfect prince, and Skelton was not the man to miss the opportunity he had here for instilling his own political opinions into the king's son, his passionate desire to root out the abuses in Church and state, while at the same time preserving the basic institutions. Bearing in mind Henry's future attitude to the Church, it is not far-fetched to perceive that in this, as in other attitudes, Skelton was, as he described himself, Henry's 'creaunser' or creator.

Unfortunately for the development of Henry's character, it was not only through formal lessons that Skelton was to influence him: Henry lived in the climate of Skelton's personality, since a tutor shared much of a pupil's day. As a guide to what this was like, we have the curriculum laid down by Edward IV for his eldest son. The day began with matins at about six o'clock – for everyone then rose earlier than they do today; then Mass in the chapel, then breakfast. On days of special Church feasts he and most of his household had to listen to a sermon as well. After breakfast he had lessons until dinner, which was as early as ten o'clock (or eleven o'clock on Fridays and other fast days, when fish instead of meat was served).

During dinner there were 'read before him such noble stories as behoveth to a prince to understand'. After dinner he returned to his lessons, then went to take part in or watch 'all such convenient disports and exercises as behoveth his estate to have experience in'. Then followed evensong, supper at four o'clock, succeeded by 'all such honest disports as may be conveniently devised for his recreation'. Having risen early, he also went early to bed, the curtains being drawn finally around the oaken four-poster at about eight o'clock; for an older child bedtime was postponed to nine.

Henry would have shared some of his lessons, his meals, religious services and some of his recreation with his sisters, Margaret and Mary, and with John St John, Lady Margaret's great-nephew, who now lived at Eltham; but although the

king believed in educating his daughters almost as well as his
sons, there were many lessons which their different ages would
have made it impossible for them to share. As for John St John,
he seems, though his birth date is unknown, to have been
considerably younger than Henry. So the king's second son
can be assumed to have spent much of the day alone with
Skelton, exposed to the influence of his eccentric character and
the bubbling salty flow of his English speech.

John Skelton was not, of course, Henry's only teacher: there
were those who taught him specialist subjects. There was the
French master, Giles Dewes. There were music masters who
taught him to sing and to play the lute. The king bought a lute
for his second son for 13s. 4d. in 1498 when Henry was only six,
suggesting that his musical talent had shown itself early.
(Eventually Henry was to become expert in all the musical
instruments of his day, as well as knowing musical notation
and theory at a time when most people could play only by ear.)
And there was a dancing master, for boys as well as girls had
to learn to contain their natural energy and awkwardness in
the 'serene and graciously undulating' *basse danse*. In this
'queen of measures' they learned to take tiny neat steps near the
ground, alternately bending the knees, then rising on the toes,
transferring weight from one foot to the other, while dancing
slowly two by two and side by side across a room to a French
tune: *Filles à Marier, Le Petit Rouen, Hélas, Madame, L'Amour de
Moy* or *La Gorrière*. Since the children were soon to dance well
enough to give a display at court, the dancing master's lessons
must have been frequent.

Finally there was one man in Henry's life who was part
junior tutor and part companion, a young nobleman who lived
on and off at the palace, and whose chief function apparently
was to instruct Henry in the gentlemanly accomplishments of
which the obscurely born Skelton knew nothing. William
Blount, Lord Mountjoy, pronounced the French way, was
thirteen years older than the duke. His birth was suitably high;
the first Lord Mountjoy, his grandfather, had married Anne
Neville, aunt of Edward IV, sister of the Kingmaker and widow

of Humphrey Stafford, duke of Buckingham. He was well connected; his step-father was the earl of Ormond. And his family
had a tradition of service to the king; one of his ancestors, Sir
Walter Blount, had been slain in the battle of Shrewsbury while
wearing King Henry IV's coat armour to mislead the enemy.
His grandfather had been treasurer of England under King
Edward IV, and his father had been lieutenant of the castle of
Hammes, jointly with his brother James Blount, and captain
of the castle of Guisnes in the pale of Calais. James Blount, who
had been actually in charge of Hammes when Henry VII invaded
England, had been the first official to declare against Richard III.

As well as this blue-blooded ancestry, Mountjoy had exceptional urbanity and presence, as we can see from his regular
selection by Henry VII as part of the welcoming committee on
important diplomatic occasions. His predeliction for women –
he was to marry four times – suggests that he was attractive,
and from a letter written by Erasmus in 1511 we know that he
was modest and serious-minded, avoiding the constant round
of dice and revelry indulged in by many young men of his rank,
while at the same time doing everything expected of a nobleman. Watching him, Henry could learn how to wear rich
clothes, how to behave gallantly to a lady at a banquet, how to
gamble, not too dangerously, at tennis and bowls, chess and
cards, and how to play at gleeke or click-clack, using cards
adorned with columbines, rabbits, roses and pinks. This elegant
lord was perfectly fitted to devise 'honest disports . . . for his
recreation'.

But Mountjoy was more than just a graceful courtier; he also
helped Henry with his lessons, particularly history, which he
read with Henry at the king's special request. While still only in
his teens, Mountjoy was an accepted member of the brilliant
English humanist circle which included Thomas Linacre,
William Grocyn, John Colet, and young Thomas More, still
reading law at Lincoln's Inn, but already known for his wit
as 'honey-tongued More'. At the age of eighteen Mountjoy
had studied in Paris, attended by a fellow of Queen's College,
Cambridge, and his own chaplain, and had become patron of

the renowned scholar, Desiderius Erasmus of Rotterdam. At the age of nineteen he had married his first wife. Mountjoy had the aristocratic *savoir faire* and knowledge of the world that Skelton so clearly lacked.

It was through Mountjoy as well as Skelton that Henry developed a veneration for learning and learned men that was soon to impress no less a scholar than Erasmus himself, and it is through Erasmus that we catch a revealing glimpse of the duke of York aged eight, while Skelton was his tutor. Erasmus was staying at a house belonging to Mountjoy's family near Eltham when two other members of the English humanist circle, twenty-one-year-old Thomas More and a fellow lawyer named Arnold Edward, came to visit him. As it was a fine morning More suggested that they should walk over to see Lord Mountjoy at the palace. Erasmus agreed, unaware that the visit had been carefully arranged beforehand.

The party crossed the moat and traversed the Great Court. Erasmus entered the hall to find not only their host's servants, but also the royal children, lined up to receive the famous scholar, Henry assuming pride of place with extraordinary maturity and poise.

'In the midst stood Prince Henry,' Erasmus noted, 'having already something of royalty in his demeanour, in which there was a certain dignity combined with singular courtesy. On his right was Margaret, about eleven years of age . . . and on his left played Mary, a child of four. Edmund [the latest royal baby born on 21 February 1499] was an infant in arms . . .'

Henry clearly dominated even his elder sister Margaret, and Thomas More, always good with children, treated him like an adult, paying his respects to him and then presenting him with some writing. Erasmus, chagrined that he had not also something to offer, promised to remedy the omission, but later he was further discomfited when, as he sat at dinner in the palace, a messenger brought him a peremptory note from this exceptional eight-year-old: the duke of York looked forward to receiving something from the great Erasmus's pen.

The child's challenge filled the Greek scholar, in his own words, with 'vexation and shame', and on his return to Lord Mountjoy's house sent him hurrying to his desk for three days of fevered composition.

It was the beginning of a fondness for humanist scholars that led Henry in early manhood to surround himself with men such as Colet, Linacre, Pace and, most loved of all, More – men of a calibre far above most of King Henry VII's poets. But it was a fondness which, like many other relationships of Henry's, had a sombre end. More, like Cardinal Fisher, Anne Boleyn and Katherine Howard, was to be executed by Henry's order; and for the dark development in Henry which made such a betrayal of friendship and love possible, Skelton cannot be held blameless.

For the poet tutor who had such a good influence on Henry's intellectual development had the opposite influence on his moral character. Skelton tried to instil a sense of moderation into young Henry, who had inherited his grandfather Edward IV's sensual passions and uncontrolled rages. He preached to Henry that his head should rule his heart, reason and a sense of proportion govern impulse and passion. He quoted to him Aristotle's words to Alexander the Great:

> You have defeated your enemies: you have annexed many kingdoms; you have subdued many empires; you have acquired sovereignty of the entire East: but all the same you have neglected to control, or have been unable to govern, the small domain of your mind and body.

This was Skelton's most deeply felt ideal, one that he doubtless voiced often, dominating the palace room from his high-backed chair behind the desk, while his royal pupil waited with hidden impatience for the too often repeated lecture to end. If only Skelton had put his principles into practice. Young Henry could not take his teacher's moral precepts seriously when he had before his eyes his teacher's contradictory example, a man full of paranoiac hate for the many enemies he made, and seething with a wild, uncontrolled vengefulness that seems scarcely contained by his poetry and leaves a bitter taste in the mouth even today.

The idealistic part of Skelton gave Henry admirable advice, as in this passage translated from *Speculum Principis*:

> Shun gluttony . . . do not deflower virgins . . . do not violate widows . . . choose yourself a wife and love her always . . . do not forget a kindness . . . listen to the other side . . . do not be niggardly . . . keep your word . . . think much, speak little, listen freely, be slow to argue . . . be always gentle, kindly, calm and humble . . . sympathize with the unhappy . . . give money to the poor . . . learn compassion . . . learn pity . . . maintain justice . . .

But there was another part of Skelton that wrote quite differently. Engaging in a poetic duel with Sir Christopher Garnish, one of the many men who had offended him, Henry's tutor wrote violently:

> *Tyburne thou me assynyd,*
> *Where thou xulddst haue bene shrynyd;*
> *The nexte halter ther xall be*
> *I bequeth yt hole to the . . .*
> *. . . ther thou xuldyst be rachchyd,*
> *If thow war metely machchyd.*

Far from listening to the other side and being slow to argue and compassionate, as he recommended his pupil to be in *Speculum Principis*, Skelton rushed at his own enemies, flinging himself into poetic invective of the utmost brutality and coarseness:

> *. . . behynd in our hose*
> *We bere there a rose*
> *For thy Scottyshe nose,*
> *A spectacle case*
> *To couer thy face . . .*

Though written after he had left Eltham Palace, these verses reveal a savagery that was already part of John Skelton when he was royal tutor and which he was accidentally to instil into his royal pupil instead of his ideal of moderation. There was, however, an even more sinister aspect of Skelton's character which was to leave its print on Henry.

The poet was as vicious to the women he disapproved of as to the men. Although, as we can see from *The Garland of Laurel* and *Philip Sparrow*, Skelton was attracted by young girls, he had taken a vow of celibacy; and he was always quick to see the blemish in the forbidden fruit. Even Jane Scroup, the heroine of *Philip Sparrow*, was not to escape his attacks. When she complained of the salacious innuendoes in this poem, Skelton retaliated by reproaching her for ingratitude and praying in a violent spurt of Latin verse that Philip Sparrow's fate might seize upon all his critics. He delighted to show up apparently respectable women as whores; so vicious were Skelton's attacks that one 'honourable gentlewoman' was driven to send this enemy of her sex a dead man's head 'as a token', a parcel that young Henry may well have seen unwrapped since it was probably sent while the poet was at Eltham Palace.

Henry's tutor was particularly preoccupied by fornication and adultery. Even the prettiest of his lyrics, *My Darling Dear, My Daisy Flower*, which Henry would often have heard sung at court, has this canker at its heart; for it is no cheerful little piece about true love, as the title suggests – it is a tale of betrayal and a girl with two lovers, the first lulled to sleep with his head on her lap.

> *Ly styll, quod she, my paramoure,*
> *Ly styll hardely, and take a nap . . .*

But the tenderness and pretty words are a cold-hearted ruse. As soon as her lover is 'all drowsy dreamyng, dround, in slepe', she is up and away, to another tryst by the river.

> *The ryuers rowth, the waters wan;*
> *She sparyd not to wete her fete;*
> *She wadyd ouer, she found a man*

That halsyd [embraced] her hartely and kyst her swete:
Thus after her cold she cought a hete.

A woman in the fifteenth century was regarded as inferior to her man; her husband was her 'lord' or 'head'; fornication and adultery were condemned by the Church and so were acceptable targets for the satirist. But Skelton's preoccupation with sexual sin went far beyond the contemporary pattern: women to Skelton were either goddesses or whores and sluts.

Later, in idealistic, erotic adolescence, Henry would read romantic literature full of gallant indulgence to the erring female, and this too would have a strong influence. But when infatuation wore thin, it was Skelton's voice rather than Chaucer's or Malory's that Henry would listen to, *Mannerly Margery* rather than *Cressida* or *Guinevere* that he would think of. King Henry VIII's treatment of his wives clearly owes much to Skelton's influence on him as a child.

Skelton's poetry has been described as 'a pitchy torchlight', a mixture of intellectual brilliance and dark prejudice. In this ambience his pupil was to live for more than three years, from the age of seven to eleven. They were the years when his father's policy was changing, becoming more ruthless, more pragmatic; and throughout this time it was Skelton's bitter tongue that counselled and interpreted for the growing prince.

When in November 1499 the king finally made a cruel decision, it was Skelton who waited beside his son to interpret the royal ethics. The boy Henry was about to receive his first lesson in political murder.

CHAPTER 7

'One Man Should Die'

'It is expedient that one man should die for the people
and the whole nation perish not.'   *William Parron*

———————————

THE little duke of York worked hard, but he played hard also,
according to the pattern of life in Tudor England which was
brightly varied by numerous holy days and seasonal celebrations when work was forgotten and both courtiers and commoners disported themselves, having first, of course, attended
the appropriate church service. Shrove Tuesday was given up
to merrymaking, cock-fights and throwing at cocks in royal
park and on village green alike, while the advent of May was
everywhere celebrated with the gathering of hawthorn boughs
and dancing round the maypole. Steel clashed and trumpets
sounded in royal tournaments throughout May and June, and
a bonfire blazed at court on Midsummer Eve. And when
palace festivities palled there were plenty of others to enjoy in
the world outside. In the summer in London on the evenings
before Church feast days, each man's door was garlanded with
flowers and herbs and lit all night by an oil lamp, and rich
citizens invited passers-by to sup with them at tables outside
their houses; while at court on feast days themselves, instead
of dining as usual in his private apartments, the king presided
over a banquet in the great hall, a banquet sometimes open to
all comers. August and September were occupied by hunting,
and Christmas lasted for twelve days.

As he grew older and more presentable, the duke of York,
with his sister Margaret, attended court celebrations more
often. They had been staying at Sheen for Christmas 1497 when,
at nine o'clock on the night of 21 December, flames suddenly

swept the rushes on the floors of the royal apartments and crackled up the costly wall hangings. Six-year-old Henry and Margaret, aged eight, roused from their beds, fled with the rest of the household into the garden, leaving precious carved furniture and gold-threaded tapestries to twist to ash in the fire. So Sheen for the second time in its history became a blackened ruin and the Tudor family had one palace less, but there were plenty more. Henry henceforward visited the court at Westminster, Greenwich and Windsor, although his base was still Eltham, with Margaret, Mary and Edmund, the new baby brother born when Henry was seven. In April and May 1498 the duke of York was staying in the same palace as the king and was often in his company, as we can see from the royal expenses. They list for these months 'to John Flee for a tippett of sarcenet for my lord of York 4s. 4d.', rewards to my lord's minstrels, including his lutanist, and 'the king's losses to my lord of York 6s. 8d.' – my lord of York had clearly won at cards; this was also the occasion when his father, fond of music himself, bought him a lute. These items from the royal account books illuminate for us the little duke's visits to court, intervals when he could taste the joys of family life, when his father would make time to play with him and talk to him, and his mother must have spent many hours in his company.

But this safe, loving atmosphere was confined to his immediate small family circle only. Outside, all around, danger lurked, danger from his other relations. When Henry rode, confident and precocious for his few years, through the gateway of one of the great palaces, he was greeted by a bevy of smiling uncles and aunts and cousins, the men in fur-lined surcoats and thick gold chains, the women in silk, satin or velvet gowns and jewelled head-dresses; but however fond their attitude to him, he knew that this was no ordinary cosy family gathering. Children are sensitive to atmosphere, and even while accepting their presents and joining in their games, Henry had quickly learned to be on his guard; these sumptuously dressed lords and ladies were part of the vast quarrelsome clan spawned by King Edward III. Who knew what jealousies and thwarted ambitions lurked beneath their silken clothes as they danced and dined and tourneyed at court, attended royal christenings and funerals, and formed flattering reception committees for visiting ambassadors? For some of these lords and ladies had a hereditary claim to the throne as good as or better than the king's.

The Tudors had altered their place in the hierarchy, made them slip a precious notch in importance, in rank and precedence. At no time was this more obvious than on the evening of a feast day when the king took part in the ceremony of the void, an elaborately formal fifteenth-century drinks party in which sweet wine in large covered cups and plates of spiced dainties were served strictly in order of rank. The king, the queen, the king's mother and any royal children allowed to stay up for the ceremony, were each presented with a gold cup by his or her own personal servant: everyone else was simply handed a cup by the king's usher. The royal privilege was not allowed even to the queen's young sisters who were often at court: twenty-nine-year-old Cecily married to Viscount Welles; twenty-three-year-old Anne married to the earl of Surrey; and nineteen-year-old Katharine married to Sir William Courtenay – King Edward IV's daughters. Two of these young women might once have reigned over a kingdom. Cecily had been promised to the king of Scotland and Katharine to the king of Castile, while Anne, according to an agreement made in 1498, was to wed Philip, archduke of Austria, son and heir of the Holy Roman emperor, Maximilian. Now they were mere subjects, walking in procession after their eldest sister who alone had become a queen. And Anne had another reason for bitterness as well: Anne's husband, the earl of Surrey, Henry's uncle by marriage, had not yet recovered the lands and title forfeited on the death of his father, the duke of Norfolk, while fighting for Richard III at Bosworth.

One of Henry's cousins was the magnificent duke of Buckingham, with his retinue of red-and-black-liveried servants. How often as he yielded precedence to the duke of York, son of Henry Tudor, did this proud and reckless nobleman recall his

own royal lineage, direct descendant through the male line of
King Edward III's fifth son, the duke of Gloucester? A dashing
performer in the tournament, Buckingham would have caught
the little duke of York's attention; and as he cannot have failed
to notice, this cousin was dressed almost as richly as the king.
Buckingham was accustomed to high places. His mother had
been the sister of a queen, Edward IV's Elizabeth Woodville. His
father had played a role in the Wars of the Roses almost as
significant as that of the famous Kingmaker; he had first
helped to place Richard III on the throne and then raised
rebellion against him. He had even planned to seize the throne
for himself before deciding to support the Tudor claim.

Another cousin of Henry's, and another dashing competitor
in the tournament, was Edmund de la Pole, later summed up by
the chronicler Edward Hall as 'stout and bold of courage, of wit
rash and heady'. Although he was the son of King Edward IV's
own sister and of John, duke of Suffolk, Edmund had been
brought so low by the advent of Henry Tudor that he could not
begin to afford Buckingham's gorgeous display. Like the earl
of Surrey, he had lost not only the family money, but also its
most illustrious title; it was the king's punishment for the
support by Edmund's elder brother John, earl of Lincoln, of
Lambert Simnel in 1486. When the old duke of Suffolk died,
Edmund was obliged to pay £5000 to inherit some of Lincoln's
forfeited lands and agree to settle for a mere earldom instead of
the dukedom he was heir to; and at court he was so constantly
and humiliatingly reminded of his loss that even a small boy
could see clearly how Edmund had fallen in the world. As a
duke he could have sat at a state banquet alone with the king
and a bishop. As an earl, if he shared the royal table, he must
be accompanied by another earl, his rating for this purpose
exactly half as good as a duke's. His scarlet parliament robe
had only three rows of ermine instead of four like the dukes'.
And when the king 'took spice and wine', in the ceremony of the
void in his great chamber, Edmund's cup was placed below
Buckingham's on the cupboard. Precedence, the duke of York
knew, to a fifteenth-century nobleman was worth even more

than money: the loss of it was equated with loss of honour. Of King Edward III's descendants Edmund de la Pole, earl of Suffolk, aged about thirty-two in 1498, had the greatest cause of all for harbouring a grudge against the Tudor power.

But there was yet another near relation with good reason to hate the king – Thomas Grey, marquis of Dorset, Elizabeth Woodville's son by her first marriage and so half-uncle of the little duke. The king had never trusted the marquis since he agreed in 1485 to leave the band of exiles in France to return to England and make peace with Richard III. Suspected of favouring Lambert Simnel, Dorset had been imprisoned in 1487. And after his release, the royal agents seized most of his lands with the proviso that, if he kept out of trouble, these would be returned to his heir on his death; the king also took possession of his eldest son's wardship and marriage, which were saleable commodities at that date.

As a further insurance against disloyalty, the wretched marquis was made to give a recognizance promising to pay nearly £1000 should he fail to fulfil all the king's conditions, and as sureties he had to find friends willing to put up between them nearly £10,000. Although by August 1499, two years before his death, Dorset had recovered most of his lands and been released from the bond, he had been tortured with financial threats for years.

Dorset's persecution was no isolated royal whim: it was part of the king's policy to put his nobles in desperate fear of being penniless and thus losing the means to support their rank, not only for their own generation but also for their children's. When the king told the Spanish envoy, Don Pedro de Ayala, in 1498, 'It is our intention to keep our subjects low, riches would only make them haughty,' he was thinking mainly of his wife's relations.

For every one of them was either a potential rival to the Tudors, or the parent of a potential rival – so much the pattern of history made clear even to a child of Henry's age. Yet these were the 'great estates' of England; their place was high in the hierarchy of society and government. The king placated and employed them; these were the people whom men respected, and he needed their support. He needed them in procession and pageantry and on the field of battle; he needed them to serve him at state banquets and underline with their titles his own magnificence. He needed the queen's sisters to attend the royal babies in the glittering grandeur of their christening ceremonies; Buckingham and Surrey to lead his armies; Buckingham and Suffolk to compete in the tournaments.

But Henry had one male cousin who was still not at court. His father's threshold of tolerance was high, but not high enough to benefit Edward, earl of Warwick; he was too near the throne. Before this son of Edward IV's brother Clarence, the king's policy of conciliation, backed with the threat of financial ruin, stopped short. One of his first actions after winning the battle of Bosworth was to send a messenger with urgent orders to the castle of Sheriff Hutton in Yorkshire – where Richard III had imprisoned the ten-year-old earl as well as Elizabeth of York. Elizabeth was to travel down to London in an eye-catching procession to take up her abode with her mother; the boy to be hustled south secretly and imprisoned in the Tower.

Although he had committed no treason and was indeed reputed to be too dim 'to tell a goose from a capon', Warwick's mere existence was a threat, as the duke of York knew well. In 1487, four years before his own birth and within only two years of his father's coronation, this cousin's name had been used to inspire Lambert Simnel's rebellion. Had it been successful, the carpenter's son almost certainly would have been replaced by the real earl of Warwick, perhaps under the protectorate of the earl of Lincoln. Simnel's forces had been defeated but the idea of rebellion lived on, as did the idea of using Warwick as its figurehead.

Since Henry VII's accession, Warwick had been seen outside the Tower only once, when he was paraded through London to prove Simnel's imposture; but the Yorkists were not deterred. Young Henry had seen Perkin Warbeck's printed confession admitting that when he arrived at Cork in 1491 the Irish reponsible for his rebellion had first suggested that he should pretend to be the earl of Warwick; only after much discussion had they decided on an impersonation of Richard, duke of York, instead. Warwick's innocence and dimness made no difference. While he lived, it was becoming clear by 1498, plots would continue to multiply. Even the boy Henry could scarcely escape such conclusions, surrounded by a family and relations who were chief actors, heroes and potential victims in the drama; and a tutor, Skelton, intensely interested in politics.

But by this year when Henry was seven, it was not so much the fear of losing his throne that aged his father with worry – though that was a fear he never lost – as the obstacles that these plots placed in the way of two ambitions. Henry VII wanted alliances with Scotland and Spain, cemented by a marriage between his eldest daughter Margaret and King James IV; and a marriage between his eldest son, Arthur, and the youngest daughter, Catherine, of King Ferdinand and Queen Isabella. If you were one of the royal family, the duke of York discovered early, your spouse was chosen for primarily political reasons. Although no marriage alliance had as yet been proposed for him, he was surrounded by talk of the desired matches for his elder brother and sister – an engrossing concern of his parents when he visited them; an equally irresistible subject for gossip among his attendants at Eltham.

Alliance with Scotland could prevent the ever present danger of the traditional stab in the back should the king lead English armies abroad, and alliance with Spain would enormously increase his status. It would be recognition that Henry Tudor was no transient monarch, but the founder of a new royal line, sire and grandsire of future kings, and it would discourage pretenders to his throne as well as providing him with an ally against the might of the two other European giants, France and the Hapsburg dominions. Many of his father's problems were too complicated for a little boy's understanding – his trade bargaining with the Netherlands, for instance, and his attempt to contain French territorial ambitions while avoiding war – but the Spanish marriage was a simpler issue. The ups and downs of the negotiations were a dominating feature in the dramatic landscape of Henry's childhood, and they would later affect his own choice of wife and his own attitude to marriage.

The prospect of the Spanish match inspired the king with special enthusiasm. It had originally been proposed several years before his second son was born. When the Spanish ambassadors first arrived in England and announced that they had power to negotiate the marriage, King Henry 'opened his eyes wide with joy', then burst out singing *Te Deum Laudamus*. Afterwards he had personally conducted them twelve miles from London to admire the prospective bridegroom, who was less than two years old, first naked and afterwards asleep. The Spaniards agreeably discovered 'such excellent qualities in the prince as are quite incredible'. All that remained was to settle the terms, in particular the amount of Catherine's dowry and the date of her arrival in England.

By September 1498, two treaties had been signed with Spain and the prince and princess had been twice betrothed, but the haggling still continued. The succession of pretenders and rebellions reminded the Spaniards of the unfortunate fates of Richard III, Edward V, Henry VI and Richard II. As one ambassador had put it in a softly courteous voice in 1488: 'Bearing in mind what happens every day to the kings of England, it is surprising that Ferdinand and Isabella should dare to give their daughter in marriage at all.' In vain the English commissioners for the alliance protested that there was not a drop of blood in existence from which any danger might arise. There was the earl of Warwick and, still unlaid, the ghost of Richard, duke of York.

Henry VII was fortunate in having an ally in the resident Spanish ambassador, Rodrigo de Puebla, a doctor of law, who believed fiercely that Spain would benefit by the English marriage and was utterly committed to it. The duke of York had often seen the little doctor who was a familiar and risible figure at court, kept so short of money that he had to live in 'the house of a mason who keeps dishonest women' and come to the king's hall to eat – while boarding his servants free in a convent of the Carthusian friars. He would emerge from the privy chamber shaken by furious royal protests at the latest Spanish terms, or cunningly flattered into smiles. And since Henry's mother, as well as his father, was obsessed by the marriage negotiations with Spain, the child cannot have failed to sense the echoes and to long also for the arrival of his Spanish sister-in-law who would make his family so much more secure, a seal of their greatness and a rare prize. Henry knew, if only subconsciously, that he too would gain in status from the marriage: if it ever took place; for unlike their ambassador, Ferdinand and Isabella kept an open mind on the subject. Already in 1497 they had gone so far as to treat secretly with Warbeck, offering him asylum in Spain.

After the pretender's capture in September 1497, the king's state seemed in the words of a Milanese envoy, 'most stable, even for the king's descendants, since there is no one who aspires to the crown', and Arthur appeared a more desirable marriage prospect. But this happy situation did not last long. One summer night in 1498, tired of being the prize court curiosity, Peter Warbeck escaped through the open window of the King's Wardrobe, leaving his guards asleep. It was the first of a trio of events that, happening in the two years after Warbeck's defeat, must have seemed to the duke of York to threaten rebellion all over again, and that when he thought of them later on would encourage him to execute his own enemies straight away. On hearing of Perkin's flight, the king at once despatched riders to scour the road, and boatmen to search the river; for two days they hunted frantically. When on Tuesday 12 June the abbot of the Carthusian monastery of Sheen (just across the river from Sheen Palace) arrived at Westminster with news of the fugitive, Henry VII immediately sent a gentleman of his bedchamber to the Spanish doctor. And De Puebla who had, significantly, omitted to inform his monarchs of Warbeck's flight, there and then lifted his quill to tell them of his capture. The pretender, he wrote, was safely secured in the monastery; at his desperate prayer, the abbot had come to beg for his life.

The request was granted – for the time being. Even the merciful Henry VII, however, would put up with no more alarms caused by Warbeck. While he continued to live – which would not be long – he would do so behind a locked door. But first the king once more put Perkin on public view as a subject for ridicule; he devised the kind of display that fifteenth-century Londoners relished, a scene of grotesque symbolism. The duke of York may well have watched this show himself, but if not, he would soon have been given a complete description – for his rival's punishment was typical of the black sense of humour of the age, the kind of cruel joke that Henry was taught by his contemporaries to enjoy.

In the courtyard of Westminster Palace carpenters built a high platform such as Warbeck would have sat on had he realized his ambition, but this was no carpeted honourable eminence nor was it crowned with a regal chair and canopy of state. This dais was ludicrously made of wine casks and hogsheads, in one of which Perkin was said to have hidden on his way to Cornwall on sighting an enemy ship. The platform was topped by the stocks. Here on Friday those crowds who might have started new rumours that he was indeed the son of King Edward IV saw the wretched pretender stand, a butt for refuse and mockery for most of the morning.

The following Monday, from ten in the morning until three in the afternoon, Warbeck stood in similar stiff discomfort at Cheap. From there he was marched under strong guard to the Tower and shut in a cell where he could 'see neither sun nor moon'. When he was taken to court in August and exhibited to a Flemish ambassador, the handsome, healthy youth imprisoned a few weeks before looked a pale, broken thing; and De Puebla, who was present, reported, 'He is so much changed that I and all other persons here believe his life will be very short.' He added cruelly if philosophically, 'He must pay for what he has done.'

While the 'pretended duke of York' suffered in his dungeon, deprived of exercise and light as well as hope, the seven-year-old real duke had history lessons in the gilded, tapestried rooms at Eltham Palace. And just at this important stage of his development, when the windows of his understanding were being thrown open, he was presented with the living spectacle of a king who abruptly changed his policy. For instead of the mocking clemency which Henry's father had hitherto shown to claimants of his throne, he suddenly used severity founded on a travesty of justice. And, as the intelligent child would see too, this new, cunning and sinisterly realistic policy was to be immediately and startlingly successful.

The king was prodded into ruthless action by the threat in 1499 of yet more trouble from two further pretenders. At the beginning of the year, as frost still limned the trees in Eltham park, there came news of a youth on the borders of Norfolk who claimed he was the earl of Warwick escaped from the Tower. Apart from a priest who preached his cause from the pulpit, he had as yet no adherents, but this time the king would take no risks. Having personally examined the boy and ascertained that he had no allies, Henry VII handed him over to the law; for this pretender there was to be no ridiculous but safe job as a turnspit. The boy, whose real name was Ralph Wulford, nineteen-year-old son of a cordwainer dwelling at the Bull in Bishopsgate Street, London, was tried and promptly condemned to death. He was hanged on a gibbet at St Thomas Watering, where he dangled in shirt and hose from Shrove Tuesday until Saturday, when sickened passers-by complained of 'annoyance'.

The Wulford incident disturbed the king out of all proportion to its seriousness. And in the weeks that followed, the duke of York might well have noticed the change in his father: the endless pattern was beginning to haunt him. Would the procession of pretenders go on for ever? Would he, like his predecessor, die violently, dispossessed of everything?

The Tudor mask of cool wisdom slipped; for once the man beneath was visible. Even De Puebla noted, 'The king has aged so much during the last two weeks that he seems twenty years older.' As superstitious as any of his contemporaries, Henry VII secretly consulted a famous prophet, a priest who had accurately forecast the deaths of both King Edward IV and King Richard III – the priest forecast that his life would be in danger all that year. It was a prophecy that seemed confirmed within a few months. Suddenly in the summer of 1499, when the duke of York celebrated his eighth birthday, Edmund de la Pole fled from England. The immediate cause was hurt pride. He had killed a man in a quarrel and been pardoned, but he had been indicted for the offence before an ordinary court of justice instead of before his own peers, and for the already humiliated Edmund this last withdrawal of aristocratic privilege was too much. Now he was on the continent. Would he take up arms against the Tudor king? Was he following in the footsteps of his brother John, earl of Lincoln, who fled to Burgundy before openly rebelling under the banner of Lambert Simnel? As yet this Yorkist sprig had made no aggressive move and no claim to the throne, but his flight was deeply worrying.

Henry VII closed the ports – so that even patently innocent men, like Erasmus, found it difficult to leave the country – and he sent out emergency orders. Edmund's associates were to be examined; all those who had accompanied him to the coast were to be put under house arrest; any suspicious person found close to the coast must be arrested likewise. And the king despatched two fair-spoken envoys, Sir Richard Guildford and Richard Hatton, to attempt to persuade the fugitive to return. At the same time, he resolved to rid himself for ever of all possible pretenders he could lay his hands on in England.

The scheme was simple. And it would certainly have been transparent to Skelton and to his pupil; for Henry was reading the English chronicles which were full of similar problems all resolved in ways no less distasteful than the one his father adopted now. Peter Warbeck, the arch escaper, was moved into a cell beneath the earl of Warwick; two former followers of Warbeck's were appointed his attendants. If the king also hired an *agent provocateur*, as has been suggested, this was an unnecessary embellishment. Soon the two young men were communicating and by mid-November there was proof of a treasonous plot. On Saturday 16 November Peter Warbeck and John Walter, the mayor of Cork, who had been a prime mover in the imposture, were arraigned in the White Hall at Westminster – before Lord Mountjoy among others – and were condemned to a traitor's death.

On Thursday 21 November the duke of York's cousin, Edward, earl of Warwick, pathetic object of the exercise, stood before his peers in Westminster Hall. He confessed to treason, submitted to the king's grace and mercy and heard his judgement pronounced by the earl of Oxford: a traitor's death. On 23 November Warbeck and Walter were drawn on hurdles to Tyburn, where the pretender mounted the scaffold and made a short speech repeating his confession of 1497 and taking it upon his death that he was not the son of Edward IV. On 29 November young Henry's cousin, aged twenty-four, was conducted to a scaffold on Tower Hill and there beheaded.

It had been as ruthless an act as any of the murders committed by the Plantagenets – and as useful. It was the solution to the problem of rival claimants to the throne that had been forced on monarch after monarch, even though these claimants were close relations. The sole difference was in the method: Henry VII's was cleverer. Not for him the mysterious death in the Tower, followed by a scandal that painted him a villain. That, he decided, was a role his victims should play. He had made Warwick's death seem legal punishment for treason, punishment that could take place for all to see in the light of day.

Murder, judicial or otherwise, was unattractive, yet for a ruler there was a certain justification. In October, weeks before Warwick had been proved guilty, the Italian court astrologer, Dr William Parron, had summed it up: 'It is expedient that one man should die for the people and the whole nation perish not, for an insurrection cannot occur in any state without the death of a great part of the people and the destruction of many great families with their property.' The same argument was voiced by other renaissance writers whom the duke of York would later read; for a king, Henry was forced to observe, ethics were not the same as for his subjects.

Murmurs of discontent at this execution of a prince in the flower of his youth soon died. But the effect of the murder lived on: a great deliverance. For the rest of Henry VII's life no battle would be fought on English soil. And the Spaniards were finally convinced that a Tudor prince offered a desirable alliance and a stable future for their daughter.

On 11 January 1500 De Puebla wrote to King Ferdinand and Queen Isabella:

> After kissing the royal feet and the hands of your highnesses, I cause you to know . . . this kingdom is at present so situated as has not been seen for the last five hundred years until now . . . as appears by the chronicles; because there were always brambles and thorns of such a kind that the English had occasion not to remain peacefully in obedience to their king, there being divers heirs of the kingdom . . . Now it has pleased God that all should be thoroughly and duly purged and cleansed so that not a doubtful drop of blood remains in this kingdom, except the true blood of the king and queen, and above all, that of the lord prince Arthur.

By March 1500 a treaty of alliance between Spain and England had been concluded and confirmed, and Ferdinand and Isabella had promised to send Catherine in about the month of May, although she did not in fact set out until the following year, when arrangements for the Scottish marriage between King James IV and Margaret Tudor were also finally under way.

On 25 August 1501, when Henry, duke of York, was ten, fifteen-year-old Catherine finally set sail for England in one of Spain's great rolling carracks.

CHAPTER 8

The Princess of Spain

'And after them rode the princess upon a great mule
richly trapped after the manner of Spain; the duke of
York on her right hand.'

MS in the College of Arms

———

By July 1501 the king had decided where his second son should
live when he was grown up. In making his decision Henry VII
clearly had in mind Arthur's safety when he should become
king and the civil wars that had arisen in the past, figure-
headed by an ambitious younger brother. The young duke's
main dwelling, Henry VII decreed, should be in Derbyshire, too
far away for him to be tempted to interfere in government.

So, for the then lavish sum of £1000, the king bought for him
Codnore Castle, built by the lords Grey in the thirteenth and
fourteenth centuries, surrounded by extensive lands and manors
and the customary deer park. At the same time, retainers who
had previously proved themselves loyal and efficient in Margaret Beaufort's blue-and-white livery were being promised a
post in my lord of York's increased household. For the king's
brother would keep a vast establishment when he grew up,
ruled over like the king's by velvet-clad officers with white rods:
chamberlain, steward, treasurer and controller. Over the many
courses of dinner, brought in in solemn procession by servants
in his colours of blue and tawny, he would preside in his hall
from a throne-like chair under his own canopy of state. Only if
the king visited him would he forfeit this seat of honour. For
my lord of York would be very grand indeed, but not quite as
grand as Arthur, and certainly not as powerful. So in the summer of 1501 Henry's resplendent but limited future seemed

firmly established.

But one bold and extraordinary man was not so sure. On 28 August 1501 in Eltham Palace Henry's tutor, John Skelton, wrote a short treatise in Latin of advice on how a king should rule; he entitled it *Speculum Principis* and presented it, not to Arthur, who was heir to the throne and about to marry the Spanish princess, but to the duke of York. Skelton's gift, hand-written in black and crimson and gold, and enclosed in leather adorned with a Tudor rose and angels, and stamped with the royal arms, can still be seen in the British Library today. At the time the gift seemed a rudely inappropriate gesture. True, in the text Skelton addressed both princes, but that did not take away from the tactlessness of his having treated Henry, as well as Arthur, as a future ruler. For Henry could become king only through successful rebellion or by Arthur's death, both of which appeared at the time most unlikely.

Arthur was cast in a smaller, narrower physical mould than Henry, but there is no suggestion at this date that he was ailing; had there been, the Spanish monarchs would not have agreed to his marriage with their daughter. Skelton's belief that Henry would inherit the throne seems to have been the result of wishful thinking born of nothing more substantial than an ambition to share vicariously in his pupil's glory.

But his vision of his pupil's future greatness had concrete effects. A younger prince, taught that he could one day become heir to the throne, could not but end by regarding his elder brother as an obstacle in his way. Living under different roofs for many years, the two boys were already estranged; Henry had probably long been jealous, and in the ceremonies about to take place in the autumn of 1501 there would be plenty to stimulate his jealousy. By mid-October the duke of York was at court.

King Henry VII had built himself a palace like a 'second paradise', fully worthy of the Spanish marriage alliance that was about to take place. On the ashes of burnt Sheen had risen Richmond, named after the earldom that the king had lost when he was a child. It was a many-storied, rose-red brick and stone creation of towers, pinnacles, and gilt-and-azure weather-vanes of the royal arms, and it incorporated an even more wonderful invention – running water in the king's chambers. Every known device to delight the senses was included: the ceilings of the royal apartments were painted azure between the timbers and adorned with the Tudor roses and Beaufort portcullises picked out in gold; and the bay windows opened on to 'most fair and pleasant gardens'. Wide paths were adorned underfoot with 'marvellous beasts . . . properly fashioned and carved in the ground, right well sanded and compassed in with lead'; the paths were bordered on either side with the fashion-able 'knots' of low fragrant bushes and herbs in elaborate patterns. At the lower end of the garden were butts for archery and 'houses of pleasure', in which to play chess, dice and tennis; and rambling decoratively here and there among the pleached alleys and fountains, were 'many vines, seeds, and strange fruit'.

In this renaissance palace ten-year-old Henry was staying with his parents when the messenger arrived with the long-awaited news from the coast: 'Your Grace, the princess of Spain has arrived at Plymouth.' Not since Henry V conquered France and wed the French king's daughter had there been an English marriage of such grandeur. It was exciting news for the whole court, but particularly so for the duke of York; because the king had decided that his younger son should accompany the Spanish princess on her ceremonial entry into the heart of his kingdom, the walled city of London. For Henry it was to be a double milestone in his growing-up – when he first felt to the full the intoxicating adulation of the crowd and when he first drew close to the girl who was to play such a crucial part in his own life.

The arrangements for the wedding were pressed ahead with speed and the pageantry was to draw in the whole royal family. No time was to be allowed Catherine and Arthur even to grow used to each other's appearance; had they not for years ex-changed stilted love letters in Latin? And was that not enough? They were to be married in St Paul's Cathedral as soon as

Catherine, travelling slowly to recover from an almost disastrously rough sea passage, could reach the capital, which since May had been preparing for her reception.

The day after the news of her arrival, King Henry with an escort of nobles, wrapped in thick capes against the pouring rain, rode out of the gates of Richmond Palace to meet the princess on her way from Plymouth. Riding post from his castle in the Welsh Marches, Arthur met him at Easthampstead, whence they rode over Salisbury Plain to Dogmersfield, where the princess rested.

Having satisfied himself that Catherine was a fit wife for his favourite son, heir to the kingdom which he had conquered by might and brain, and that Ferdinand the Catholic, more aptly nicknamed Ferdinand the Fox, had not tricked him, the king rode back to Richmond on 9 November to reassure his queen and prepare for the next stage of the ritual. He had brought back with him the prince of Wales. That same day Arthur, now a slim, fair, tallish boy of just fifteen, rode up Fleet Street 'with a goodly escort', through Ludgate into the city, to take up residence in the King's Wardrobe, a building which was conveniently almost in the shadow of the great spire of St Paul's. On 10 November 1501 the king and queen also took up residence close to the cathedral, in Baynard's Castle on the north bank of the Thames.

On 12 November it was my lord of York's turn. Over hose, shirt and pourpoint, attendants helped him into a fur-lined coat with a heavy gold chain over the shoulders. Henry's clothes denoted high rank at a time when rank was universally respected (for Edward IV's sumptuary laws had forbidden the wearing of certain colours, rich materials and furs to men below a certain social status); so instead of the self-conscious discomfort of a modern ten-year-old, Henry felt a satisfying vanity. Tall and brawny though he was for his age, he still resembled a renaissance angel, his pink and white face just touched with hauteur by the incipient Roman nose, his auburn hair curling nearly down to his shoulders, and all of him

radiating vitality and good humour. His mount was no less
magnificently dressed than he in gold bit and gold jewel-
encrusted stirrups, its trappings flowing back below knee
and hock as Henry's gold spurs made the horse leap forward.
Accompanied by the archbishop of York, the duke of Buckingham, the earl of Surrey, the earl of Kent and many other lords,
Henry rode to St George's Field on the south bank near
Lambeth Palace where Catherine was staying.

It is not difficult to guess the boy's thoughts as he waited
there for the princess of Spain. Mingled with the excitement of
his role in the pageantry, his delight in the open air and the
feeling of his splendid well-schooled horse beneath him, would
be a pricking dart of envy at his brother's good fortune.
Marriage to this daughter of one of Europe's most powerful
monarchs. A girl who had left that sunny land and braved
shipwreck to reign as queen of England. A girl who had brought
with her in her procession from Plymouth down the country
roads of England wagons full of tapestries, fine clothes and
beautiful carved Spanish beds, as well as a sparkling collection
of jewels and plate for her dowry. In the competitive Henry lust
for other people's possessions was a basic trait, but Henry's
moods always appeared to wash over him quickly, so that no
one divined the dark feeling that often lingered beneath; now
he was agog to see this foreign princess from a country that he
himself might never visit.

Not only Catherine's country, but her parentage also was
wrapped in glamour. She was the daughter of the formidable
Isabella, queen in her own right of Castile, who, married to
Ferdinand, king of Aragon, had united Spain, and had herself
ridden with her army to battle against the Moors and thrown
them out of Spain. When he grew up young Henry would
write music, lyrics and a 'tragedy'; his imagination was
always keenly romantic although inevitably blunt concerning
people's feelings.

From Lambeth Palace came the sound of a Spanish tune
stirringly played by trumpets, shawms and sackbuts. Abruptly
Henry brought his mount to a decorous standstill. Like some

marvel from mythology, the procession came in sight – gold chains, fine silks and velvets of English lords vying in splendour with Moorish brocades of Spanish dignitaries, and in the centre rode the princess herself, small for a grown girl, with an air of courage. Not for Isabella's daughter the shining gold-and-white litter provided by King Henry. She was perched on a high, cushioned side-saddle on a huge, gorgeously caparisoned mule, a broad-brimmed hat on her head, shaped like a cardinal's hat, above a carnation-red coif, a gold lace under her chin; and her long, light auburn hair hung loose down her back. Behind her, Spanish and English ladies rode in pairs, each facing a different way like book-ends; but the Spanish ladies' hair flowed loose under broad-brimmed hats like Catherine's, while the English ladies wore conventional gable head-dresses. All were gowned in brilliant cloth-of-gold, except for the princess's duenna who rode in black as befitted her solemn status. Behind these riders came the horse litter which Catherine had scorned, and chariots full of court ladies. Henry was at an age when most twentieth-century boys look with scorn on girls – but surrounded by this aura of rich strangeness, Catherine was no mere girl; she was a princess out of a magic tale.

The formal words with which the duke of York, aged ten, suddenly stiff and shy, greeted the princess of Spain, aged fifteen, have perished. They were probably learned by heart in Latin, for Catherine understood Latin but no English, and just a little French. So though she was now close to him physically and had, as we know from contemporary descriptions, an exceptionally sweet, friendly smile, the real Catherine was still mysteriously remote; Henry could communicate with her in only the most distant way. Much of Henry's feeling about Catherine, who was to be first the delight, then the bane of his life, can be traced to these first impressions of her.

The greetings over, Henry took up his place on Catherine's right and the procession set off again. They clattered triumphantly through Southwark and turned on to famous London Bridge, the street bordered with houses that spanned the river. Windows and archways were hung with tapestries and carpets; and crowds, almost as anxious to see my lord of York as the princess of Spain, pressed against the railings. Henry, relaxing against the high cantle of his saddle and smiling at the onlookers with adult ease, could see his magnificence reflected in their eyes, before becoming the next moment a little boy again, fascinated by the spectacle before him.

The city had prepared seven marvellous pageants, groups of allegorical figures standing on the many conduits that produced the city's fresh water or on any other spot which would elevate them above the crowd. But the pageants today had one recurrent theme which every now and then jarred the delight for a jealous ten-year-old. On the drawbridge itself stood a group of 'virgins in white', above them two 'saints'. In learned verse they announced themselves to be St Catharine, the princess's name saint, and St Ursula, one of Catherine's ancestors. Both these saintly ladies, the 'virgins' proclaimed, were descended, like Catherine herself, from King Arthur. Throughout the pageants the King Arthur theme, linking the most famous English hero with the bridegroom, would be heavily accented.

A remarkable small figure in the centre of the procession, Henry rode beside Catherine on and up Gracechurch Street. Everywhere there were cheering crowds and pageants which the citizens had prepared for months, with the help of their best versifiers and a great deal of gold, white, blue and red cloth and paint.

Opposite the Falcon Inn, carpenters had built a 'castle' in which stood Policy, dressed like a Roman senator, Nobleness, dressed like the richest courtier, and Virtue, inevitably yet another white-clad 'virgin'. Cornhill had been transformed. Here, where only a few weeks ago, on 28 September, a merchant sat in the pillory for selling short-weight coal, while his offending sacks were burnt beneath him, an archangel glittered and shone. On top of the conduit a representation of the zodiac showed 'the increase and waning of the moon with many other conclusions of astronomy'. Above stood the archangel Raphael with golden wings 'and feathers of many colours', while beneath sat King Alfonso the astronomer, Boethius the philosopher, and Job, the interpreter of God's will, each in turn declaiming the complex reason for his presence. Each in turn flattering and focusing attention on Arthur in a way the most generous-hearted of younger brothers would have found it hard to forgive. And generosity was never to be a marked trait in Henry's nature.

Near the end of Soper Lane in Cheap – now cleared of its market stalls and lined with richly draped railings and members of the city guilds – there was yet another tribute to Arthur. The great conduit ran with free wine and above was a 'celestial place', painted with the twelve signs of the zodiac, surmounted by a figure in a golden chariot who represented, as he explained in rhyme to the duke of York and Catherine, Arthur fully armed in justice.

But running through the pageants was another theme which was to colour Henry's view of matrimony with eventual tragic results for Catherine. The pageants celebrating her union with Arthur stressed its prime purpose: children and the continuation of the Tudor dynasty. No less a person than 'the father of heaven' put it bluntly as he sat enthroned at the Standard in Cheap, candles in golden candlesticks burning before him to represent the Catholic Church. In impressive tones and doggerel verse, he declaimed:

> Loke ye; walke in my precepts, and obey them weel,
> And here I geve you that same blissing that I
> Gave my wilbeloved children of Isarell;
> Blissed be the frute of your bely.
> Your sustenance and frutes shall encrease and multiplye,
> Your rebellours enemyes I shall put in your hand,
> Encreasyng in honour bothe you and your lande.

The father of heaven did not mince words: a queen's first duty was to increase and multiply. Young Henry was left in no doubt of that. He was left in no doubt also that Catherine would amply fulfil her task; she was desirable in every way.

The last pageant was perhaps the hardest for a competitive

younger brother to take. Unlike the other pageants which had
been designed and paid for by the city of London, it had been
especially ordered by the king at the huge cost of £100 and
stood outside the west door of St Paul's – a splendid image of
King Arthur in a tower. Henry saw it as he escorted Catherine
to the Bishop's Palace where she was to lodge until the wedding,
proof of his father's personal involvement and a painful
reminder that Arthur was his father's favourite.

Henry, however, was a fighter. In the marriage festivities
which now took place he would strive to outshine the heir to
the throne and succeed incredibly. For in descriptions of the
ceremonies it is clear that the duke of York played the more
prominent part.

It was the sturdy, cherub-faced, elaborately clothed Henry
who took the bride to church. Two days after the procession
through the city, he waited at the gates of the Bishop's Palace
while Catherine seemed to float towards him, wearing a wide-
sleeved gown of white satin flowing over the graceful graduated hoops of an early Spanish farthingale, her face misted by
a long white veil. The queen's young sister, Lady Cecily,
carried the train. Arm-in-arm and two-by-two, a procession of
high-born gentlemen preceded the bride; also arm-in-arm and
two-by-two, a hundred high-born ladies fell into place behind
her. As the minstrels struck up, young Henry took her hand in
his own perhaps suddenly shaky smaller one and led her to the
west door of the cathedral, where onlookers were packed even
into the rood lofts.

Slowly, with boyish steps, Henry led the romantically
mysterious princess along the aisle on a specially constructed
platform seven feet high. On and up to a still higher platform,
brilliantly carpeted in red, on which Arthur in white satin, like
a celestial figure from one of the pageants, waited to take
Catherine from him.

Watching the ancient ceremony and automatically translating the Latin words, 'in sickness and in health till death do us
part', did it occur to Skelton's pupil that his elder brother might
not live to inherit? The previous year in June Henry had seen

his little brother Edmund, aged just over one year, carried away in a black-and-gold funeral procession, like his sister Elizabeth. But Arthur was fifteen, and life-expectancy for a child increased with age.

When at last the wedding, followed by high Mass, was over, Arthur slipped through a door in the consistory and across to the Bishop's Palace to await his bride. It was his brother Henry who led her ceremonially from the church into the palace for the wedding feast which preceded the customary public bedding: a ritual which also emphasized for Henry the nature of a queen's first duty.

At about five o'clock in the afternoon the king sent the earl of Oxford 'to take the assay of the bed', a procedure that consisted of rolling a long stick-like implement over the four-postered expanse of feather mattress resting on 'litter', to ensure there were no bumps or – far worse – hidden weapons. Then the bed was decked out in the finest linen sheets, rich fur and velvet covers, and sprinkled with holy water. Led away by her ladies, Catherine was disrobed, veiled and 'reverently laid and disposed' in the marriage bed. To a merry tune of shawms, viols and tabors, a vast laughing crowd of courtiers escorted Arthur in his nightgown into the bridal chamber, where the music ceased while bishops ritualistically prayed for a fruitful consummation of the marriage. Henry was probably one of the half-ribald, half-awed party, and he would have heard Arthur's famed boast the next morning: 'Bring me a cup of ale, for I have been this night in the midst of Spain. Masters, it is good pastime to have a wife.' With such an introduction to Catherine, it is not surprising that Henry should see her as the perfect wife and queen, a vision which gained an extra glow of magic from the court entertainments that followed.

With the rest of the royal family after the wedding, he went by river to Westminster for more than a week of tournaments and banquets. Normally so careful with his money, the king had lavished it on this public display – part chivalric romance and part carnival – which ever afterwards was to be for young Henry the ideal outward face of kingship. The twenty-four-year-old duke of Buckingham rode into the tiltyard in a pavilion of white-and-green silk surrounded by Tudor red roses, this whole contraption carried by servants on foot wearing jackets of black-and-red silk. Henry's uncle by marriage, Sir William Courtenay, rode into the field enclosed in a red dragon – the manuscript does not explain how – led by a giant with a tree in his hand.

On the evening following the first day's combats Henry sat on the dais with his parents near a massive exhibition of the royal wealth, a cupboard with seven shelves, all shining with gold or silver-gilt pots. He watched a disguising whose theme was that knightly fantasy of love that was to surround him as he grew up and to set him searching in middle age for an impossible ideal. It was clothed, of course, in allegory.

Three floats entered and stopped before the dais. First a castle drawn by four fantastic beasts, a gold lion, a silver lion, a hart with gilt horns and an elk; eight fair ladies, four dressed in the Spanish fashion and four in the English, looked haughtily out of the casements of the castle, while in the turret at each corner a child sang. Next came a lady dressed like Catherine, in a wide-sleeved gown over a farthingale, standing on a ship in full sail from which descended two men: Hope and Desire, ambassadors – they explained in verse to the audience – from the Mount of Love to the ladies in the castle. Alas, their humble diplomacy was in vain: the ladies refused to listen to them, for a little suspense was necessary even in a disguising. Then in came the third float, the Mount of Love itself, on which stood 'eight goodly knights' brandishing banners. When the ambassadors explained that they had been spurned by the ladies, the knights exclaimed with fury and stormed the castle with sugar plums. The ladies graciously submitted, descended to the floor and danced with the victors; again the actors mounted their floats, which then withdrew from the hall.

This pretty device of love conquering all was followed by a wonderful chance for Henry to outshine his brother. The young royals were about to entertain the assembled courtiers.

In turn the children descended from the platform and danced to the dramatic music of fife and drum, first, of course, the heir to the throne. Arthur danced two of the stately, graceful basse dances with his young aunt, Lady Cecily. They returned to the dais and Catherine, with one of her Spanish ladies, danced in their place. At last it was young Henry's turn and he made the best of it. Clutching his sister Margaret by the hand, he came down from the platform, and the entertainment livened up. Determined to outdo everyone else, Henry danced so energetically that he suddenly flung off the gown that hindered him and danced on in his doublet and hose, a sight that delighted the onlookers and was to the king and queen 'right great and singular pleasure'. When he again sat down on the platform and the great cups of wine and plates of spiced cakes were passed, Henry had already set the mark of his own extraordinary vitality on the history of England, for the incident found its way into the official description of the wedding.

The celebrations came to an end with a final disguising at Richmond Palace, a spectacle even prettier than that of the first day. Into the hall packed with courtiers and ambassadors, trundled a chapel two stories high 'full of lights and brightness', drawn by sea-horses; on one side of the chapel was a huge painted mermaid, on the other a huge merman, and inside each of these legendary creatures a Child of the Chapel sang 'right sweetly and with quaint harmony'. From inside the chapel gallants and ladies flung white doves and coins; the courtiers scrambled for them.

The wedding was now over and the Christmas season approached. It was time for Arthur to ride off towards his castle at Ludlow with his bride; and for Henry to return to his strenuous lessons.

To protect the precious heir to the throne, a special carol had found its way into the court song-books. Young Henry probably sang it himself, forgetting his jealousy in the delight of hearing his clear voice rise and fall perfectly to the notes.

According to this song, Arthur (denoted by the ostrich feather badge of the prince of Wales) had a claim now not only to the thrones of England and of France but also to that of Spain.

> *Wherfore, good Lord, syth of thi creacion*
> *Is this noble prince of riall lynage,*
> *In every case be his preservacion,*
> *With joy to rejose his dew enerytaunce,*
> *His ryght to optayne,*
> *In honor to rayne,*
> *This eyre of Brytayne,*
> *Of Castell and Spayne,*
> *Ryght eyre for to be;*
> *Wherefore now syng we:*
> *From stormy wyndis and grevous wethir,*
> *Good Lord, preserve the Estrige Fether!*

Arthur's marriage and departure had underlined the wide gap in status between him and his younger brother. That winter of 1501 to 1502 Skelton's vision of his pupil wearing the crown seemed a mere frivolity and, despite the solemn words of this hymn, the future of 'the ostrich feather' looked far more secure than that of the duke of York. Arthur might become king at any moment, to judge by past history. Richard III had been killed at the age of thirty-three; Edward IV had died at the age of forty; Henry VII looked thin and old for his forty-four years and his sight was already failing. When his father died and Arthur succeeded, young Henry would exchange the comfortable niche of king's treasured son for a dangerous role.

Then Henry's superior gifts, his good looks, high spirits and popularity, would make him an object of suspicion. From his reading of the chronicles, he already knew how easily disaster could overtake a king's brother. His great-uncle George, duke of Clarence, handsome, popular, but unable to resist the lure of the crown, had been finally condemned as traitor and murdered in the Tower, drowned ingloriously in a butt of Malmsey wine. Richard, duke of Gloucester, faithful during Edward IV's lifetime only to usurp the throne after his death, had been in his turn betrayed and slain on Bosworth Field. To be a king's brother, Henry knew, often meant to become a king's uncle also, an even more hazardous role, a relationship that in the past had brought with it the dreadful choice: kill or be killed. Had Richard III not seized power, the queen's Woodville relations would almost certainly have disposed of him as that other duke of Gloucester, Thomas of Woodstock, had been disposed of – murdered it seemed by order of King Richard II.

To make life harder for him, Henry alone among the surviving royal children appeared unlikely to occupy a throne, for his father had arranged impressive marriages for both his sisters as well as for his brother. On 25 January 1502 in the queen's presence chamber in Richmond Palace the duke of York, with six-year-old Mary and a glittering audience of courtiers, saw Margaret 'married' to the king of Scots, with one of the Scottish ambassadors, Patrick, earl of Bothwell, dressed in a gown of cloth-of-gold, acting as proxy for King James IV. Henry heard the archbishop of Glasgow ask Margaret whether she was marrying of her own free will and Margaret lift her child's voice in reply, 'If it please my lord and father, the king, and my mother, the queen', followed by a hasty reaffirmation of his consent by Henry VII. Margaret was twelve, while King James IV was already in his mid-twenties and notorious for his many love affairs, but Henry had been taught that unhappiness was a small price to pay for such a great gain in status.

For six-year-old Mary an even grander marriage was in view. A match had been proposed for her with the infant Charles, heir through his mother Joanna to the kingdoms of Spain, and through his father Philip to Burgundy and Austria.

Although for three of his children King Henry VII's dynastic ambition had soared high, there was no future sovereign in sight for his second son; and so far only one marriage had been considered – to Charles's sister Eleanor, a fact that may have encouraged Lord Herbert of Cherbury to believe that the boy was intended for the Church. The lack of further marriage plans for Henry again underlined his inferior status. The king was in no hurry to make future trouble for Arthur by creating a rival branch of the royal family. As if to discourage the young duke from hankering after power that was unlikely ever to be his, in the early months of the new year 1502, there came a spate of political drama. Inevitably it involved close members of his family.

His cousin Edmund de la Pole, earl of Suffolk, who had fled across the Channel in the summer of 1499 after killing a man in a quarrel, had some months later made his peace with the king and returned to England. The summer before Arthur's wedding he had fled once more, no one knew why; and this time, ominously, he had taken his brother Richard with him. With Maximilian's agreement they had settled in Aix-la-Chapelle. Since the De la Poles, unlike the previous pretenders Warbeck and Simnel, had a real claim to the throne, they were a potential source of great danger. Maximilian gave them very little help, but he also refused to agree to Henry VII's request to extradite them. So King Henry VII could do nothing more than copy a medieval rite: at St Paul's Cross, Suffolk and six known confederates were publicly denounced as traitors, excommunicated and cursed with bell, book, and candle. But what of the unknown confederates?

The king suspected all Suffolk's friends, all his relations, anyone of Yorkist blood, and that included many of the most prominent courtiers. In March young Henry's uncle by marriage, Sir William Courtenay, he who had made such a sensational entry into the jousts that followed Arthur's and Catherine's marriage, was thrown into the Tower; with him went Edmund's brother, William de la Pole, and Sir James Tyrell, governor of Guisnes in the pale of Calais, who had sheltered the pretender when he fled first in 1499. Sir William Courtenay, attainted for treason the following year but spared the axe, would not set foot outside the Tower again until after King Henry VII's death in 1509. William de la Pole would remain in the Tower until his death thirty-eight years later.

Tyrell, with a fellow traitor, Sir John Wyndham, would be executed in May 1502, after making, so it was said, a momentous confession: it was he who, under Richard III's order, was responsible for the murder of the two little princes in the Tower in 1483.

But before Tyrell's alleged confession there had occurred in young Henry's life an even more momentous event that removed the shadows from his future and flooded it with glorious light.

CHAPTER 9

'The Ostrich Feather'

'From stormy wyndis and grevous wethir,
Good Lord, preserve the Estrige Fether!'
Fayrfax MS

———————

IN the night of 2 April 1502 the gates of Richmond Palace 'of
double timber and heart of oak, studded full of nails right thick
and crossed with bars of iron', opened to a messenger with a
letter from the prince of Wales's chamberlain in Ludlow to the
king's council.

Arthur was dead.

The event that would wholly change the duke of York's
future was an agonizing and probably unexpected blow for
his father, although Arthur had been ailing since Shrovetide.
The council kept the prince's death secret until the following
morning, when as usual the royal confessor knocked on the
door of Henry VII's bedchamber. Alone with the king, the
friar raised his voice and intoned the pious words: '*Si bona de
manu Dei suscipimus, mala autem quare non sustineamus?*' (If we
accept good things from the hand of God, why do we not also
sustain misfortunes?) Then he told the king. Henry VII
insisted on hearing all the melancholy details of his son's
death – perhaps from the sweating sickness. And only when he
had dismissed the friar and imparted the sad news to Elizabeth
did this tightly controlled man allow his grief to show.

The queen, knowing where the sharpest pain lay, knew also
how to apply a healing balm. Even if Arthur was dead, on whom
all Henry's hopes had rested, his dynasty would continue, she
reminded him. 'My Lady, your mother, had never no more

children but you only and God by his Grace ever preserved you. God has left you yet a fair prince . . .'

Later in the morning the king had to remind his weeping queen of her own good counsel and they both knelt to thank God for the blessing that still remained to them – their fine young son Henry.

Was the boy present at Richmond Palace during this scene that sheds a softening light on the bronze effigies of Henry VII and his queen in Westminster Abbey? Regrettably, the chroniclers do not tell us, any more than they tell us what grief Henry showed at the news that his brother had died, aged fifteen, and was already embalmed with spices, and coffined. But behind any display of sorrow and the shock of losing yet another member of his family, there must have lurked joy. For when, after three weeks' lying in state, the funeral procession at last set out from Ludlow Castle, labouring through mud and rain to Worcester Cathedral, it carried with it the chief threat to young Henry's future: he was freed from the risk of his own premature death as rebel and pretender to the throne. As dirges were sung at the king's command in churches throughout England, who knows what glad tune sounded in Henry's heart?

No one any longer stood between him and the throne after his father's death. As for Catherine, she was not even pregnant. Indeed, her duenna, Doña Elvira Manuel, had written to Spain insisting that her mistress was still a virgin.

By the summer of 1502 when he celebrated his eleventh birthday, Henry had achieved the position of splendour for which nature seemed to have fitted him, although he would not be formally created prince of Wales for another two years. This late date is certain from the royal accounts which list for 23 February 1504 'to the heralds at arms for their largesse at the creation of my lord prince 100s.'. Only then would he be invested with the insignia of his new rank, the ring on the third finger of his left hand (a symbol, according to Margaret Beaufort's ordinance, that he was 'married to do justice and equity and to show right wisdom to all parties') and the verge of gold ('in token he shall have victory and deprive and put down his enemies and rebels'). And only then, so the parliament rolls for 1504 inform us, did he inherit the prince of Wales's 'great and notable possessions', while at the same time forfeiting to the king those that he had inherited as duke of York from Jasper Tudor. Henry VII, it seems, could not bear to take part in an earlier ceremony of creation for fear it might remind him too poignantly of the death of his favourite child. But in every other way the grieving father allowed his second son to slip almost at once into the empty place. The wording of a document dated 22 June 1502 is revealing: it granted 'to our dearest son Henry, prince of Wales, the office of guardian and capital judiciary of the forest of Gaultres in the county of York'.

And, of course, the extra flattery began at once too. Dr William Parron, who claimed that he could cure the new disease of syphilis as well as foretell the future, presented to the king a Latin horoscope of the new prince of Wales. Adorned with a map of the world (leaving out America) and illustrations of the influence of the twelve houses of heaven, it predicted wonderful things: the prince would be a devout churchman, a triumphant ruler and the father of many sons; his mother would live to be eighty.

Not for Henry the cloudy awareness of most boys who inherit titles and who, because their lives continue in the same way, scarcely realize the implications. Sixteenth-century etiquette made it apparent in every facet of his existence that he was the most important person in the kingdom after the king and queen. He now became the nucleus of a vast household – including gentlemen ushers, chaplains, footmen and guards – with proportionate appetites and attendant needs noted in the patent rolls; and a number of extra luxuries were added to his diet. Royal commissions were issued to purveyors of not only 'rushes, coal, fuel and straw, mutton, beeves, calves, pigs, small pigs and lambs, capons, pullets, hens, geese' and 'coneys', but also of 'swans, cranes, partridges, pheasants, larks and other fowls and all kinds of fish'; besides 'hay, oats, horsebread, beans, peas, litter and harbourage for the horses'. There can have been few empty rooms and little silence left round the courtyards of Eltham.

On his visits to court Henry's importance was marked by the gourmet aroma and long succession of dishes carried to his chamber. Only the meals of the king and queen were more expensive and cunningly cooked. To consume in his own private apartments he was supplied twice a day with no less than twelve loaves, six dishes of meat, eight gallons of ale and one 'sextarie' of wine – rations liberal enough, one would have thought, for an entire household – although it did not have to satisfy more than the prince himself and ten of his servants – ten being a mere fraction of his entourage, as we know from ordinances which allowed the prince of Wales twenty servants in the palace, ten of whom could eat in hall, while the rest of his household must be boarded outside the court.

This lavish increase in food, wine and servants was only one of the many signs of Henry's new status. Now when he went in procession to celebrate a Church festival he walked alone, like the king. And when his father generously licensed a rich subject to found a chantry – that is, to pay a chaplain to pray in perpetuity for certain people's souls – the list usually included the prince of Wales, as well as the king, the queen and the king's mother, before the name of the founder of the chantry. So as Prince Henry sat at his narrow sloping desk at Eltham – reading a handwritten vellum manuscript or book newly printed by Caxton – he could warm himself with the knowledge that he had been singled out for divine protection, that in chapels all over England priests earned their living kneeling on flagstones and lighting long white candles, praying for his salvation.

Apart from these recorded changes in Henry's life, there were inevitably many more. As heir to the throne he would one day have power to grant titles, estates and lucrative jobs. A man could make or lose his living by pleasing or offending a king; the right word, the right smile, a cap doffed at the right moment might make a man rich, while the wrong gesture might mean a loss of office or worse. Such power draws adulation even from men who do not mean to flatter, and the effect of becoming heir to the throne on the already vain, self-confident Henry was to make him even more egotistical.

But Henry's new importance did not bring with it any relaxation of routine: quite the reverse. His lessons increased with his elevation to prince of Wales, although the tutor whose lively ribald utterances entertained him was to be banished from his society.

John Skelton had at last been too tactless even for the tolerant Henry VII. His recently written allegory *Bouge of Court** was infuriating – in it, the poet had had the gall to portray Henry VII's courtiers as rogues, deceivers, flatterers and cheats, a view of the seat of government very different from the picture of sober worth that the king was trying so hard to paint. But this was far from being Skelton's only crime. His quarrelsome nature was by now as well known as his bawdy poems set to music. The popularity of such songs with certain courtiers did not make them suitable for a future king. Even such a royal libertine as Prince Henry's grandfather, Edward IV, had insisted that nothing but the most edifying language should be used in the hearing of his young heir, and Henry VII, as well as Margaret Beaufort, possessed a vein of puritanism that in part his son would inherit.

So after five years Skelton was dismissed from his post as royal tutor, given an extra forty shillings on top of his yearly stipend, and sent to Norfolk to become rector of Diss, a parish in the king's gift, where he was to write his most famous and shocking satirical poems.

Into his place in Prince Henry's household, with precious books and quills and a bundle of modest gowns, moved William Hone, a man so discreet that his personality has left no record at all on history. If Hone attempted to combat his pupil's excess pride his efforts were unsuccessful. This was a problem that Skelton, for all his faults, would have lost no time in

* Allowance according to rank of food, drink, candles and fuel.

tackling; as we can see from his poetic drama *Magnificence* with which in about 1516 he roundly took the king to task for indulging his fancy at the expense of common sense and moderation.

Under Hone's regime Henry rarely emerged from the schoolroom; his programme of study seems to have been interrupted only by sleeping, eating, religious worship and sports. There is no record of his ever having attended a council meeting, although occasionally he would act as witness to an official document. He set his signature on a charter to the earl of Ormond granting him the right to hold a weekly market and on a grant of certain revenues to the dean and canons of St Stephen's Chapel in Westminster Palace. His name appeared frequently on commissions for the peace, as Arthur's had from infancy, and also once on a commission of *oyer and terminer* at Westminster on 16 January 1503. But this was a formality only. It was not necessary for the prince of Wales in person to exercise judicial authority either at the sessions of the peace or at the court in Westminster to enquire into and punish more serious crimes.

But that did not mean that Henry VII was not preparing his son for government. The king subscribed to the sixteenth-century humanist belief that it was more important for a future ruler to learn the theory of government than to practise it; and that could be best learnt from books. So Prince Henry continued to study Latin grammar and literature, to pay lip service to the humanist ideals of peace, the importance of avoiding war, and the value of scholars.

To his knowledge of Latin, French and music, he was soon adding Italian, Spanish, medicine and theology, as well as three new subjects from the quadrivium, astronomy, geometry and arithmetic. Astronomy and mathematics were particularly fascinating subjects now that they were helping men to discover new lands across the seas – the West Indies in 1492, Newfoundland in 1497, Venezuela in 1499 – the first indications of a whole continent whose existence most of medieval Europe had not even suspected before.

As well as receiving instructions from Hone, Henry still enjoyed the company of Lord Mountjoy. This accomplished nobleman had become governor of Hammes in the pale of Calais in 1503, but he still spent much time in England, reading history with the prince and improving the boy's Latin composition by showing him Erasmus's letters, sent in hopeful profusion by the perpetually needy scholar to his patron. There is no doubt that Henry was given for special study Erasmus's essay in favour of marriage, originally written for Mountjoy when that nobleman had been a student in Paris.

In view of Henry's future six marriages this essay and the circumstances surrounding it are worth considering. Years later Erasmus himself would tell the story: after presenting the essay to Mountjoy, Erasmus had asked how he liked it. 'I like it so much that I have made up my mind to marry,' the young nobleman replied with enthusiasm, and when Erasmus pointed out that there was another side to the question, added with a smile, 'I pray you, keep that to yourself. I am quite content with the first side.' So without bothering to think them out, Erasmus simply tacked on to the original essay a few commonplace arguments against marriage and published the whole treatise, at Mountjoy's insistence, as an example of letter-writing in his book *De Conscribendis Epistolae*. Thus Henry, like Mountjoy, received the full force of the original argument for matrimony. When Mountjoy had married, and outlived, no less than three wives, Erasmus claimed only very limited responsibility, since it was easy, he insisted, 'to upset the coach on the side to which it already leans'. Erasmus's essay, reinforced by the example of Lord Mountjoy's amorous disposition, would help to upset young Henry's coach in the same direction.

Among his other studies Henry worked particularly hard at his music. There were two celebrated musicians at Henry VII's court, Dr Robert Fayrfax and William Cornish Junior, whose help he could call on; and he reached a high standard. Henry was himself to compose not only the words and accompaniment of a number of court lyrics but also two Masses which are still sung today. And he learned to play skilfully on the organ, lute and harpsichord, becoming indeed so versatile a musician that in 1515 a Venetian ambassador would describe him as playing 'every instrument'.

The new prince of Wales did not suffer this demanding if exciting course of study entirely alone. Apart from his sisters, Margaret and Mary, who continued to share the same roof with their newly elevated brother, and John St John, Lady Margaret's great-nephew, other boys and youths known as henchmen or children of honour, would share some of the prince's lessons and recreations.

These children of honour, chosen for their high birth, handsome appearance and manner, were used as pages and educated at the royal expense in 'grammar, music and other cunning and exercises of humanity, according to their births and after their ages'. Later at court they were promoted to other posts in the royal household. And when the time came, they would play their traditional role in the king's funeral and coronation ceremonies: they rode on great coursers, clad in mourning black or in blue velvet powdered with gold fleurs-de-lis, and bore the symbols of the king's achievement and titles.

Four of these boys, the prince's companions, varying greatly in age and background, were to play a key part in his life. Charles Brandon, some seven years older than Henry, was already in 1502 a young man. Impressively tall, black-haired and extrovert, Brandon was later to become the nearest to a best friend that Henry ever had. Henry would create him duke of Suffolk and even forgive him when he secretly married Henry's own sister. Two qualities made him specially attractive to the young prince: Brandon was a fine athlete and, as the son of Henry VII's standard-bearer killed at Bosworth, he was reassuringly unrelated to the royal family. Brandon was also an irresistible ladies' man and was to initiate Henry into at least one early amorous adventure.

Sir John St John, who was also not too closely related to kings, would continue to enjoy Henry's favour throughout his reign, becoming – according to his epitaph in Bletsoe parish church – guardian to one of Henry's daughters, the future Queen Mary, and chamberlain to the other, the future Queen Elizabeth.

But two other companions of the prince in his childhood would not be so lucky. Edward Neville, with his tall brawny physique, blue eyes and auburn hair, was so like Henry that they were sometimes mistaken for brothers. And as young men they would enjoy the same spectacular lively pastimes, competing in tournaments and dressing up in exotic costumes in disguisings, which often ended in dancing and the chance to chat up the prettiest girls at court. But Neville came of the rebellious blood of Warwick the Kingmaker. Henry would first knight Neville, then, when both were middle-aged, execute him for treason.

Neville was the particular friend of Henry Courtenay, who was first cousin to the prince and about five years younger. This little boy, son of the prince's aunt, Katharine, first joined the royal household in 1502. He brought with him into the peace of the schoolroom the spectre of rebellion and death; for his father was that Sir William Courtenay who, under suspicion of favouring the traitor Edmund de la Pole, had been suddenly arrested in March and thrown into the Tower, where he remained in danger of execution. Since the arrest the queen had supported her sister's children.

From the beginning the relationship of the two Henries was ill-omened. Each boy knew that his father's death might be caused by the other's father; yet some kind of friendship seems to have grown between them. For Henry when he came to power would release William Courtenay from captivity, restoring to him his hereditary title of earl of Devon, and also create Henry Courtenay marquis of Exeter. Not until many years later, in 1538, would the cousinly relationship reach its almost inevitable conclusion, when Henry Tudor signed the warrant for Henry Courtenay to die a traitor's death. It was a fruition for which the ground was already preparing in 1502. For at the age of eleven Henry Tudor learnt from Henry Courtenay a useful lesson, one he would remember all too well: how to live untouched by the sufferings of a close companion while he himself basked in fortune's warm golden beams.

Prince Henry's companions were not ideal. They introduced into his apartments a sense of troubles in the world outside. But some boys near his own age were necessary, not only for the prince's happiness, but also for his education in military skill, which now began to take up many of the hours that had been set aside for sport. King Henry VII had won his throne by conquest and was proud of it. His will instructed that when he died, a gold-plated image of him in armour was to be set kneeling upon a table of silver and gilt in the shrine of St Edward in Westminster Abbey, holding between its hands 'the crown which it pleased God to give us, with the victory of our enemy in our first field'. Henry VIII also must be prepared to fight, to defend his inheritance.

From early boyhood Henry had practised shooting with the longbow. It was time for him to learn to use spear, poleaxe and sword, the most important being the sword. Strong, sharp-pointed and between forty-five and fifty-five inches long, with a handle which a man could wield either with one hand or two, Henry would attempt in battle to thrust it through the chinks in an opponent's armour; and if this tactic failed, he would follow up his attack with the poleaxe, a long-handled axe with a sharp blade on one side, hammer-head on the other and often a spike on top, to make it even more deadly. The aggressive, competitive Henry, like all boys of gentle birth, was trained to kill.

He learned to fight on foot and on horseback, practising first by hacking and thrusting at a quintain, which was a man-high target set up on a post, sometimes in the form of a brightly painted Saracen's bust, with fierce black eyes and dangerous scimitar. (At the beginning of the sixteenth century it was not yet realized that Christendom would never again ride with holy banners on crusade.) Prince Henry gloried in such physical exercise and in the admiration his skill aroused, but fighting also appealed to the burgeoning romantic in him; for the real ugly purpose of weapon play was prettily wrapped in chivalry. To fight well was part of the ideal of knighthood embodied in popular medieval literature, in heraldry and the tournament. As a young man in years to come, Henry would genuinely see himself at times as the perfect knight – how brightly then must the ideal have burnt before his blue eyes when he practised sword-play, as an eleven-year-old, beneath an instructor's critical gaze in the royal park.

Soon Prince Henry knew the excitement of being fitted for his first suits of armour, gleaming plate armour in the smooth, rounded Italian fashion, that would enclose him from helmet top to broad metal toes – one suit for fighting on foot, another for fighting on horseback. The armourer's craft had reached its peak, the steel cunningly jointed to echo every movement and made as comfortable as possible, lined and worn over a doublet of leather or quilted canvas, a padded under-collar (or 'arming partlet') and a bolster at the waist. But even with these aids to comfort, wearing armour took practice; the prince had to learn to mount and dismount without assistance and to move swiftly under a weight of about sixty pounds, even when the sun made the metal torturingly hot.

Gleaming encouragingly before the prince as he sweated in his armour and battered at the quintain was the prospect of eventually playing the hero's part in the brilliant scene of the tournament, surrounded by trumpet notes and heraldic banners.

Tournaments were no longer staged only on special occasions. They were now part of the May and June festivities in Greenwich park, although the costumes of the combatants seem to have been less elaborate than those used for state celebrations. On 22 May on the wide lawn before the palace gates Prince Henry could see heralds erect a 'green tree' and, hanging from it on a green lace, a white shield. On this virgin surface two challengers wrote their names, and, with two gentlemen 'aiders', on every succeeding Thursday and Monday until 20 June, from six in the morning until six at night, they fought any men bold enough to answer the challenge by inscribing their names beneath.

The contests, which the ambitious young prince watched with excitement and envy on his visits to court, consisted of 'one cast with the spear . . . seven strokes with the sword'. And the opponents fought 'at the barrier', which meant through or over the top of a wooden fence, usually with blunted weapons. Fighting at the barrier, either mounted or on foot, was to become one of Prince Henry's favourite pastimes; but he also loved the joust with its sensational canter down the lists, bent fiercely over a red-and-white lance, in honour of some fair lady.

It would be some years yet before the heir to the throne would be allowed to risk himself in such a game. For although the lance* was not particularly heavy, to score a hit on an opponent needed lightning judgement, and for the man unlucky enough to be thrust by lance from his saddle, a painful and dangerous fall might follow. Meanwhile Prince Henry could practise by running at the ring – the popular test of skill which consisted of galloping towards an upright post with horizontal bar from which hung a detachable ring; this he would carry off, if he could, on the tip of his lance.

At the same time as he acquired these equestrian skills, the prince was developing his physical strength by 'casting the bar' and wrestling, both traditional knightly accomplishments. He was also perfecting himself in the less energetic courtly pastimes of tennis and bowling. For Henry VII believed in the renaissance ideal that a superior body added to a superior mind could create a whole superior man deserving of his subjects' obedience.

This almost remorselessly demanding programme might have broken another boy. Did he ever have time to play? But to Henry's competitive nature, each activity was something to be mastered, and in this there was pleasure; eleven is an age when a bright child can appreciate his exceptional

---

* It was held in the lance rest on the right side of the breastplate, while a long hook, stretching under the right arm, steadied the lance butt.

ability. Looking back on Henry's boyhood through knowledge of the grown man, it is impossible not to conclude that while the rigours of his education might sometimes have bored him, they mostly brought a happy sense of achievement, while his physical education and his music lessons he loved for their own sake. At the same time one can understand why, when he eventually became king, he spent so much of his days enjoying himself, delegating the tiresome details of government to his ministers.

Such was the pattern of eleven-year-old Prince Henry's existence when suddenly, in February 1503, while logs in the wide fireplaces filled the air with fragrance, tragedy struck his family yet again. His mother, the queen, died in child-birth, and her death made bleak Henry's happy winter world and scarred the emotional side of his developing personality for ever.

It was ten months now since his mother, the magnet of the boy's gentlest feelings, had comforted his father after Arthur's death by reminding him, 'We are young enough yet to have more children.' It was a suggestion that the king soon put to the test. By Christmas the broad-sleeved, black or crimson velvet gowns especially favoured by Elizabeth revealed that the thirty-seven-year-old queen was once again heavily pregnant. She arranged to 'take her chamber' at the splendid new palace of Richmond, an appropriate birthplace for the baby boy that she hoped would heal the king's grief.

On Saturday 4 February 1503 – Candlemas Day, according to the calendar then in use – the king and queen were staying in the royal apartments in the Tower of London. Henry VII had donned his velvet robes to join in the candlelit procession in honour of the Purification of the Virgin, although he did not so demean himself as to carry his own candle, which was carried instead, according to his mother's ordinances, by a gentleman of high rank on his right. The flickering light had scarcely faded into the darkness when, unexpectedly, weeks before her time, the queen's pains began. That night in the

Tower, chaplains murmured hopeful prayers in a nearby room while she was delivered of a girl, a frail child hastily christened Katherine in the chapel of St Peter Ad Vincula on Tower Green. Within a few days the queen herself was fatally ill. A week after the christening, in the morning of 11 February 1503, her thirty-eighth birthday, Elizabeth died. Katherine 'tarried but a small season after her mother'.

A mother's death is always traumatic for a young child. And although Henry had seen little of her in his early infancy, she had always been a gentle goddess-like figure in his mind; as he grew older and saw more of her, their mutual affection had grown too. Mother and son had in common not only their Plantagenet characteristics but also their powerlessness compared with the king and Lady Margaret Beaufort. To Henry, tossed by the waves from these busy domineering personalities, Elizabeth must have seemed a harbour of peace. Now this resting place had suddenly vanished. His mother, like his two brothers and his sister, was dead, and the drawn-out funeral rites perpetuated her death. Coffined in lead, then in wood, and draped in black velvet with a white cross on top, she lay in state in the chapel for eleven days, while in London priests interceded with the powers of heaven for her soul. The king had paid for no less than six hundred and thirty-six Masses to be said in the city; but this can have been no comfort to her son as he knelt by the velvet-covered box that, incredibly, contained the person he loved best. In adult years tears would come with suspicious ease to Henry's eyes, but the tears he wept for his dead mother we know came from his heart. The death of 'my dearest mother', he wrote in a letter to Erasmus four years later, was 'hateful intelligence'.

Although the royal family at this date did not take part in funeral ceremonies, they usually watched public processions from a successful merchant's gabled house in Cheap. And it was from here that young Henry may have leaned out to see his mother's funeral cortège, but whether he saw it personally or only heard it described, it was a sight to burn itself into his mind.

From the plain little church of St Peter Ad Vincula, eight nobles carried the queen's coffin into a black-draped carriage, topped by an effigy of Elizabeth in her crown and state robes, a glow of colour among the hundreds of black-hooded and black-gowned mourners who formed the procession, in carriages, on horseback and on foot. Eight horses wholly enveloped in black, except for their eyes and their hooves, drew the carriage through the city down the Strand towards Westminster Abbey.

First rode the crimson-clad nobles, then the mayor with his gold and crystal mace next the royal funeral carriage. Although Henry VII's affection for his queen has often been called in question by historians, we are told by a contemporary chronicler that when she died, he 'privily departed to a solitary place and would no man should resort unto him'. And the lavishness of her funeral is further proof of his love; it cost more than £3000 and was a tribute to her virtue and piety. All round the carriage gentlemen carried torches, and banners of 'Our Lady', 'the Assumption', 'the Salutation' and 'the Nativity'. On one side of the streets stood the craft guilds in their brilliant coloured liveries, on the other, a row of white-gowned men with flaming torches. Along Fenchurch Street and Cheapside, as a last tribute to Elizabeth's 'chastity', the torch-bearers were thirty-seven 'virgins' wearing green-and-white garlands. These were unforgettable images for the young prince of Wales, and ever afterwards his mother's memory would wear a saintly glow.

Elizabeth's death left a sudden terrifying vacuum in his affections. A modern psychologist has suggested that he never grew out of an Oedipus complex, a desire for but horror of incest, a suggestion which seems borne out by his future sexual relations with three women of the same family, the Boleyn sisters and their first cousin, Katherine Howard; for the mature Henry too sex and death would be strangely linked. But far more than his sexual development was affected. With Elizabeth's sudden death, Henry was deprived at once of a gentling influence and of a reality; for even so good and kind a woman as Elizabeth had faults. But Henry had not yet been old enough to perceive them and learn to accept the whole human being, and Elizabeth left him picturing her as the perfect wife and queen, modestly obedient to her husband; an impossible standard against which Henry was later to measure his own wives to their disastrous disadvantage. Even more damaging, his mother's death further crippled Henry's capacity to love, which had already been weakened many years before by a love-starved infancy followed by the loss of his nurse, Anne Oxenbrigge. It was a bad time for Henry, especially as, unlike more ordinary families, his could not draw together for mutual comfort. Royalty cannot indulge its grief at the expense of policy, and policy that summer meant fulfilling the Scottish treaty.

Elizabeth's disappearance from Henry's life was followed a few months later by that of Margaret. In August 1503 he escorted his thirteen-year-old elder sister by horse and litter in a splendour of new velvet gowns, plumed harness and trumpet fanfares on the first stage of her journey to meet James IV of Scotland. Margaret, tempestuous and self-willed, was too like Henry for him to find her always compatible, but she shared the special apartness that in the sixteenth century isolated those of the blood royal from other companions. Her present journey would take her far away from her brother in spirit as well as body, since marriage would unite her to a kingdom that was England's traditional enemy. Henry escorted her as far as his grandmother Margaret Beaufort's house at Colyweston before turning back towards London and the two remaining members of his once large family: his little sister Mary, younger than he by nearly five years, and his father, the king, who was exhaustingly preoccupied by state affairs.

From now on the main female influence over Prince Henry was that of Margaret Beaufort, who oversaw many of the details of his education and household although she never resided there permanently. She had been intensely fond of him since his early childhood, but she was divided from him by two generations, different interests and temperament. Had

Henry's other grandmother, the fascinating, fallible Elizabeth Woodville, survived instead of dying in 1492, she might have understood her grandson better.

At fifty-eight Lady Margaret was all intellect and spirit. Her flesh honed away from her narrow bones and deep-set eyes, she now wore always on her small thin body the black-and-white attire of a vowess, her only vanity a badge of rank. She wore the 'barbe', or lower part of her headgear, well up to her chin, a fashion allowed by her own mourning ordinances to no one below the rank of baroness; beneath these nun-like garments she wore a 'shirt' or 'girdle' of hair. She rose every morning at five, an hour before the usual time, and occupied herself until dinner with religious devotions, including four or five Masses, which she heard kneeling, although this position hurt her back. After dinner she organized her household, actually washed the feet of the poor, comforted and studied the dying – hoping herself to learn from them how to die well – or translated some French religious work. A further sign of great piety, by contemporary standards, she often wept in penitence for her sins. And when she attended a court banquet – for she could not resist the delight of seeing her beloved son and grandchildren in their glory – she ate very sparingly. She was therefore hardly the woman to understand her sensual grandson with his romantic, insecure need to possess the best of everything: beauty, riches, excellence.

One interest, though, Lady Margaret did share with Prince Henry: a strong grievance against the French. The French king owed Lady Margaret a large sum of money which had been advanced by her mother, the duchess of Somerset, to the duke of Orleans when he was a prisoner in England. But despite Lady Margaret's constant applications she had not received a penny of this debt, and eventually she made a gift of her rights to Henry VII in the hope that he would recover them by force. We still have his letter of thanks, reminding her gently that the present was not a good time to war against such a powerful nation. Lady Margaret's indignation about this debt reinforced Prince Henry's romantic desire to repossess lands lost to the

French in the Hundred Years' War; young Henry, too, with surprising tactlessness, would express his hatred of France many times in his childhood and youth. But this one shared interest was not enough. Margaret Beaufort could not give the prince the loving companionship that he so badly needed after his mother's death. And the intensity of his grandmother's love for him blinded her to his faults.

CHAPTER 10

My Lord the Prince

'It is quite wonderful how much the King likes the
prince of Wales. He has good reason to do so, for the
prince deserves all love.'   *Hernan Duque de Estrada*

AT the beginning of 1504 Henry was twelve, an age by which a
prince of Wales could normally expect to be sent to live near
his principality. Long before this, both his predecessors, his
brother Arthur and the unfortunate little Edward V, had
taken up residence in Ludlow Castle on the borders of Wales.
For a boy of Prince Henry's precocious ability and ambition
the prospect of residing in Ludlow was exciting.

In the castle with its narrow windows and enticing views of
river and distant hills, for the first time he would be beyond the
rigid care of Margaret Beaufort, and also for the first time he
would be living in his own dwelling; as a change from the
castle itself, he could move to palatial Tickenhill, near Bewdley,
which had been built by King Henry VII for Arthur. Although
his life would be ordered by a governor, Henry himself would
still be the most important person there, for he was nominally
head of the Council of the Prince of Wales, which not only
administered his vast estates in Wales, Cornwall, Chester and
Flint, but also exercised wide judicial and military powers in
Wales and on its borders. Thus he would learn how to govern
an extensive region, invaluable experience when he came to
rule the kingdom. And his power need not be merely nominal
for long. The council was ruled by its president – at this date
a bishop, William Smith. King Edward IV had planned that his
son should be president of the council at fourteen, and although
Arthur at fifteen had still not achieved this honour, Henry

being more capable might perhaps be given a responsibility denied his elder brother. With his growing power, in Ludlow Castle, with the finest tapestries from Arras and cupboards gleaming with plate, he would seem a prince indeed, half-way to the golden attainment of kingship.

So in the spring and early summer of 1504 Henry, studying in his apartments at Eltham, waited for the king's order that would send him to Ludlow and make him a prince of Wales in deed as well as name. He would probably have borne the delay with impatience, unable to understand why his father hesitated. Yet the king's reasons were vital: Prince Henry was now the sole survivor of four sons; on this one boy's life depended the king's whole achievement, the Tudor dynasty and the peace of the kingdom.

Threats were again gathering round the growing boy. As Prince Henry knew from his reading of history, his succession would be very uncertain should the king die soon. The people of England were tired of the disorder that invariably came with a child on the throne, they wanted no repetition of the power struggles that had taken place during the minorities of Richard II and Edward V. But King Henry VII had more recent and immediate evidence of the dangers surrounding his son, evidence of which Prince Henry was almost certainly ignorant.

There is still in existence a letter which depicts the atmosphere of fear in which the king made his decision about Prince Henry's future. The letter came from John Fleming, an important official in the high-walled, well fortified little town of Calais, and it reported words that had passed at a secret meeting between himself, the king's deputy in Calais, Sir Richard Nanfan, the treasurer Sir Hugh Conway, and the master porter Sir Samson Norton. They had discussed what would happen if the king died. For he was, Hugh Conway had said, 'but a weak man and sickly, not likely to be no long lyvis [*sic*] man'. This was obviously the prelude to a grave allegation; for to predict the death of the king could be treason, and a matter of treason the king always examined as closely as he examined the books of payments kept in the royal treasury.

Now one can visualize the way his eyebrows ridged together as he bent low in his high-backed chair, softened with cushions, his weak grey eyes almost touching the desk on which rested Fleming's report.

About four years ago, Fleming wrote, when the king lay ill in his manor of Wanstead, Sir Hugh Conway had been present when 'many great personages' discussed what would happen were the king to die. 'There were some,' he told the little group of Calais officials, 'who spake of my lord of Buckingham . . . others there were that spake . . . of your traitor Edmund de la Pole, but none of them that spake of my lord prince.'

Fleming's letter was disturbing and distressing news for a king who had spent many years trying to root out rebellion, and as Henry VII read on, the information was of a kind to make his already thin mouth set harder.

From Conway's remarks it seemed that, on the king's death, everything that he had built would break into chaos. Since coming to Calais, Sir Hugh added, he had spoken of the future to Sir Nicholas Vaux, lieutenant of the English castle of Guisnes, and to Sir Anthony Brown, lieutenant of the castle at Calais, both of whom had smugly replied that they would be safe in their strongholds whatever might happen. But, Sir Hugh asked, pausing and gazing emphatically at his listeners, the little party of Calais officials gathered in secret discussion, what would happen to *them* if the king were to die? They had no castles to shelter in. Calais would fall if the castle fell and, with the king dead, would not Sir Anthony Brown's wife, cousin and adherent of Edmund de la Pole, open the postern gate to him in the middle of the night? The king was bound to die soon, Sir Hugh insisted; he had proof. He could show them a book of prophecy in which it was written that Henry VII would reign no longer than had King Edward IV, which was just over twenty-two years.

That part of the letter invited the king's frown too. Unless granted the royal licence, books of prophecy had been forbidden by law, since they could be used to sway the superstitious to rebellion.

Then into Fleming's letter a ray of light broke briefly. Sir Hugh's mention of the illegal prophecy had caused quick nervous protests; the master porter told him to burn the book, the king's deputy to 'leave this prophecying for ye speak of things that . . . I never hear nor see . . .' And all swore that they would rather suffer death than see the king's son deprived of his inheritance. But the ray of light was soon extinguished. For Sir Hugh's other remarks had brought a heartfelt rumble of response; every official there, beginning with the deputy himself, mentioning some dangerous man they would 'rid the world of' when the king died.

Fleming's letter suggested that seeds of a new civil war lay ready to sprout beneath the surface order of King Henry VII's kingdom, a situation in which it would be foolhardy to send Prince Henry to Ludlow. For living there, he would be perilously far from his father's protection and, should the king die suddenly, he would be too many hours' riding from London to be sure of seizing the throne before a rival usurped it. Recent history had proved as much. When Edward IV died in 1483, had twelve-year-old Edward V been at Westminster instead of Ludlow, he might have lived to be king in fact as well as in title.

In such uncertain times King Henry VII decided that his only son, Prince Henry, could be safe nowhere except at court and under his own watchful eyes. This decision, typical of Henry VII, who preferred personally to oversee everything important, doubtless had the approval of the nervous Margaret Beaufort, who ruled the schoolroom. The judgement of this adoring grandmother, survivor of the feuds and murders of the Wars of the Roses, could not but concur with the king's: keep the prince of Wales safe at all costs.

So Prince Henry was told that he was not to go to Ludlow – a decision that at his age would have been maddeningly disappointing and also unintelligible. For how could he, at twelve, comprehend his father's dynastic anxieties? He would not be able to do that until he himself was king – but a king with no son at all to succeed him – when he would burst out in anguish, 'Am I not a man like other men?' furious, and pathetic in this one aspect of life where he was not all-powerful. But that time was still hidden. In the summer of 1504 he was still a young boy seeing his future self as predicted by Dr William Parron: father of many sons. The boy's problems were in a different key from the man's, but still painful.

Some time in the long light days of 1504, Prince Henry received, instead of the order telling him to ride to Ludlow, a command to journey to reside at Westminster. As the prince rode magnificently forth, preceded by trumpeters and followed by a long line of green-and-white-liveried servants, he must have ached inwardly with humiliation and anger. Instead of gaining in independence and importance, he was losing greatly; for to live at court he needed to sacrifice a large part of his own personal household. It was a sentence almost of imprisonment, and Henry's indignation stoked the fire of his hatred against all rivals for the crown, those pretenders whose threat had robbed him of his right as prince of Wales. It probably also stoked the fire of his hatred against his father, who had shown so little understanding.

But for a high-spirited, curious boy there were many exciting distractions as he rode down the Strand and through the gates of the Thames-side palace of Westminster, this noble sprawl of stone and timbered two-story buildings, guarded by tall yeomen, sharp halberds in their hands, their tunics embroidered back and front with the red rose of Lancaster encircled by gold vines. Westminster, where the prince was now to reside for much of the year instead of visiting it only occasionally, was at the centre of government. The king took his chief councillors with him when he visited his other palaces but the law courts of Chancery, King's Bench and Common Pleas always sat at Westminster Hall, which stood next to the palace, facing on to the forecourt with its clock tower and conduit.

The forecourt was a kaleidoscope of shifting colour – nobles in silken clothes with gold chains mingled with successful merchants in fur-lined gowns, judges in crimson or mustard robes, abbots in purple mantles, physicians in black. There were foreign ambassadors, Burgundians in great-brimmed, bright ostrich-plumed hats, Frenchmen in neat black velvet 'bonnets', widely copied by the English, Italians in the new skirts called bases. And interspersed with these, a sober warp for the brilliant colours of the gentry, ordinary citizens in the browns and greys considered suitable for the lower classes brought presents to the king: cherries or fish or a promising child to serve in the royal household.

Inside, the palace was even more interesting. Beside Westminster, Eltham was provincial. Here were halls built for the grandest ceremonies: the White Hall; the hall with a gallery of sculptured kings, built by Richard II; and the king's own bedroom, which was big enough for a banquet and known as the Painted Chamber, so called from the biblical scenes which had been frescoed in bands round the walls by order of King Henry III, the frescoes interspersed with angels bearing crowns and tall figures personifying virtues and vices. Upstairs, where all the king's private apartments and offices were located, the tiled corridors bustled with retainers, either in the royal green and white, or in the liveries of the many noblemen and gentlemen entitled to a room at court and a specified quantity of servants, food, wine, candles and fuel, according to their rank.

Occasionally, the scent of musk and ambergris would indicate the approach of some particularly wealthy nobleman – the duke of Buckingham, the earl of Surrey, the earl of Essex, or Lord Giles Daubenay perhaps, chamberlain of the exchequer and of the royal household and now the most influential of the king's ministers. Daubenay, with Thomas Lovell, chancellor of the exchequer, Richard Fox, bishop of Winchester and keeper of the Privy Seal, John Riseley and Richard Guildford, most frequently sat on the select committees of the council which assembled behind the tapestry-hung doors. At Westminster Palace also, the king kept 'dressed like Englishmen' his chief curiosity: the three wild men discovered by the explorer John Cabot in Newfoundland, 'clothed in beasts' skins', eating raw flesh, 'and in their demeanour like to brute beasts'.

But Prince Henry is unlikely to have had long to look around him. Because here, to Westminster, came all 'the great ones' of England who, according to Fleming's letter and the lessons of history, were not to be trusted, the prince would have been escorted swiftly to his rooms. Having personally sifted the evidence in Fleming's secret report, the king decided to penalize no one mentioned in it, perhaps because so many had been involved; but that decision implied that he must keep his only son doubly safe. Hence it was that Prince Henry found himself ushered into lodgings that led directly out of the king's privy chamber.

It does not mean, as some biographers have suggested, that he lived henceforth in just a single room. He still retained, we know, some servants of his own, including a gentleman usher, footmen, and a groom of his privy chamber who later swore on oath that Henry, like Arthur, received 'dignities proper to a king's sons'; he kept his own minstrels and even his own company of players. All this indicates spacious apartments where, safely hidden, he could keep his own miniature court, with Mary, five years younger than himself, his companions, playmates and tutors, apartments where he could eat his meals sitting under his own canopy of state, while his servants ate at tables lower down the room; although he himself probably carved on occasions for his father.

But impressive though all this might seem to his entourage, from the boy's point of view his authority was maddeningly limited. To enter the main body of the palace he needed the king's permission. Anyone visiting him must first pass the two yeomen of the guard always posted, with their gilded halberds, one on each side of the main door leading to the king's apartments. And even when Prince Henry went into the royal park for his afternoon sport no one, except his specially sanctioned companions, might speak to him 'for fear of his life'. The very occasional mention of such an important person as the prince in ambassadors' despatches during the year 1504 to 1505 indicates that these gossip-hungry envoys were rarely fortunate enough to see him; that when he moved with his long retinue

to Richmond, Windsor or any of the other royal houses, he
was as closely kept as at the mighty palace of Westminster.
Only so could the king feel that his heir was safe from treason
among 'the great ones'.

In view of Fleming's report it is easy to see why as late as
1504, when Henry VII had contrived successfully to 'cleave
fast to the crown' for eighteen years, he still acted as though
he believed he was sitting on gunpowder. He bound his lords
to loyalty with the shackles of bonds and recognizances;
any man he did not trust he made to promise in writing to
pay a large sum of money should be fail in his obligations to
the crown. The victim of the royal suspicion had at the same
time to find other men willing to guarantee his good behaviour,
also for large sums of money.

Any infringement of the peace among 'the great ones' led
to the signing of one of these dreaded documents, as the
'magnificent earl of Northumberland' discovered. For engaging
in a dispute with the archbishop of York this vain young head
of the Percies (father of the youth who later wooed Anne
Boleyn) was forced to promise in a recognizance to pay £2000
should he ever offend against the peace again. And the following
year the king increased the threat. For disposing of the marriage
of one of the king's wards – then a saleable commodity and one
of the king's most profitable perks – the earl was fined £10,000
which was a fortune at that date. And although in fact the earl
had to pay only about a tenth of this amount while the rest of
the fine was suspended, the document with the earl's signature
remained in the king's possession, and the earl lived in fear that
he might be required to pay the whole crippling sum at a
moment's notice.

Northumberland was not alone in his fear. It was shared,
it has been estimated, for some part of Henry VII's reign by
more than two-thirds of the nobility. 'Great ones' who did not
themselves offend, so did not have to sign a recognizance for
their own good behaviour, were drawn into the king's wide net
by being forced to act as guarantors for a friend or relation.
By such methods, as Edmund Dudley (one of the chief officers

Richmond Palace, detail from a drawing by
Anthony van den Wyngaerde

The roof of the Great Hall at Eltham Palace, where Henry VIII
spent much of his childhood

Henry's tutor,
the poet John Skelton.
Woodcut in a manuscript
of *Speke, Parrot*

Perkin Warbeck:
from the *Receuil d'Arras*

Philip the Fair,
by Jean of Flanders

Catherine of Aragon,
by Michel Sittow

The family of Henry VII with St George and dragon. A votive painting of 1505-9, possibly an altarpiece for St George's Chapel, Windsor

Henry VIII and Catherine being crowned beneath their respective badges of the Rose and the Pomegranate. A symbolic portrayal of 1509

of the King's debt-collecting agency, 'the council learned in the law') wittily wrote, the king kept his subjects 'in a loving dread'.

The atmosphere of fear and suspicion spread into the school-room, where Prince Henry learned that his father did not even trust Lord Mountjoy, tutor-companion to the prince since he was eight years old – Mountjoy, who was all enthusiastic admiration for young Henry, and who treated him with the affection of an elder brother. But how could the king be sure of the loyalty of any of his nobles, when they were so inter-related? Was not Lord Mountjoy the son-in-law of Sir William Say, who was a cousin of the traitor Edmund de la Pole, earl of Suffolk? When in 1503 the king made Mountjoy governor of the fortress of Hammes in the pale of Calais, Mountjoy was obliged to sign a recognizance promising to pay 10,000 marks should he not be able to keep the castle safely and also to find no less than twenty-eight guarantors to put up sums of money should he fail in his obligations. To tangle the web further, Mountjoy had himself to promise to pay a further 10,000 marks should he be unable to find a substitute on the death of one of these guarantors. Mountjoy's pupil cannot have failed to know of his youngest tutor's financial anxieties.

Prince Henry had lived all his childhood in an atmosphere of suspicion, ever since, when he was three years old, Sir William Stanley had been executed for treason. He had learned to suspect his own relations, and he had learned, too, that even when they were innocent they might have to be beheaded to safeguard the peace of the realm. Now, through his father's financial policies, he learned in his teens that a close and loving companion of many years must also be watched and doubted. Recent research has shown that a child can outgrow the effects of harmful early childhood experiences. But in Henry's case they were repeated. Thus already his ability to love with enduring affec-tion had been almost fatally blunted. Now the king's treatment of Mountjoy confirmed the lesson that Henry had learned from the Stanley episode: take anyone else's love at face value only. In the grown Henry in later life, after the generosity of youth

was over, there would be a deep contradiction – romantic idealism on the surface, and beneath, a dark and dangerous cynicism
about all human relationships. This increased his sense of
standing wholly alone, apart from and above the rest of
mankind.

Married and Unmarried

'With this ring I thee wed, and with my body I thee
honour and with all my gold I thee dower.'

Sarum Missal

———

FATE had decreed that the single parent Prince Henry still possessed when he reached his teens came from the cool intellectual Tudor side of his family with which he had least in common. Although loved by both his father and his grandmother, he was the odd one out in this family threesome. Margaret Beaufort and Henry VII were both physically and mentally similar and bonded by deep affection. Lady Margaret wrote to Henry VII as 'My dearest and only desired joy in this world'. In return for this devotion, the king lavished on her lands and houses, including the great house of Cold Harbour in London, which under Edward IV had belonged to the heralds. He wrote to her in his own hand, although bad sight had now made this a long task, asking her to let him know what else she might like and assuring her tenderly, 'I shall be as glad to please you as your heart can desire it; and I know well that I am as much bounden so to do as any creature living for the great and singular motherly love and affection that it hath pleased you at all times to bear towards me . . .' And he signed himself 'Your most humble and loving son'. The sympathy between young Henry's father and grandmother, this evidence suggests, was far closer than that between either of them and the prince, who took after the sensual, hot-blooded Plantagenets.

Henry VII was not unaware of sensual pleasures. His palace of Richmond delighted the senses in many ingenious ways. And his chamber expenses reveal a suspiciously large reward

of £30 paid on 25 August 1493 'to the young damsel that danceth' and another of £12 paid on 13 January 1497 'to a little
maiden that danceth'. But such delights were far down in his
scheme of priorities. It is true that he lavished money on his
robes, appearing before ambassadors 'leaning against a tall gilt
chair covered with cloth-of-gold' in a 'violet-coloured gown,
lined with cloth-of-gold, and a collar of many jewels, and on his
cap . . . a large diamond and a beautiful pearl'. But the money
was spent with a political aim: to convince men who equated
riches with power that he owned a fortune. He does not seem
to have taken particular pleasure in the clothes themselves.
Not for King Henry VII long discussions on fashion with his
robe-makers. His gowns varied little in style; he left the new
Italian bases, the slashed sleeves and side-tilted plumed hats to
young courtiers, and he sat for his portrait by Michel Sittow
with his shoulder-length grey hair uncurled. There is no trace
in Henry VII of the voluptuous vanity and ostentation of his
son, the future Henry VIII, whom a Venetian envoy would
call 'the handsomest potentate I ever set eyes on'. It is impossible
to imagine Henry VII, even in his youth, joining in his own
revels dressed as a shepherd or a Moor or a Turk.

The temperamental gulf of difference between father and
son was widened by the contrast in their upbringing. Prince
Henry had grown up in luxury, the precious son of the ruling
royal family: Henry VII had had to fight for almost everything
he possessed. And now he found himself in a predicament that
still causes trouble between parents and children today. How
could this self-made king understand his indulged thirteen-
year-old son, with his fine tastes and education, his sophisticated ideals and fancies, his dawning physical vanity and love of
fashion – luxuries the elder Tudor had been unable to afford?
How could this spoilt thirteen-year-old understand the anxieties
and austerities of the father? In the years to come this gulf of
misunderstanding would be widened into a ravine by the king's
attitude to Prince Henry's marriage.

Ever since the middle of 1502 Prince Henry had expected to

inherit his brother's exotic widow along with his title and lands. On hearing of Arthur's death, Ferdinand and Isabella despatched unsentimentally and immediately an envoy to the king of England; he had instructions to propose a marriage between their daughter and 'the prince of Wales that now is'. Henry VII seemed content with the new arrangement. And by the summer of 1503 money wrangles over the unpaid half of the dowry from Spain and the marriage allowance due to Catherine from the king of England appeared to have been resolved: Henry VII was to retain the first instalment of her dowry, the second instalment – to consist of 65,000 crowns in money and 35,000 in Catherine's plate and jewels – was to be paid before the prince completed his fifteenth year. Meanwhile Catherine was to renounce her dower rights in exchange for a promise of similar dower rights when she should marry the prince.

On 24 June 1503 Prince Henry, then four days short of his twelfth birthday, had found himself the focal point of a palace betrothal ceremony, graced with the customary lords and ladies. He stood beside the seventeen-year-old Catherine, who was now about the same height as he, an intimidatingly grown-up girl in a strange beautiful dress, her skirts bell-shaped over a hooped petticoat instead of falling in folds, like English gowns. But the child's natural awe of the adult would have dissolved as he saw her smile.

Catherine's kind looks were no accident. Had not her parents written ordering her to marry the new prince? Catherine was first and foremost a dutiful daughter and she knew that the English alliance was essential to her parents' plans to oust the French from Italy. She knew, too, that unless definite arrangements were made for her to marry young Henry, she would not be able to continue to pay for her household of fifty servants in Durham House, the mansion between the Strand and the Thames where the king allowed her to live. Directly after Arthur's death Henry VII had given her £100 a month. On this she could just manage, although without paying her servants' salaries or buying herself new dresses. But now even this allowance had stopped and her parents sent her nothing.

She was an exile, but her parents did not want her back. They had paid good money for an English marriage and they expected one; no other marriage was possible for her – they had made this quite clear to Catherine. 'Some persons have advised the princess of Wales not to accept what the king offers,' they had written. 'The advice is bad. She must accept whatever she can get.' What she could get, it seemed in June 1503, was the prince of Wales.

The betrothal was *'per verba de praesenti'* which meant that it should henceforth be binding, and included words from the actual marriage service. When the king and the Spanish ambassador, on behalf of Ferdinand and Isabella, had formally consented to the betrothal, Prince Henry took Catherine's right hand in his right hand and spoke his carefully learnt lines. 'I am rejoiced . . . to contract matrimony with thee Catherine and take thee for my wife and spouse and all other for thee forsake during my and thine lives natural. And thereto I plight and give thee my faith and truth.' It was a fantastic, moving moment for the boy when his own flow of words stopped and they began again in heartfelt tones from the lips of the young woman at his side. She was now his fate, his partner for life according to the laws of the Church – whether he liked or hated her. And while it is difficult to be sure of the feelings of a nearly twelve-year-old boy, the signs are that he certainly liked and would soon be indulging in romantic dreams of her.

Catherine at seventeen was a fitting subject: she was slim with long reddish-gold hair, bright grey eyes in a pale face and vivacious ways that created the illusion of beauty. And she was determined, with all the strength of her nature and the desperation of her plight, to please him; he was her salvation and her attitude to him during the next few years would be one of possessive affection.

For his part Prince Henry, too, as he reached puberty was soon ready to 'fall in love', the unphysical adoration of the very young, forced into premature bloom by the fashions of his time and society. Romantic love was for the small extravagant palace society what sex is for many people today – ubiquitous but lacking in any real emotion. When during dinner the Children of the Chapel raised their pure piping voices in the minstrels' gallery, it was usually on this theme, as were the songs sung by the courtiers after the final course. It was an abject love, that of a knight for his lady who could command him in all things, the gallant fiction which has come to be called courtly love and which began in twelfth-century Provence.

Prince Henry's mind was awash with the plaints of faithful swains rejected by unkind mistresses, full of words like 'heart, alas, truth, woe, unkindness', love imagery that clothed even the songs about religion, politics and the vagaries of fortune. There still survives in the British Library a little volume of court songs in red and black notation, a book that Prince Henry himself may have handled. It includes the songs that he sang in a voice which, though deepening, was to remain surprisingly light; the songs are full of exaggerated descriptions of the power of love.

> *Benedicite! Whate dremyd I this nyght?*
> *Methought the worlde was turnyd up so downe,*
> *The son, the moone, had lost ther force and light;*
> *The see also drownyd both towre and towne:*
> *Yett more mervell how that I hard the sownde*
> *Of onys voice sayyng, 'Bere in thy mynd,*
> *Thi lady hath forgoten to be kynd.'*

In the ocean of love contained in this little volume the few ribald lyrics were a mere drop. But songs were not the only means of being in fashion – every court pastime was spiced with dalliance. The prince learnt from the amorous Lord Mountjoy to flirt with words while card playing and dicing, and to flirt with his eyes on a candlelit evening when courtiers and their ladies sat on cushions listening to the latest romance read aloud.

The civilized half of Europe was in thrall to love. In Italy, France, Spain, as well as in England, the new printing machines pressed out new romances and new versions of old romances:

Orlando Innamorato, Orlando Furioso, Amadis de Gaula, La Belle Dame Sans Merci, La Morte D'Arthur, Chaucer's *The Knight's Tale* . . . stories in which love, although often destroying the knight errant who pursued it, was important, dramatic, exciting.

Other entertainments echoed the theme. In the disguisings Prince Henry saw fair ladies 'in their hair' gaze enticingly from thin board castles about to be stormed by knights. No tournament was complete unless embellished with an audience of fair ladies, eyes beaming down passionate messages to the knight of their choice – a convention whose romantic essence is caught in a famous sixteenth-century lyric.

> *My soverayne lorde for my poure sake*
> *Six coursys at the ryng dyd make,*
> *Of which four tymes he dyd it take;*
> *Wherfor my hart I hym beqwest,*
> *And of all other for to love best*
> *My soverayne lorde.*

Even the game of tennis, in which Prince Henry was learning extraordinary skill, was used as part of the game of love, as the poet Henry Howard, earl of Surrey, would later describe:

> *The large grene courtes, where we were wont to houe,*
> *With eyes cast up into the mayden's tower.*
> *And easie sighes, such as folke drawe in loue.*

For the courtier at the beginning of the sixteenth century a lovelorn look was as essential as the curl in his hair, the rings on his fingers and the perfume on his body; married or unmarried, he must appear to be in love – preferably with someone whose name he was too honourable to utter. A suggestion of a secret affair lent a man glamour. Such heights of sophistication could not yet be scaled by a teenage boy – but he could begin to be in fashion by expressing devotion to the most convenient object to hand. And that was Catherine.

In the summer of 1504 Prince Henry's romantic feelings for Catherine suited the king well; for Spain was winning its wars against the French in Italy. Henry VII treated her as his 'beloved daughter' and provided her again with £100 a month. He even sent her a splendid new head-dress and 'a St Peter in gold', presents identical to those he had sent his mother and his eldest daughter Margaret, queen of Scotland. And when Catherine fell ill, he offered magnificently to 'convoke all the physicians in the kingdom' to make her better.

So far, Prince Henry had seen little of his 'wife', sequestered as she was with her duenna among the bead curtains and Spanish trinkets of Durham House on the Strand. But in 1504, when he himself had come to live permanently at court, he had the pleasurable excitement of her company on a royal progress. In August when, as usual, the king rode off to spend the remaining summer days in his deer parks, he took his son with him for the first time. Little Princess Mary, aged eight, and Catherine came too. They rode from Richmond to Windsor, then on beside the ever widening river to Greenwich. Freedom from seclusion and his lessons, long days of sport surrounded by sunlit beech and oak trees and deep cave-like shadows, the delicious *fête champêtre* atmosphere, all seemed designed to make thirteen-year-old Prince Henry fonder of his eighteen-year-old wife. Sometimes they waited with bows and arrows on a hidden platform until the horn's blast warned that the prey was being driven towards them; or, if they preferred, Henry and Catherine left their leafy sanctuary to gallop after the deer, assisted by great dogs. It was wonderful to be a superb rider, a precociously expert marksman, to see his arrow fly off through the green light, hold his breath with hope, then see his skill reflected, as the arrow hit, in the admiration of his grown-up 'wife'. Catherine was secretly instructed by her father to do everything she could to preserve the love of the prince of Wales.

These weeks of hunting offered both the convivial pleasures of a party and occasional thrilling chances for privacy. Did Catherine in some glade as they rode along together, with sudden Spanish volubility, speak passionately of her financial troubles? If she did – and she was clever enough to do so and to beg Prince Henry's help – it would have made the boy feel already a man. Just as the slight fading of Catherine's once gorgeous tissue and brocade dresses, and even her illnesses that kept her some days from the hunt, would make him feel already, by comparison, powerful and protective.

Those summer hunting days of 1504 brought a happiness that spilled over into the relationship of father and son. It even found its way into the triumphant despatch of Hernan Duque de Estrada, the new Spanish ambassador who had been sent to England especially to finalize the marriage and who was one of the hunting party at Windsor. He wrote to Queen Isabella: 'The prince of Wales is with the king. Formerly the king did not like to take the prince of Wales with him, in order not to interrupt his studies. It is quite wonderful how much the king likes the prince of Wales. He has good reason to do so, for the prince deserves all love.'

However, the ambassador's next remark sounds a less festive note in the relationship. 'It is not only from love that the king takes the prince with him. He wishes to improve him. Certainly there could be no better school in the world than the society of such a father as Henry VII. He is so wise and so attentive to everything, nothing escapes his attention.' The time had come, Henry VII had obviously decided, when he himself should supplement Hone's schoolroom instruction on the theory of government with some lessons in diplomacy, but through Estrada's lines, we begin to see the king as a pedant, a father who instead of listening to his son and enjoying his company, lost no opportunity to lecture him, even when they were hunting.

At the age of forty-eight the king's sense of duty overrode all more human emotions. He was becoming a slave to the function of monarchy; and in the king's obsessive state about the future of his kingdom, even his only son was a pawn to be moved this way and that according to political necessity. Events were now suddenly to make the Spanish match appear much less attractive.

In November 1504 Prince Henry was yet again enjoying the carefully chaperoned society of his 'wife' in the palace of

Westminster when news arrived that her mother, Isabella the Catholic, had died. With Isabella's death, Catherine's status changed – everything that she had taken for granted shifted. She was no longer the daughter of the monarchs of Spain. Isabella had been queen in her own right of Castile, Ferdinand merely her consort. Now Ferdinand, though still *de facto* governor of Castile, was no longer its rightful king. He was king only of Aragon. Isabella's heir was Catherine's pretty but unbalanced elder sister, Joanna, who was married to Maximilian's son, Philip, archduke of Austria and duke of Burgundy. It was soon apparent that Philip intended to rule Castile in his wife's name.

Thus Philip and Ferdinand became rivals and their mutual friends must choose between them. Henry VII had for some years been growing closer to the Hapsburgs. In 1500 he had personally met Philip just outside the town of Calais. In April 1504 Maximilian had sent Henry VII a precious relic, a leg of St George enclosed in silver parcel gilt, and on St George's day Prince Henry had ridden in procession with his father, from Baynard's Castle through London to St Paul's Cathedral, the relic carried aloft before them by the bishop of Chester. Now it was clear to Henry VII that alliance with Philip was the more valuable, since Philip would be ruler of half Spain as well as of Burgundy. In the light of all this Ferdinand's daughter was no longer a very eligible bride for the heir to the crown of England. Although Henry VII probably himself played the fashionable game of love at tournament and banquet, sending longing glances from his weak grey eyes across the tiltyard and the roast peacock, he left such pastimes out of politics. In 1505 he treated Catherine most ungallantly.

Prince Henry was old enough to appreciate the changed political situation, and also the change in his 'wife's' status. But he was not yet hardened enough to perform without damage the action that the king now demanded of him, an action of a kind that might lie for ever on any ordinary man's conscience. It is often forgotten that, arranged though royal marriages were at the time, they nevertheless paid lip service to love; Arthur had for years before his marriage written 'love letters' in Latin to Catherine. Prince Henry too had been encouraged to show 'love' for Catherine by sending her tokens.

He had learned to distrust the love of friends, relatives and ministers, but romantic love was still an untarnished ideal. What the king now demanded of him was an act of complete cynicism towards Catherine. This thirteen-year-old boy must absolve himself from his promise to marry the girl to whom he had plighted his troth and whom he already believed to be his wife. But he must make his protest secretly; Catherine was not to know of it until he decided to marry someone else. Meanwhile she, of course, would consider herself bound to marry him.

According to the treaty made in 1504 with Spain, Prince Henry was to marry Catherine as soon as he had completed his fifteenth year, provided the second half of her dowry was ready in London and waiting to be paid. It was the day before the prince was fourteen, when a boy was considered to reach the age of consent. Secretly, Prince Henry, the bishop of Winchester, a notary, James Read, and a trusted group of councillors slipped away from the luxurious upstairs apartments down to a little room below the kitchens where no one could see them even through a window. Here in a west wing of the palace of Richmond, they assembled. Presiding in his robes in a ceremonial chair was the aptly named Richard Fox, bishop of Winchester, who had earned the royal trust long ago as one of the little band of exiles in Brittany, and who was now used by Henry VII for his most subtle negotiations. Before this resourceful prince of the Church and the black-gowned notary beside him, Prince Henry was made to stand up and in his newly broken voice read a long legal manuscript in Latin.

In the name of God, Amen. Before you, reverend lord and father in Christ, Richard, by the grace of God and the apostolic see lord bishop of Winchester, I, Henry, prince of Wales, duke of Cornwall, and earl of Chester, declare, announce and in this document proclaim that although I while of tender years, and being to all knowledge below the age of manhood, contracted a de facto marriage with her most serene highness Catherine, daughter of the king of Spain; and although that contract, because of the impediment of my minority is in itself already invalid, imperfect and of no effect or force; nevertheless because, with the onset of my years of manhood and my mature age, the contract might in itself now be thought or seem to be clearly validated or confirmed by reason of tacit consent, mutual cohabitation, the exchange of gifts or tokens, or in any other way lawfully declared; therefore, I, the aforesaid Henry prince of Wales, being now on the verge of manhood and attaining the age of manhood, declare that I do not intend in any way to approve, validate or ratify that pretended contract by anything I have said or may say, or have done or may do. But now, in these presents [document], induced by no force, trickery or prayer, but willingly and freely and in no way compelled, I denounce any contract of the kind and dissent therefrom; and I wish and fully intend in the best mode and manner, and in the best, most valid and most efficacious legal form that I can or could employ, to withdraw completely from the same matrimonial contract and expressly dissent from it; and accordingly in these presents I denounce it and dissent therefrom. And I aver that by no word, deed, act or behaviour, spoken, done, performed or displayed in future by me, or in my name by anyone at any time, whatever it may be, do I wish or intend to acquiesce in the aforesaid matrimonial contract, or in the said lady Catherine as my spouse or wife. Of which I wish, require, ask and beseech you all to bear witness.

Then with the quill that was placed in his hand, the boy signed 'per me Henricum Walliae principem' (under my hand, Henry prince of Wales). And the king's councillors, including Giles Daubenay (another of that little band of exiles in Brittany), Charles Somerset, earl of Worcester, and Thomas

Ruthall, the king's Latin secretary, hastened to sign their names beneath.

The king intended the protest – so his subtle servant Fox insisted years later – as a precaution only; he always meant his son to marry Catherine. If this was the story that Henry VII told the prince it must have seemed to the boy as unlikely then as it does to us today. For, living in apartments next to his father's, he often saw admitted into the privy chamber ambassadors in wide-brimmed Burgundian hats – signs of Henry VII's growing friendship with Philip, already proclaimed king of Castile and known as the king archduke.

By October 1505 Henry VII was sending him secret messages discussing marriage once more between Prince Henry and Philip's young daughter Eleanor, the match proposed for him originally in 1501. The king apparently did not take into account the strongly romantic feeling in his son, now beginning to see himself as a knight errant from the fashionable romantic tales.

The behaviour forced by his father on this teenage boy was traumatic. Henry the prince was being made to act in a way repellent to Henry the hero of romance. Having rescued the princess – and with her ragged court, her widowhood and exile, Catherine was in need of rescue – he must return her to the dragon's lair. In deciding on such an act, a realist like King Henry VII examined, then chose his priorities, clear-sightedly accepting the responsibility. Not so Prince Henry. Brought up softly, surrounded by images of idealism, he could not bear to admit that he did not match them. Young Henry, as the world would soon discover, had a vigorous conscience; he could not bear to accept the blame; it must be someone else's fault. His father's or Catherine's own perhaps, never his. Self-deception was to become one of the adult Henry's least lovable characteristics and the manner in which he prepared to shed his guilt after the protest has all the marks of being his own plan, approved by his father.

Prince Henry wrote to the pope, then Julius II. He complained of a threat that his 'wife' had made (perhaps as a result of learn-

ing of the secret protest). She had threatened, he said, to make a
vow dedicating herself to a life of prayer, fasting, pilgrimage,
and abstinence of a kind that would endanger the health of her
body and the uses of marriage – and she had done this without
her 'husband's' permission. He begged the pope to forbid
her to make this vow. And as usual in Henry's childhood, the
papacy was obedient to the English demand. On 20 October
1505 Julius set his seal on a brief which gave the fourteen-year-
old boy authority to tell his 'wife', aged nineteen, what she
might and might not do with her body in case he might want
to marry her. As a commentary on the kind of domination a
husband of the day, even a lad of Henry's age, might have
over his wife, it is here given in full:

Greetings, beloved son, and our apostolic blessing.
    Although it is sufficiently clear, according to divine and
human laws, that a wife does not have complete authority
over her own body apart from her husband, and that her
vows and fasts, so long as they are considered to interfere
with her bodily health, the procreation of children, and the
customary usages of her life, can be revoked and undone
by her husband; and whereas we have heard that our beloved
daughter in Christ, the lady Catherine, princess of Wales,
your wife, fired by extreme religious fervour, makes and
keeps many vows and proposals for prayer, fasts, abstinence
and pilgrimages, and wishes to continue in them without
your permission; wherefore we have been humbly petitioned
on your behalf that we should give you permission to restrain
her from the said vows and purposes – which seem, taking
into account the opinions of doctors and the condition of
her constitution and of the realm, to be an impediment to
the health of your said wife, and your marital intercourse and
the procreation of children – and that you may annul all
these on our authority: we, therefore, considering that the
husband is the lord and master of the wife, and that the
bringing up of children is among the especial blessings of
matrimony, being disposed in favour of petitions of this kind,

grant you permission to restrain the aforesaid Catherine, your wife, and to compel her not to observe without your permission any vows or purposes of prayer, fasts, abstinences or pilgrimages, or do any other act which, as is manifest, may interfere with the procreation of children; and to prevent her, for the future, from entering upon any other such vows or purposes; and if she does so without your permission, to prevent her from carrying them out; or as formerly, if you prefer they may be commuted by our apostolic authority for other good works in accordance with the advice of her own proper confessor, notwithstanding apostolic regulations, ordinances and anything else whatever to the contrary.

Possessed of this strange document, Prince Henry would have the beginning of a reason, should he further require it, justifying a refusal to marry Catherine. How easy in a year or two's time to insist that she had indeed impaired her ability to bear children and so made herself unfit to be his queen.

Prince Henry's request for this papal brief curiously foreshadows the pattern of some of his nastiest future acts, the ingenious dance steps with which, when he became king, he would extricate himself conscience-clear from close personal relationships that had become inconvenient. This request, coupled with his protest against his earlier betrothal, may well have helped to create that habit of double-think of which the future King Henry VIII would be unrivalled master. By the summer of 1505 Prince Henry, pupil of humanism, reader of romances, had learned a most useful lesson – how to live with his conscience, simply by believing that it was the other person who was always guilty. Henceforth Henry would see his victims as their own executioners. He had learned to use the method of judicial murder for other necessary endings.

But his complicated relationship with Catherine was still only just beginning.

CHAPTER 12

Lessons in Kingship

'There could be no better school in the world than the
society of such a father as Henry VII.'
Hernan Duque de Estrada

DURING the three years from 1505 to 1508 Prince Henry grew
into a young gallant taller and broader than his father, his
incipient whiskers close shaved by his barber, who also used
curling tongs to bend the prince's locks into the new short bob
in line with his chin. He was clad in velvet, satin, cloth-of-gold
or tissue, in colours chosen to enhance his auburn hair and
pink-and-white skin. Probably he was already wearing the latest
knee-length base from Italy to reveal his fine calf, topped by a
doublet with puffed and slashed sleeves, and adorned by a belt
with dagger, purse and gloves suspended from it by laces.
But while her fast maturing young husband thus indulged
his flair for fashion, Catherine wore the same gowns that she
had brought with her from Spain – the tissues until they were
threadbare, and the brocades which, though shabby, being
thicker, lasted a little longer. For King Henry now gave her
only just a very little money for food.

The prince still referred to her possessively as 'my wife' and
gazed at her from his small blue eyes with calf love. Yet at
the same time as Prince Henry felt these adolescent yearnings,
another more ominous pattern of his relationship with
Catherine was forming in his mind. Little by little he was
growing used to the idea of her as a creature with no rights of
her own except what the English monarch chose to give.
She was his to marry if Henry VII chose, so cunningly had the
prince's father outfoxed Catherine's. 'My son and I are free . . .

while Ferdinand and his daughter are bound if we choose to have them so,' Henry VII boasted.

Now that England had at last firm government, Prince Henry was one of the most desirable matrimonial prospects in Europe. French ambassadors brought proposals to marry him to Marguerite d'Angoulême, sister of the dauphin Francis. Flemish ambassadors continued to suggest Philip's daughter Eleanor. Both princesses would have larger dowries and more powerful connections than Catherine.

The king was not unique in thinking along these lines. For it was an age when dynastic marriages were the fashion, when they not only seemed the way to important alliances, but also another means of conquest: whole kingdoms could be annexed simply by marrying the heir to the throne. Countries whose people regarded with xenophobic hatred the foreign merchants in their midst would nevertheless accept a king or queen of a foreign nationality. The Hapsburg family's cleverly chosen marriages – Maximilian's to Mary of Burgundy, and Philip's to Joanna of Castile – had brought both the Netherlands and half Spain into the Hapsburg dominions; on Ferdinand's death Philip's little son Charles would be heir to all Spain. Why should not Henry VII achieve similarly triumphant arrangements for the Tudors?

So Prince Henry grew up in an atmosphere of matchmaking, with marriage constantly talked of, both his own and his father's. For King Henry VII, aged only forty-six at Elizabeth's death in 1503, was determined to marry again, for political advantage and for sons; and also just a little for his own pleasure.

Prince Henry, ever since 1505, had heard the physical merits of his prospective step-mother discussed, as well as her political suitability. King Ferdinand and Queen Isabella had suggested the young queen of Naples and King Henry VII sent his ambassadors to her with embarrassing instructions. They were to note and describe for him every detail of her body and appearance: 'her face . . . whether painted or not, fat or lean, sharp or round . . . cheerful, frowning or melancholy . . . clearness of

skin . . . colour of hair . . . eyebrows, teeth and lips . . . nose and
forehead . . . complexion . . . arms . . . hands . . . neck . . . breasts
. . .' They were to note particularly 'whether any hair on her
lips' and to 'endeavour to speak with her fasting . . . so that they
may see whether her breath be sweet . . .' For primitive dentistry,
combined with a diet of highly spiced food, made sweet breath
something that could not be taken for granted even in a young
girl.

The ambassadors returned to say that, as far as they could
tell without undressing the lady, her appearance was in every
way delightful, according to sixteenth-century standards. Her
face was 'unpainted . . . amiable, round, fat . . . eyes greyish
brown, brows like a wire of brown hair, teeth fair, clean,
well-set, lips somewhat round and full . . . complexion fair,
sanguine and clean, arms . . . in length of a good proportion,
hands . . . full and soft . . . breasts somewhat great and full and
trussed somewhat high'. There was 'as far as could be perceived'
no hair on her lips and her breath was 'of a sweet savour'.

But when they added that she was virtually without estates
or money, that her property in Naples had been confiscated and
she was dependent on Ferdinand for a small yearly jointure,
Henry VII promptly lost interest in her sweet breath and high
bosom and transferred his matrimonial attentions to Philip's
rich sister Margaret, archduchess of Savoy. He visualized a
grand triple dynastic alliance according to which he would
marry Margaret, his daughter Mary would wed Philip's son
Charles, who had become heir to the two kingdoms of Spain
as well as the Hapsburg lands, and Prince Henry would marry
Eleanor. It was a glorious grandiose vision in which England
would gather to herself, so her king hoped, the alliance of the
Empire, the Netherlands and Spain; and at the same time stop
the bolt hole for Yorkist pretenders to the English crown.

A king must think of his kingdom first: marriage was an act
of state. When, growing up in such an environment, Prince
Henry nevertheless still chose to love Catherine, he could not
but look on his choice as an act of magnanimous condescension
and more than Arthurian gallantry. (The psychological cause

of his feeling for Catherine, which is thought to have been stimulated by the obstacles now put in the way of its fulfilment, would not have occurred to him at a time when the term Oedipus complex was yet to be invented.) As a young prince Henry flaunted his ideals just as he might flaunt the latest fashions: the voluminously topped surcoat to make his own broad shoulders appear even wider, the finest Spanish black embroidery on the low neck of his white shirt that just showed above his quilted doublet, the softest kid boots and loops of gold lace on his velvet cap to echo the high-lights in his hair. But he could not live close to a man like King Henry VII without realizing, if only reluctantly, that as with fashionable clothes there came a time when ideals must be shed. He might feel hostile to his father for his ill-treatment of Catherine but he learned from him the lesson of kingship: politics before people, pragmatism before personal relationships, practical considerations a long way before principles.

As King Henry VII admitted in a letter to his mother Margaret Beaufort, courteously asking her leave to promote her confessor John Fisher to a bishopric, 'I have in my days promoted many a man unadvisedly and I would now like to make some recompençon [recompense] to promote some good and virtuous men . . .' But promotion of unvirtuous but able politicians, like that of Richard Fox to holy office, was only one of the many realistic actions required of a sixteenth-century ruler.

Throughout Prince Henry's adolescent years Catherine's image for him was that of a figure very far below him in the hierarchy, the butt of misfortune. The widow of one prince of Wales, she yet had no widow's jointure; the betrothed of another prince of Wales, she had no regular allowance and no certainty of marrying him – and that was not the fault of the English king alone.

Henry learned the lessons of kingship from Catherine's father too. Although Ferdinand swore he loved Catherine 'more than ever a father loved his daughter' he would do nothing to help her except send angry messages to Henry VII, accusing him of not providing for her. But Ferdinand himself would not fulfil his own side of the marriage treaty by producing the second half of Catherine's dowry. Prince Henry, on hearing ushers announce, not very respectfully, 'Dr De Puebla', soon came to know that the shabby, gout-crippled ambassador's visit usually but incredibly heralded yet another request from Ferdinand to be allowed to postpone payment of the rest of the dowry. In turn, Ferdinand pleaded press of business, Isabella's death, Philip and Joanna's accession to the crown of Castile and his own absence in Naples. He promised to pay eventually, but later. Ferdinand's excuses were accepted by Henry VII. After all, though he wanted the money and was irked by the delay in payment, it was an arrangement that suited him well enough, since it left him free in the eyes of the world to marry his son where he wished; now he would have no need to use Prince Henry's protestation. Not the king of England, but Catherine, was the loser. With every postponement her position became more wretched.

Ferdinand's behaviour was due to the fact that he did not trust the English king. He suspected that if the rest of the dowry were sent Henry VII might find some pretext to hang on to it and still not marry Catherine to his son. Even for his child's sake, Prince Henry learnt, a king would not risk losing 65,000 crowns; money and statecraft were worth more than love. His own father protested affection for Catherine, and he referred to her as his 'daughter', but he did not intend to exchange his only son for any but the best possible bargain – and he was not going to give Catherine a penny more than he had to. Ferdinand felt the same. Only once did he send Catherine even a small sum; it was, he claimed, the English king's duty to provide for her as he had retained half her dowry. Henry VII impatiently disagreed, insisting that anything he chose to give was charity. And while these two monarchs bargained in letters exaltedly endorsed 'To the most serene and excellent King Ferdinand' or 'To the serene prince Henry', letters in which each referred to the other as his 'brother', Catherine's household nearly starved. Her coffers were full of valuable plate and jewels, but these she had been ordered by her father not to sell; they were part of her agreed dowry and if she lost them she might lose for ever her chance of remarriage.

When in the spring of 1505, a few weeks before Prince Henry made his secret protest against his betrothal, Dr De Puebla had been ushered upstairs into the royal presence, it was with a message from Catherine, a message whose fierce desperation even the obsequious Spanish ambassador could not obscure. She was so poor, she had told him to say, that she had been forced to borrow money. Had she contracted debts for luxuries, the king might have had reason not to pay them. But that was not the case; she had had to borrow simply to pay for food. If he continued utterly to abandon his 'daughter' it would reflect dishonour on his character. Unfortunately for Catherine, her obstinate pride had led her to tackle the king in the least tactful way possible.

Henry VII could be kind, especially to women in trouble. Warbeck's wife had fared well at his hands; reverting to her maiden name of Lady Katherine Gordon, she lived at court where she attended on the queen and enjoyed all the privileges of an earl's daughter. Had Catherine simply pleaded with him for a small regular allowance, he might have softened. But instead here was Catherine, not yet twenty, telling him, the king, that it was his duty to treat her better. He would not be scolded in this way by a penniless princess. Henry VII, wifeless and troubled by worsening bad sight, was also becoming increasingly irascible, and Catherine's attempt to fight him with moral arguments only succeeded in setting him against her. Later in her life Catherine would use the same tactics on her husband with the same unfortunate results.

During the next three years Prince Henry was to observe his father treat his 'wife' with increasing cruelty. Living next door to his father's apartments, Prince Henry must often have heard her Spanish-accented voice voluble and passionate as she wept over her poverty. She complained that her servants were ready to beg and she herself was all but naked. But she continued to lecture the king on his duty and so to alienate him. And although Prince Henry might sympathize with his 'wife' – it was, after all, his property that was being ill-treated – he could not protest. For a child in the sixteenth century did not criticize his father, and no one could safely criticize the king. Instead, Prince Henry had to listen, with apparent approval, to his father's exasperated comments about Catherine – and to watch him also court her father's rival Philip.

Few of the king's actions were hidden any longer from the son, because these days they were often together. 'I keep the prince with me because I wish to improve him,' Henry VII had told the Spanish ambassador, Hernan Duque de Estrada, in August 1504. The prince was aware that his father had multiple reasons for desiring alliance with Philip, including the need to protect England against France, which not content with annexing the duchy of Brittany in 1491, had since sent her armies into Italy. English merchants needed more reasonable terms for their wool and cloth trade with the Netherlands – and to make the alliance even more tempting to King Henry VII, still nervously protecting his dynasty, in 1505 Philip now had in his dominions 'the prey which Henry VII most desired', the White Rose, Edmund de la Pole. To gain Philip's goodwill, King Henry VII had lent him in April 1505, £108,000 'for his next voyage into Spain', a euphemism for aid against Ferdinand; in September he lent Philip a further £30,000. With such expenses, how could he afford to pay for Ferdinand's daughter Catherine?

But Henry VII's policies were not all the result of cool reason. Certain incidents, it seems, had caused him to dislike Ferdinand. In 1505 he had badly failed the English merchants trading with Castile. Eight hundred of them had sailed some fifteen hundred miles with a cargo of cloth, intending to sell it in Seville and bring back olive oil and wine. When they arrived they found that Ferdinand had been unable to persuade the council to grant them the special privileges that they had enjoyed in Isabella's lifetime. They had not been allowed to sell their cloth. Back in England, in August 1505, they rode in a furious troupe to Richmond Palace and complained to the king:

they were 'all lost and ruined'. Henry VII was furious with
Ferdinand over this, and he was constantly irritated also by the
endless haggling over Catherine and the realization that the
great prize he had won for his heir had turned out to be worth
very little.

When in December 1505 Catherine once more complained
passionately, and unwisely begged for a refuge from her
misfortunes, Prince Henry learned that his father had played
one of his characteristic sardonic jokes on her. She was invited
to court for Christmas, and when she had installed herself
there with only a fraction of her usual number of servants,
the king informed her that he had granted her request; this
was her refuge; her household was an unnecessary expense,
to be dissolved; he had already sent her carriage and horses
away. She was no longer to return to Durham House. So Prince
Henry's 'wife', still styled the princess of Wales, but robbed of
her own home, must henceforth live at court like a poor
relation, to be attended by only five of her ladies, Alonso de
Esquivel, her Master of the Hall, Juan de Cuero, her treasurer,
and a physician. Already her cook had been sent back to Spain,
captured on the way and enslaved by the Moors of Barbary –
but what mattered most to the pious Catherine, at twenty,
far from kin and country, she was left with no Spanish
confessor.

The prince's feelings when Catherine came to reside permanently at court were probably mixed – pity for his damsel in
distress, joy that she was at last living in the same palace with
him. Any hope that he had, however, of frequent intimate
meetings with Catherine was to be disappointed. The king
must prevent not just any physical love-making between his
fast maturing son and the girl desperate to marry him, but any
verbal love-making also; because even a promise to wed between
a man and a girl could constitute a legal pre-contract invalidat-
ing any future marriage, as Edward IV's children had discovered to their cost.

In a palace as spread out as Westminster and divided by

courtyards, it was easy to keep even lovers apart. Catherine was allotted rooms at the other end of the sprawling palace, so vast a distance from Prince Henry that he rarely saw her, except with bowed head and prettily grave expression on Church festival days when the king went in procession and the whole palace gathered for religious worship. She lived almost entirely hidden in her apartments – she slept, ate, read, played the lute, embroidered and prayed here, and practised those modified forms of religious penance allowed to her by an English confessor whom she could barely understand. This secluded existence was varied only when the king, relenting, invited her to join the English royal family for some special entertainment. And even then it was not easy for Prince Henry to talk to her, for Catherine's English was still as halting as his Spanish.

The difficulties of their meeting and the distance which the king kept between them preserved a hazy romantic charm round Catherine that hid from Prince Henry her unyielding nature and fixity of purpose: to marry him as her father had ordered, or to die in England.

But although separating Catherine from the prince by rooms and galleries, corridors and courtyards, King Henry could not stop members of the prince's household from whispering to him of her misfortunes. He was bound to hear how Catherine, convalescing from a tertian fever, had been refused the meat her physician ordered because it was Friday and a fast day. How she was denied even a little saffron that she had sent for from the king's kitchens. How her ladies could not marry because she had no money to provide them with dowries. How her servants vainly tried to maintain the appearance of a court in Catherine's cramped chambers; and, since she could not afford to pay them, her Master of the Hall and her aged treasurer had had to sell their best silk and velvet clothes. And the prince would hear, too, shocked hints of Catherine's own growing shabbiness – how even her chemises were patched, and in order to buy just one new dress, a black velvet, she had had to sell some of her bracelets. But what could she do with

no money? And besides the king had recently said, with charac-
teristically cruel humour, that he would not accept her jewels
as part of her dowry; they were her personal ornaments, and
what would people think of him if he took away a lady's
ornaments? Catherine's plight was indeed desperate.

CHAPTER 13

'Best Beloved Brother'

'And you, my son of Wales, you see that we are old and
that in years to come you will need good friends.'
Henry VII

———————

ON 15 January 1506, soon after Catherine came to live at court,
a sudden terrible wind arose out of the south-west and blew
across London for twelve hours. From noon to midnight it
tore up trees, sent tiles spinning from roofs. It struck the brass
weathercock from its socket on the towering spire of St Paul's
and blew it across the churchyard into a neighbouring huddle
of houses where it shattered the sign of the black eagle; the
black eagle was the emblem of the German emperor. Superstitious Londoners who declared this a bad omen for him were
soon proved right. The same violent wind hurtled across the
Channel, where it seized and buffeted an imposing fleet sailing
off the English coast. The emperor's twenty-eight-year-old
son Philip, unable to reach Castile by land because of a treaty
King Ferdinand had made with her erstwhile enemy France,
had decided to journey to his wife's kingdom with his army by
sea. Customarily at this date kings kept their armies safely
at home in winter, but the king archduke, known also as Philip
the Fair, was both impatient and bold, qualities that were to
make him especially impressive to Prince Henry when fate
brought them together.

Philip had left the Netherlands accompanied by his queen,
a large army and many courtiers. With bravado and a fair
wind he had sailed past Calais by night, 'shooting guns,
having great torches lit in his and divers other ships, trumpets
and minstrels playing and singing, with great pomp passing

179

the narrow seas'. At midnight of the second night of his journey the mighty wind sprang and scattered the fleet, sending some ships to Wales, some to Dartmouth, some to Falmouth, and some to the bed of the sea, and leaving the king archduke's ship alone in the black storm. The distinguished passengers got ready to die. Joanna embraced Philip and swore she would die with him; Philip, shaking off Joanna who bored him, embraced his nobles and swore he would die with them.

Two days later, as rain and floods swept England, a black-clad Spaniard arrived suddenly at the English court, King Philip's secretary with a letter from his master to King Henry VII. With the rest of the court Prince Henry was soon alight with the news: Philip had come ashore at Melcombe Regis, near Weymouth in Dorset. The storm at sea had been terrible: people, horses, furniture and all the wheat supplies had been swept overboard into the boiling sea; thousands had been drowned; a husband had seen his wife washed away. It was a tale as grimly dramatic as Prince Henry had read in Latin versions of the *Iliad* and *Odyssey*, or in medieval romance. And it concerned a prince like himself, a prince who had been hero of the hour. King Philip had given a noble speech (although how anyone heard it while the storm raged so noisily is mysterious). Now in his letter, with a flourish of loving courtesy reminiscent of his former manner to Henry VII at their meeting at Calais in 1500, King Philip asked permission of his 'father', the king of England, to visit him. At this unexpected present from the hand of fortune the king sent back an effusive invitation to Philip to come to Windsor.

The warm relaxed happiness of that summer of 1504 once more suffused the court. Prince Henry saw his father change from his usual introverted mood to his occasional flowery expansiveness as he ordered an extravagant welcome. Philip's visit, Henry VII decided, was to be a 'triumph' such as there had not been since Princess Margaret's marriage.

No gift was too generous for the king to send to his new 'son'. To Philip he despatched rich clothes, horses, litters, food, and a selection of lords spiritual and temporal to escort the king archduke on the first lap of his journey. The court too was to shine in the luxury Prince Henry equated with happiness. To decorate the grey walls of Windsor Castle, the king sent rumbling over the bad roads carts full of plate and tapestry and silken hangings, cushions and cupboards and carved beds. He had allowed the court to grow shabby. Now the whole place and everyone in it was to get a face-lift. Tailors hastily stitched up new green-and-white liveries, while Prince Henry was despatched to meet Philip at the old palace of Winchester.

It has generally been supposed from reports of Spanish ambassadors that Henry VII kept his heir in the background and perpetually at his studies, but the task the prince was now allotted shows that by 1506 this was no longer always true. For he was to spend a night and a day with Philip in company with Richard Fox, bishop of Winchester. Although Henry VII was not yet ready to expose his fourteen-year-old son frequently to public view – he is very rarely mentioned in the chronicles – this mission suggests that the king was now ready to trust him in diplomatic encounters with envoys from all rulers except Ferdinand – a situation that is explained by the boy's dangerous partiality for Catherine.

Prince Henry set off for Winchester on 31 January and reached the palace at the time of vespers, primed with flattering speeches. But when he saw Philip's tall figure striding towards him, genial and smiling, it seems he had no need of flattery. According to an account of the meeting by an anonymous Fleming, thought to have been a member of Philip's suite, it was friendship at first sight. Philip, in the words of the chronicler Edward Hall, 'amiable and lovely . . . quick-witted, bold', a man of strong physical appetites, extrovert and jovial, was exactly fashioned to please the adolescent Prince Henry.

That night's banqueting was uninhibited by the presence of Queen Joanna, who was already subject to those bouts of melancholy that would enable her husband and father when it suited them to claim she was mad. Her possessive love embarrassed Philip, who preferred more ordinary women; he had left her behind in Wolverton Manor in Dorset with the excuse that she was exhausted by the storm. Over the table laden with pastry, game and goblets of wine from the bishop's cellars, Philip and Henry, discoursing in French, discovered that they had much in common besides the mutual attraction of their lonely high birth.

Each saw and admired in the other a male of similar type – large, athletic, sensual yet pious. Philip had spell-binding stories to tell a young boy about the recent disaster at sea – how it had seemed as if the waves and the wind together wished to swallow them, how day had dawned as dark as night, hiding from them the nearby shore, how the sails were all torn and Philip with his companions had huddled together in freezing cold on the deck, barefoot and bareheaded. How he, Philip, giving himself up for dead, had nevertheless prayed frantically into the storm, to God, to the glorious Virgin Mary, promising that if she would intercede for his life he would go on pilgrimage to her churches at Montserrat and Guadalupe and offer in each church before her image his own weight in money. She must have heard him because a miracle had then happened. No sooner had he made his vow than the sky cleared slightly and they could see the shore, enabling them to sail their tattered ship into a tiny harbour. But even then their dangers were not at an end. For the inhabitants, thinking them invaders, nearly shot them full of arrows. One can hear Philip's engaging laugh ring out.

This marvellous adventure still casts a spell today read in the Flemish contemporary account in L. P. Gachard's *Collection des Voyages des Souverains des Pays-Bas*. How much more spellbinding must the story have been when told by the king archduke himself to the fourteen-year-old boy, in the candlelight and deep shadow of the tapestried room, agleam with firelight, jewels and silver-gilt cups full of wine.

It is not surprising that when after dinner the next morning Henry and Philip rode forth towards Windsor, they appeared to their Flemish observer 'good friends and brothers'. Although the Spaniards were all in black – Philip's hood, gown and harness of black velvet, and his company of less than a dozen

nobles in black 'tawny', a less luxurious fabric – it was nevertheless a cheerful party that rode through a countryside whose
floods had suddenly turned to ice. In a frosty stubble field a
couple of miles from Windsor, King Henry waited to give the
official greeting, wearing a purple velvet gown and hood,
topped by both a cap and a bonnet, and riding a bay mare in
embroidered trappings, his splendidly mounted nobility lined
up on either side.

King Henry and King Philip each courteously swept off his
cap and bonnet, but retained their hoods against the cold.
Then King Henry welcomed his guest in a short speech –
there was no point, he remarked drily, in giving a long speech
in a field on a cold day – in which he further drew King Philip
and Prince Henry together. 'You are as welcome to me as my
own son here,' he told Philip. 'I and my son and my whole
kingdom are at your disposal.' Then, with Philip between them,
royal father and son rode towards the newly decorated Windsor
Castle where, as they entered the first gate, 'minstrels and sackbuts played'.

Although it was to last not quite a month, King Philip's
visit to the English court was one of the high points in Prince
Henry's development. For the first time he was to attend one
of the rare summit meetings of the day between monarchs, to
have a front row view of his father's cunning and ruthless
diplomacy, and to be included in the secret conversations as
though he were an adult; and for the first time he was to enjoy
the company of a young man of even higher rank than his own.
To add to these pleasant and stimulating new experiences,
Philip's visit was made more memorable for Henry by its very
special political significance: Philip held in his power the man
who more than any other cast a shadow over the prince's future,
the only one of the pretenders so far to escape Henry VII's net.
Repeatedly Maximilian had refused to extradite De la Pole, on
the grounds that Aix-la-Chapelle, where he resided, was a free
city. But in 1504 the White Rose was forced to flee from his
debts, to be captured first by the duke of Guelders, then by

Philip, who now had him semi-imprisoned in his castle of Namur. For Prince Henry it was even more important to have this pretender safely back in England than it was for King Henry VII; for it was the young prince's claim to the throne on Henry VII's death that the White Rose was most likely to contest. So beneath the delight of Philip's company, the gaiety and pastime that Philip brought with him to court, there was for Prince Henry an undercurrent of excitement, a dramatic question mark. Could Philip be persuaded to hand over Cousin Edmund?

To impress his important guest, Henry VII scattered the carefully collected wealth of his coffers, like a figure from one of the romances. And on their arrival at Windsor Castle Henry VII insisted on himself showing Philip to his rooms. He escorted the king archduke up the steps of the new tower and through three magnificent state chambers, shining with silken hangings and splendid with carved canopied beds covered in silk, velvet and fur. (For beds, being rare and precious, were a feature of most of the royal rooms.) But it was not until Philip stood in the doorway of the final chamber that he understood what sacrifice his host had made. This room, according to an anonymous Englishman, probably a herald, was 'hanged with rich cloth of gold, the border above of crimson velvet and embroidered with the king's arms, with other royal devices . . . roses, portcullises etc.' Such lavishness could belong only to the bedchamber of a king; Henry VII had relinquished his own apartments to his guest – the medieval virtue of courtesy could be carried no further. And at the same time as he sacrificed his own comfort for Philip, Henry VII fed and housed all his retinue as well and promised to pay all his expenses when he should depart again for the English coast. Frugality seemed to have fled the court. Now everything was plentiful, even kindness.

The following afternoon, after dinner, Prince Henry had the rare experience of seeing Catherine treated as though she was Henry VII's 'daughter' in fact as well as figure of speech. In her black velvet dress, a foil for her youth and her jewels, she helped to entertain Philip: Mary played the lute and the regals and danced, partnered by an English lady; Catherine danced before him partnered by a Spanish lady. As though equally favoured, both princesses then went to join the king and the king archduke on the carpeted dais. This compliment to his possession, his 'wife', would presumably have pleased the enamoured Prince Henry, although Catherine's pleasure was slightly marred by a snub she received. When, anxious to put in a word for her father King Ferdinand, she bravely asked her brother-in-law to dance, he refused with a light quip, jokingly referring to his experience at sea, 'I am a plain sailor, yet you would have me dance?' And he turned away and resumed his conversation with Henry VII. But if the prince observed this incident he is unlikely to have held it against Philip. Was this not, after all, the accepted way to treat women who attempted to interfere in politics, a man's preserve?

Encouraged by his father, Henry was to use Philip the Fair as his model, and this charming but callous royal guest was as a result to have an influence far greater than the length of his stay. The king deliberately threw his son and the young monarch together. Together they hunted and played tennis, the king archduke using one of the new pear-shaped rackets instead of batting the ball with the palm of his hand, which was then the usual method of playing. Together they watched the contemporary 'sport' of horse-baiting, a variation on the popular bear- and bull-baiting, in which a horse was tied to a post, set upon by dogs and forced to try to defend itself with teeth and lashing hooves. And together they shared in elaborate ceremonial. On 9 February under the painted and gilded ceiling of St George's Chapel, Prince Henry took part in a magnificent exchange of compliments. First King Philip was created a Knight of the Garter – with the prince kneeling to fasten the symbol of this English order round Philip's athletic leg; then Prince Henry was in his turn invested with the crimson velvet robes and mantle, the collar and pendant of the Burgundian order of the Golden Fleece. At the same ceremony in the same opulent and sacred surroundings, the two kings signed a treaty which they swore on 'the real wood of the cross of our saviour' should 'last for all time to come', and in which each promised to be 'a friend of a friend and an enemy of the enemies' of the other and swore, if finding the other's rebels in his dominions to have them conducted in chains to prison. After that, although the White Rose was not specifically mentioned, surely Philip would feel obliged to yield him up. As an especial bonus, Philip also signed a marriage treaty, according to which King Henry was to marry Margaret, archduchess of Savoy, with a large dowry of 30,000 crowns.

Afterwards Prince Henry dined with the two kings in the privy chamber. Henry VII was euphoric. He delivered one of his most flowery speeches. 'This dinner is a symbol of the new amity between England and Castile,' he declared. 'Our enemies shall have nothing to rejoice at in this meeting. This table where we dine shall become as famous as King Arthur's round table at Winchester. We shall have it put on display as a memorial to the perpetual friendship and alliance which has been made at it.' Then, according to our Flemish contemporary narrative, he turned and said to his son:

And you, my son of Wales, you see that we are old and that in years to come you will need good friends. And consider that what I do now for my good son, the king here, I do not do because I hope to get some reward from him, but I do it for the honour of his person and his virtues and so that he will always look with favour on you. And I conjure you always to be loyal to him and that you take care always to think of him before yourself and that you prefer his needs and affairs to your own.

It was a deeply significant occasion for Prince Henry. These were words to make him feel the reality of his approaching kingship with all its responsibilities and pleasures, his own rapidly coming importance; for his father had made for him the first foreign alliance of his approaching reign.

This delightful little dinner *à trois* was interrupted by a palace official bearing an insistent message from a French envoy who had just arrived at Dover and begged an audience of the king. Wishing to keep in with France, Henry VII at the same time feared to offend Philip, and his solution to this problem was an instructive lesson in political balancing. He issued a grudging invitation to the Frenchman to attend a banquet at court, but delegated the rest of the envoy's entertainment to his son: Prince Henry spoke good French, he could take the French envoy hunting. The prince, taught by Margaret Beaufort to hate the French, protested; but this was a mere gesture to please Philip. Because his father's order was in fact a compliment; it showed – and before Philip – what confidence Henry VII already placed in his son, a confidence that seems to have been merited.

Prince Henry was by nature an affable host, with the high spirits that shed delight over the most ordinary pastime. But standing with the French envoy on a hidden platform in the deer park, he could not resist making one jibe. His arrow had brought down a stag. 'Well shot! Well shot!' cried the envoy, with diplomatic enthusiasm. The prince, his fair skin bright with triumph, turned his head, looked at him with hard blue eyes and said gracefully, 'Yes, good enough for a Frenchman,' which the envoy took as a compliment to the skill of French archers, but which, the prince afterwards revealed to Philip, really meant: 'I wish a Frenchman rather than the deer had had the shaft inside his body.'

This remark reveals the precocious duplicity beneath the courteous bearing of Prince Henry at fourteen. But duplicity surrounded him; and at no time more poignantly than when Philip's wife Joanna arrived at court.

On 10 February 1506, a fine winter's day, the prince waited on the stone steps of the new tower at Windsor, with his father, Philip, Catherine and Princess Mary to receive the queen of Castile. Suddenly in the frosted park a brightly-coloured little group trotted out from under the white oak trees: Joanna with her ladies and an escort of English noblemen led by Lord Mountjoy. It was the nearest that Prince Henry was to come in his teens to being part of a family reunion. Henry VII stepped forward to embrace and kiss her (for Joanna was still very pretty with a disturbingly direct way of talking). Catherine and Mary followed suit, then the whole group went up into the warmth of the tower. But beneath this loving welcome, lit up by Joanna's dangerously frenetic gaiety, less loving feelings lurked. The ambitious Philip had contemplated formally declaring his wife mad and putting her under restraint, thus being able to seize all her inheritance of Castile for himself. As for Henry VII, who was afterwards to express the greatest affection for Joanna, he treated her at this moment with outward courtesy, but no true consideration; for he was secretly plotting with Philip to remove power from Ferdinand. As Catherine was intensely loyal to her father, he dared not leave the sisters together, so although they had not seen each other for four years, Henry VII allowed them only one night in each other's company. The day after the queen's arrival he sent Catherine and Mary to Richmond and he himself rode there with the prince a day later. Joanna remained a further three nights with her husband at Windsor to satisfy convention and to sign the treaties. Then, having sent her in a litter paid for by Henry VII to Exeter safely out of the way of his policies, Philip also rode gaily off to Richmond. Thus both by his father and his hero, Prince Henry had set before him yet another example of cruelty in personal relations; he was to follow it himself in later life.

It was at Richmond on Sunday 15 February that King Henry VII received the expected dividend on his huge investment, a formal promise from Philip to send to England the last Yorkist pretender, Prince Henry's second cousin, Edmund de la Pole, in exchange for a written undertaking from King Henry that he would spare De la Pole's life and pardon him – an undertaking however that did not bind his successor.

Henry VII was now willing to let his visitor depart. From Philip's point of view the weather was milder, the sea less rough, it would soon be time to sail.

On Thursday 18 February the two kings and the prince rode, hawking as they went, to Baynard's Castle, the Thames-side

palace inside the walled city of London; on Friday they rode
to the Tower; on Saturday, in procession through the city of
Westminster; and on Sunday back to Richmond – there to
watch a display of wrestling between Englishmen and Spaniards
and – variation of Philip's apparently favourite brutal sport –
'baiting between horse and bear'. Finally, on Saturday 28 February they rode again to Windsor, past a row of cheering Eton
schoolboys standing along the churchyard bars. On Sunday they
took savage joy in another barbaric horse-baiting and on
Monday 2 March 1506 Philip took his leave after Henry VII
had made an emotional speech, attempting to bind together
his son and Philip in perpetual amity. According to our
anonymous Flemish reporter, he begged his guest:

> for your virtue, franchise and nobleness to become the father,
> guard, protector and friend of my son of Wales who is here.
> And I beg you, if he needs your assistance, to do for him as
> I have for you. And my lord if you have any trouble in Spain
> you know I have no son but this one, nevertheless since I
> know the love that he has for you and to help you, I shall
> send him to you . . .

As usual in his flowery speeches, Henry VII had overdone it,
but, according to the Flemish chronicler of the scene, it was
an emotional occasion for everyone there.

The speeches ended at last, the black-clad Spaniards moved
away, taking the king archduke, who was Prince Henry's new
idol, with them. As Philip and his entourage trotted off there
were tears, the chronicler reports, in men's eyes. Prince Henry
was given to wild swings of emotion often unrelated to any
lasting depth of feeling, but that his sorrow at parting from
Philip was genuine we have evidence. Prince Henry all his life
would find letter-writing tiresome, despite Mountjoy's early
coaching, and either dictate his correspondence or leave it to a
minister. Two rare letters that he wrote himself concern
Philip. The first, in French, was written on 9 April 1506 when
the king archduke, delayed by illness on his journey to the coast,
was still in England, waiting at Falmouth for a favourable

wind. This letter in Henry's own youthful handwriting can be seen in the British Library; here is the English translation:

> Most high, most excellent and mighty prince,
> I commend myself to you in the most affectionate and hearty manner that I can. Whereas the chamberlain of my most dear and well-beloved consort, the princess my wife, is going at present to you for certain matters which he says he has to transact in that quarter, he has requested me to write to you in his favour. I pray you very heartily, most high, most excellent and mighty prince, that you will hold him recommended in his said affairs, and that you will apprise me from time to time and let me know of your good health and prosperity, which I particularly and with all my heart desire to be of long continuance as I would my own. And for my part, whenever I can find a fitting messenger I am determined to do the like to you.
> Moreover on your intimating to me if there be anything here in which I can do you honour or pleasure, I will take pains to satisfy you in it with all my heart, by the good aid of Our Lord, whom I pray to give you, most high, most excellent and mighty prince, good life and long. Written at the manor of Greenwich the 9th day of April.
> Your humble cousin,
> HENRY PRINCE OF WALES.

The excuse for the letter – a request for patronage for some favoured servant – was a fairly usual request from one prince to another – although the fact that the servant concerned was Catherine's, reveals the extent of her influence at this early date over Henry. What was not usual, however, was the addition of the request to Philip to write back. Sandwiched in the middle of this formal letter, it was a cry for continued friendship, a proud and lonely boy's plea for companionship with a man of high rank who had stirred him to admiration and gratitude.

For the gratitude there was good cause. Philip had sent orders for Edmund de la Pole to be sent to Calais. And here on 16 March this last of the pretenders to haunt the reign of

King Henry VII was handed over. On 24 March the controller of the town, Sir John Wilshire, with a guard of nine fully armed soldiers brought him across the Channel. At Dover he was met by Sir Thomas Lovell and conveyed by night to comfortable but secure apartments in the Tower with a secrecy that suggests Henry VII feared to give Londoners another focus for rebellion. At last the man who more than any other might have menaced Prince Henry's chance of peaceful succession was, thanks to his hero King Philip, safe behind thick walls and narrow barred windows.

The reply Philip made to Prince Henry's letter, perhaps through Mountjoy, who at the king's orders kept Philip company at his departure port of Falmouth, has not survived. There was however to be little time for friendship.

The rest of Philip's life was like a moral tale. After he left England and arrived with his army in Spain, everything seemed to go Philip's way. Ferdinand, who had sworn in 1505 that he intended to rule Castile to the end of his days 'and not for to diminish or lose therein of his honour and profit the value of a bean', surprisingly retreated peacefully to Aragon. Philip and Joanna were jointly crowned king and queen of Castile in the gold-encrusted cathedral at Burgos. Then, at the peak of his good fortune, on 25 September 1506, Philip died suddenly after a brief illness – poisoned, scandal whispered, by King Ferdinand, and a story came out of Spain that Joanna, to whom Philip now belonged in death as never in life, had his coffin carried about with her wherever she went – a macabre ending for the handsome young king for whose friendship Prince Henry had tried so hard. It was more evidence of the inconstancy of fortune, the fleeting quality of life of which he had already had too much. By the age of fifteen the prince had lost two sisters, two brothers, his mother and now the king to whom his heart had turned in friendship; for him indeed love and death seemed intermingled. Word of his grief travelled over the sea, probably through Mountjoy, to Erasmus, who wrote Prince Henry a letter of condolence in Latin. The prince wrote an elegant reply, also in Latin, beginning with one of the pious tags in fashion at the time:

Jesus is my hope

I am greatly affected by your letter, most eloquent Erasmus, which is at once too elegant to be taken as written in haste, and at the same time too plain and simple to seem premeditated by a mind so ingenious. For in some way those epistles which by a mind thus endowed are brought forth with the more designed elaboration, in like manner carry with them a more studied difficulty. For while we apply ourselves to a purer eloquence, that open and clear manner of speech escapes us almost unawares. But this your epistle is to be esteemed as much for its evident perspicuity, so that, in fine, you seem to have achieved every point. But wherefore do I determine to laud your eloquence, whose renown is known throughout the whole world? Nothing that I am able to fashion in your praise can be worthy enough of that consummate erudition. Wherefore I pass over your praises, in the which I think it the more fit to keep silence than to speak in manner too niggard.

The news of the death of the king of Castile *my wholly and entirely and best-beloved brother*, I had reluctantly received very long before your letter. Would that the report thereof, had either reached us much later or been less true! For never since the death of my dearest mother, hath there come to me more hateful intelligence. And to speak truth, I was the scanter well-disposed towards your letter than its singular grace demanded, because it seemed to tear open again the wound to which time had brought insensibility. But indeed those things which are decreed by Heaven are so to be accepted by mortal men. Continue, therefore, if in your country there be any tidings to advertise us by letters, but may they be of happier sort. May God bring to a fortunate issue whatsoever may happen that is worthy thus to be remembered. Farewell.

From Richmond, the 17th day of January.

This quite extraordinary letter by such a young boy foreshadows Henry's manhood – his belligerent keenness to accept a challenge and to prove himself equal to the best, his intellectual vanity, his egotism – and his exceptional ability. For when Erasmus suspected that such a young boy could not have composed the letter by himself, Lord Mountjoy – who had access to the prince's papers – showed Erasmus a corrected first draft of this letter that proved Prince Henry well able to write polished Latin without help.

But beneath the mannered phrases is the cry of defiantly real grief for 'my wholly and entirely and best-beloved brother' with whom no other companion could compare. Now he had no one left of similar rank except Catherine, whom he was rarely allowed to see, little Mary his sister, his grandmother and his father.

The prince had developed a companionship of a kind with his father. Through the *Great Chronicle* we catch a glimpse of them walking along a gallery in Richmond Palace in 1506, the king a thin faded figure beside his already bigger heir, with his fresh pink-and-white and auburn colouring and young vigour. But the companionship was bound to be an authoritarian teacher-pupil one, and the king's failing health did not improve it. In the spring of 1507 the king was stricken by a mystery illness during which, for six days, he could neither eat nor drink. His black-robed physicians thought he was dying, but to their surprise, he recovered, though the illness left him for several months more thin and worn than ever, and he grew impatient even with his loved only son. While old King Henry's abilities declined and young Prince Henry's grew, obedience became increasingly hard for him to give. As the months passed the causes for friction between them multiplied.

CHAPTER 14

Love and Conflict

'He scolded the prince as though he would kill him.'
Gutierre Gomez de Fuensalida

———

EVEN the proudest of fathers feels a twinge of jealousy when he sees his son grow stronger and more potent than he, and the aging and ailing Henry VII had never been as physically splendid as the prince, who by the age of sixteen was portrayed in a poem describing the May and June games at Greenwich as already 'most comly of stature' and of 'parsonage'. Fast approaching his final height of six feet three, his body was so superbly muscled from the constant demanding exercise he loved that in future years men would remember him as a youth in terms of classical heroes. The author and diplomat Sir Thomas Chaloner, born in 1521 and sent on embassy to Charles V in 1540, wrote:

> Even Hercules of old could hardly have bent the yew bow so well with the sinewy strength of his arms . . . and, in wrestling, Pollux would have been no match for him in striving for the wreath of oak leaves. Whenever he sought to turn the powerful neck of a warhorse, controlling it with cunning voice and hand, you would think he was Castor himself; and if he put on his shining armour, his splendid helmet with nodding crest, and his gilded breast-plate he would excel even Trojan Hector. When he hunted deer through the woods with nets and a pack of hounds, not even Hippolitus . . . could have surpassed him in glory.

Chaloner exaggerated, but not much.
That summer of 1507 the May and June games at Greenwich

consisted of 'jousts, archery, tourneying on foot with sword and spear, wrestling and casting of the bar'. One of the challengers on both occasions was the prince's companion Charles Brandon, whom Henry admired as much as he could admire anyone of humbler rank. The May games were in honour of Princess Mary, who presided in a green dress as Lady May, but the June games were performed at young Henry's special request, the poet tells us.

> Syth our prynce . . .
> Is desyrous to the moost knyghtly vre [use]
> Of armes to whiche marcyall auenture
> Is his courage.

From this poem we gather that at these games young Henry was a gracious spectator only:

> It pleaseth hym of his benygnyte
> To suffre gentylmen of lowe degre
> In his presence
> To speke of armes and of other defence
> Without doynge vnto his grace offence.

But if he was a mere spectator at the tournament in 1507, it was for the last time. At the age of seventeen and in the year 1508, the prince of Wales began to appear regularly in the contests himself – a sensational competitor. Head and shoulders taller, according to Chaloner, than the average sixteenth-century Englishman, he was clad in the finest Italian armour, his splendid horse caparisoned in rich cloth embroidered all over with the ostrich plume emblem of the heir to the throne. And to the audience of courtiers, who were well aware that any day now this shining boy would hold the fate of each one of them in his strong hands, he would indeed have looked heroic. At every flamboyant feat of the tournament – at running at the ring and at fighting on foot with sword and spear, as well as at jousting in the tiltyard, they saw him excel. And after he had won, when he lifted his helmet from his exultant boyish face, he looked so handsome that he seemed not just heroic but fully 'divine'; two years later his face would be described as 'fair and bright' and 'so very beautiful that it would become a pretty woman, his throat being rather long and thick'.

Yet despite his growing maturity and the kingdom's clear need for a second heir to the throne, he was still no nearer to living with the woman who according to their betrothal ceremony in 1503 was already his wife. Coolly assessing her 'husband's' libido in September 1507, Catherine wrote to her father, 'He is not yet so old that delay is disagreeable.' But Catherine had not taken account of the romantic in young Henry, which would always be stronger than sexual desire. In the sexual hothouse of the English court, the delay would have become progressively less bearable for the youth divided from the object of his love by a royal rabbit warren of chambers and corridors.

It was not as though Prince Henry was allowed to distract himself with other women. Apart from a much later rumour of an affair with Lady Elizabeth Boleyn (daughter of the earl of Surrey and wife of Thomas Boleyn, then esquire of the body to Henry VII), a rumour which was probably based on very little foundation, there was in a court alive with gossip no suggestion of Prince Henry having any sexual liaison. His attraction to Catherine, so rarely and tantalizingly glimpsed, was bound to strengthen with the months; although he was still kept hard at his lessons by his father and his small thin grandmother.

Lady Margaret in her black-and-white robes, continued to visit court and organize the domestic affairs of her beloved son. But her hands and knees had become agonizingly crippled now with arthritis and her attention was more than ever focused on religion, as can be seen from two scholarly works she interested herself in: a treatise on the seven penitential psalms published by John Fisher at her request in 1505, and *The Mirror of Gold for the Sinful Soul* which Lady Margaret herself translated from French and had published in 1507. It was too late in her life for Henry's grandmother to feel sympathy with young love.

For his part, the king observed with typical lack of sentiment that Catherine was 'full of virtues and good qualities but similar attributes could be found in many ladies, some richer than others'. He was still bent on an alliance with the Hapsburgs. Now that Philip was dead Henry VII negotiated directly with Maximilian, who wanted the prince to marry Eleanor. The King of the Romans was also trying secretly to persuade Henry VII to help him to drive Ferdinand from Castile and substitute as ruler 'mad Joanna', or her son Charles, under imperial domination.

It cannot have been pleasant for Prince Henry to know that his marriage was at the mercy of his father's devious foreign policy, but to make his situation even more unhappy, he had before his considering blue eyes what would have seemed to a boy so young a ridiculous spectacle. His father who was fifty-one, thin, yellow-faced, with sparse teeth and white hair, his body wasted by illness, appeared to be in love.

In the summer of 1506 Margaret of Savoy, having seen the portrait of her elderly lover painted for her by Michel Sittow, seemed disinclined to marry Henry VII although both Philip and Maximilian tried to make her change her mind. Inconclusive negotiations for the marriage would continue until 1508, but at the same time, Henry VII searched for a new bride. Philip the Fair's death in September 1506 had left the legal sovereign of Castile a widow and so apparently again a possible match. Beneath his rational practical behaviour Henry VII hid a dream of empire. His daughter Mary's projected marriage to Maximilian's grandson Charles should enormously extend the Tudor dominions, but that was unlikely to happen until after Henry VII's death. His own marriage with Joanna opened the prospect of instant empire in his lifetime. And why not? His 'brother', 'the most serene and most excellent King Ferdinand' of Spain, had married a young wife, Germaine de Foix, niece of Louis XII, in March 1506. By marrying Joanna, Henry could become king of Castile and add a second kingdom to the one he had conquered.

It was a delightful thought; and so too was Joanna herself,

the key to this treasure. He remembered her as 'dignified in speech and manner'. She had for him the appeal that a beautiful woman of twenty-eight can have for an older man.

Catherine's sister Joanna became the English king's latest quarry, and his imagination gave way to pent-up sexual longings. He longed to protect her against unhappiness. If she were mad, as they said, he would not marry her for three kingdoms like Castile, but when he had seen her in England she was sane; he did not believe she was mad now. Philip's treatment of her, his well-known infidelities, his threat to imprison her in a fortress, the way first he, then Ferdinand, had usurped from her the government of her kingdom, would make anyone mad. Through the glow of his new feelings, he imagined himself during her visit to England in 1506 intervening between husband and wife, pressing her to come to Richmond and making Philip treat her more kindly. 'If when she was in England I had acted as I secretly wished,' he swore in 1507, 'I would by every possible means have prevented her leaving my court. But I was prevented by my council.'

Such was the kind of passionate unlikely sentiment that Prince Henry, in love himself, was forced to listen to from his fifty-one-year-old father, to listen to without protest, while facing the prospect of a queen and step-mother whom some people believed to be mad.

This last strange matrimonial dream of his father's is one of the threads in the woof on which the prince's own life in the years 1507 and 1508 was woven, and later the experience would be the pattern for his own middle-aged search for the perfect wife. At the time, ridicule and indignation must have fought in him with joy at one of the fringe benefits of his father's romantic longings: the negotiations brought him on several occasions within a chamber's width of his 'wife'. For Ferdinand had cleverly taken advantage of the situation, replying to the English king's proposal of marriage that, if Joanna married anyone, it would be his beloved brother, and authorizing Catherine to act as his ambassador in the matter. To press his suit the enamoured king was willing to risk Catherine's coming closer to his son and he summoned her to his privy chamber for repeated audiences. Moodily bent over his studies next door, the prince was ironically aware that, while his own 'wife' was forbidden to speak to him, she was at present listening to his father's expressions of ardour for her sister. But there was hope. To marry Joanna, Henry VII seemed eager to offer almost any bribe. He would even, he fervently promised Catherine, join her father in a crusade against the Moors in Africa. Cunningly encouraged, might he not also agree to conclude Catherine's marriage to the prince?

Prince Henry owed it to his father's new friendlier feeling towards Ferdinand that his 'wife' was temporarily better treated. Setting forth at the end of August 1507 on six weeks of particularly strenuous hunting, followed on a litter by the gout-ridden but determined De Puebla, the king eventually agreed to the Spanish ambassador's repeated requests for an audience to discuss Catherine's as well as Joanna's marriage. On 7 September Henry VII sent Catherine £200 and an affectionate note, saying reassuringly that he loved her so much that he could not bear the thought of her poverty and insisting that he himself was in perfect health and enjoying a very agreeable life. When for a few days' delightful sport the court went to Winchester, Catherine was invited to ride with them – a sight that filled Dr De Puebla, ill as he was, with optimism and hyperbole. From Winchester he wrote this description of the prince: 'There is no finer youth in the world than the prince of Wales. He is already taller than his father, and his limbs are of a gigantic size. He is as prudent as is to be expected from a son of Henry VII.' He added, 'The princess of Wales is well and her health constantly improves,' a note which suggests that Catherine too was blossoming in the leafy parks and the unwonted company of her husband-to-be.

But Catherine was not a girl to lose her political opportunities in enjoyment. It was her determination to marry the prince; it was also her duty to bring England to the aid of Spain. Young Henry's remarkably pro-Spanish attitude on foreign policy when he came to power, suggests that Catherine used every one of her rare chances, including this one, to influence him. Already he dreamed of riding like Henry V at the head of a conquering army through France. The alliance between Ferdinand and expansionist France had now worn thin. If the prince allied himself with Ferdinand, Catherine would advise him, Ferdinand would help him against France. 'Indeed, if the king were dead,' she would soon be informing the Spanish ambassador, 'I should have no difficulty with the prince.'

For the rest of the year 1507 the prince watched his father – that normally most realistic of men – living in a fool's paradise as negotiations continued for his marriage with Joanna which everyone else at court knew was impossible. Catherine, hoping that these audiences would enable her to persuade Henry VII to conclude her own marriage, hoping she might glimpse the prince and perhaps exchange tokens with him, cunningly humoured the English king as ordered by her father.

The only obstacle stopping the marriage plans of his 'best beloved brother of England', Ferdinand told Catherine to say, was that Joanna still refused to have Philip buried, and no one dared to take the coffin from her, an argument that fortunately for Catherine's and young Henry's hopes seemed unanswerable, although Joanna's refusal is now considered to have been an invention of Ferdinand's to enable him to retain power.

In March 1508 it seemed that the young couple's hopes might soon be realized. Nervous that he might lose Castile now that Henry VII was becoming too friendly with Maximilian, Ferdinand actually forced himself to send the second half of Catherine's dowry to England. A Genoese banker, Francisco de Grimaldo, brought it at the end of February. With Grimaldo came a new ambassador, Don Gutierre Gomez de Fuensalida, Knight Commander of the order of Membrilla, a nobleman with a grand manner for whom Catherine had asked, believing paranoically and mistakenly that De Puebla was sabotaging her marriage. A little forceful speech from a new ambassador, she believed, would soon persuade Henry VII to solemnize her match with the prince.

When Fuensalida stepped proudly on to the shores of England Henry VII was ill again, this time 'with a disease of the joints'. He was exhausted and in pain, but nevertheless ordered his knights of the body to wrap him in his royal robes. With cloth-of-gold and ermine flapping about his thinness, he received the new ambassador at Richmond Palace with compliments flowery enough to nourish the hope in the young lovers' hearts. He loved Catherine like his own wife, he declared. She could command what she pleased of him in his kingdom. Admittedly many other ladies of high birth and much greater dowries had been offered to him for his son, he added thoughtfully, but never for a moment had he considered accepting them; he was a man who kept his word.

For the following day he had ordered a tournament in the tiltyard to celebrate Maximilian's final execution of the treaty of marriage between his grandson Charles and the princess Mary. King Henry VII invited Catherine and the new Spanish ambassador to watch Prince Henry joust.

Walking haltingly out of the palace towards the royal box, he took both his daughter Mary and Catherine each by a hand and paid them compliments in the rambling unsteady speech of a sick man. 'See, ambassador,' he enthused. 'Have I not reason to be proud standing between two such princesses?' He looked at Mary – 'The princess, my daughter . . .' then his mind and heart jumped as he caught sight of his heir Prince Henry resplendent in the tiltyard ('that God hath joined such a pair as she and the prince my son are, from whom I hope, God willing, to have fine grandchildren') . . . He turned gallantly to Catherine – 'and the princess of Castile, my daughter.' Here with a fresh spurt of energy he remembered his newly acquired son, Charles. 'And the prince of Castile. They are also fine creatures.' He took a tighter grip on the hand of the smiling, blushing Catherine. 'Look at her here! And you know the prince of Castile well, whom they say is a lovely creature.'

This appearance of family affection however – as far as Prince Henry's 'wife' was concerned – was short-lived, as were hopes of a speedy conclusion of their marriage. In April

1508 King Henry VII's weak eyes were given an upsetting glimpse of Spanish double-dealing as crafty as his own. His envoy in Spain, John Stile, wrote to say that he had obtained several interviews with Queen Joanna which showed that Ferdinand had cheated and had no intention of again losing the government of Castile by marrying his daughter to anyone. Meanwhile he was treating Joanna cruelly.

The news from Spain plunged the ailing king into such fury that no one dared to speak to him, but it was Prince Henry's bad fortune to be summoned to the royal chamber at a moment when jealousy already lay between them like gunpowder awaiting the spark. As gossips later reported, their words quickly led to the edge of violence and it is not difficult to guess their tenor. Henry VII told his son the contents of Stile's despatch, then paused, expecting the boy to console him, to exclaim indignantly against Ferdinand or against Catherine, who had simply used the Joanna marriage as bait to help along her own.

But the prince remained silent while behind the angelic face anger struggled against self-control. For he too had had his bride snatched away from him – by the king! By his own father, the very man who was now demanding *his* sympathy! Prince Henry's anger burst wildly forth. What did the news from Spain matter? Joanna was mad anyway, and his father too old for love.

In the king's disappointment and desiccated exhaustion it needed less than such adolescent tactlessness to explode answering fury. 'He scolded the prince as though he would kill him,' one of the court ladies reported with horrified gusto to Fuensalida, who hastened to hand on the titbit to Ferdinand.

So heart-broken and infuriated was the king by the news from Spain that, after his son had left, according to Fuensalida's gossiping court lady, he 'sat in a chair as though transfixed, eyes shut, for two or three hours, neither awake nor asleep'. But even though his father's anger had been only partly caused by young Henry, it would have given the boy a shock, reminding him that a king's fury had teeth, that his

father was also his sovereign lord, who could take from him
his lands, his servants, his horses, his beloved sports, his newest,
most fashionable clothes. Not surprisingly, the ambassador's
letters to Spain never again mention a quarrel between the
prince and the king. Prince Henry had learned a useful lesson.
Henceforth his hostility to his father must be hidden behind a
smiling face, like a turbulent underground stream beneath an
agreeable landscape. At the age of sixteen he had acquired a
lifelong habit: to hide his anger and jealousy until the opportunity came for revenge.

King Henry had learned a useful lesson too: to preserve the
distance between all Spaniards and his emotionally vulnerable
young son. Fuensalida, reporting on an interview that he
managed to obtain with the prince at this time, described him
as cowed and complained that the boy would answer none of
the questions put to him unless invited to do so by the king.

In succeeding months Fuensalida would try in vain for a
second interview with the prince only to discover he was 'as
carefully chaperoned as a young girl', either shut away in his
own apartments or exercising in the park with the companions
that the king had chosen for him. It was a situation in which
Prince Henry was powerless to defend Catherine from the
many extra, spiteful unkindnesses that Henry VII showered
on her in revenge for her deception.

There were no more presents of £200. Now the princess had
from the king once again food for herself and her servants
only – nothing on which to clothe herself or them, nothing
for wages or for ordinary household expenses. So she was
forced to sell still more of her dowry plate.

When in May the king was better and the court plunged into
the customary seasonal festivities at Greenwich, Catherine was
not invited to join the royal party. Her troubles made a sad
backcloth to the brilliant foreground of the prince's own life.
He competed in the tournaments every day while the king
watched from a silken pavilion, with Mary beside him.
Catherine was obliged to watch all alone except for her tiny
band of shabby Spanish courtiers, with whom she formed a

forlorn, ostracized, alien group. All those present could see that she was out of favour.

In the balmy evenings the king took his family and chosen courtiers on the river to glide pleasantly in the royal barge between the meadows while listening to the miniature orchestra of tabors, recorders and other medieval instruments that he had luxuriously ordered on board. Prince Henry knew the music would float through the clear air and the orchard blossom to Catherine, who sat deserted in the close little room that she had been allotted over a stable after having been made to give up her more airy and spacious apartments to Lady Margaret when she came to stay at Easter. On days when there was no tournament the royal party would set off on delightful rides, passing at the king's orders, between the fruit trees in front of Catherine's room, presumably to torment her with his power over her.

At mealtimes, while a vast procession of aromatic dishes travelled mouth-wateringly down the long corridors to Prince Henry and Princess Mary, those that arrived in Catherine's apartments were few and carelessly prepared. They humbled her before every scullion and footman who had seen them cooked or carried, and Catherine indignantly often refused to eat any of the food, declaring that she and her ladies – somewhat unfairly on her ladies – would die sooner than eat such swill. A princess walking in the fields or woods was normally followed by a servant with an elegantly harnessed horse, in case she tired; but since the king had had Catherine's horses removed from her, if she tired she had now to hire the best mount she could from some passer-by, and perhaps bear the humiliation when she returned of being seen on some peasant's overworked mule. In a society that clothed status in many more outward symbols than it does today, a society in which these symbols were admirable and important, the king's cruelty was obvious: he was depriving Catherine of her identity.

Henry VII was regarded by the rest of Europe as a clement king. Throughout his reign he had been markedly reluctant to shed blood. But to this one young girl he was merciless. Prince Henry was accustomed to seeing his Catherine looking pale and thin. It was the result partly of her refusal to eat poor food, partly of humiliation and anxiety, worry over money, worry about whether her marriage would ever take place. Indignant as he might feel about Catherine's treatment at the time, powerless in face of it as he was, this lesson of cruelty inside the family would sink deep into young Henry. And like many another son, when the time came he himself would eventually follow the example set by his father.

There is evidence that Prince Henry's feelings for his father were a conflict of hostility and admiration, an uneasy mixture that can be seen in the famous Holbein cartoon for the fresco which many years later he ordered painted in his palace of Whitehall. Here the son revenged himself on his father, having him portrayed an impotent, ghostly figure in the background while, swashbuckling and huge, young Henry himself possessed the foreground. And yet the mere fact that he ordered Holbein to include Henry VII in the fresco at all argues some affection and pride, affection because he could not but recall with an answering glow his father's protective love, and pride in his father's exceptional personal achievements. To have won the kingdom by conquest, established strong government despite repeated rebellions, and also gained the respect of other European kingdoms, was an awesome achievement. The prince's admiration made Henry VII's example all the more dangerously influential in this crucial year of 1508 when illness widened the flaws that existed in his character.

Prince Henry had before him the spectacle of both cruel harshness and moral dishonesty. To add to Catherine's troubles, Henry VII was now, contrary to the original agreement in the marriage treaty, insisting that the whole dowry must be paid in coin, that he would accept none of Catherine's plate or jewels. He was attempting to blackmail Ferdinand, not only into agreeing to the marriage with Joanna, but also into ratifying the treaty of marriage between Joanna's son Charles and Princess Mary, a guarantee which Henry VII knew he needed to safeguard this much-desired match. At the same time, he was smoothing the way for his son to marry a Hapsburg princess, if this continued to seem politically best.

Henry hovered, with what unhappiness we can imagine, on the fringe of it all. When on 24 July 1508 at Greenwich Palace, Henry VII summoned Catherine to his privy chamber for an hour and a half's discussion, he sent the prince from the room like a schoolboy, an experience that can hardly have flattered the seventeen-year-old heir. But the king had presumably no wish to shame himself before his son; this greedy haggling over Prince Henry's 'wife's' dowry had to be done in private even in the coldly practical sixteenth century. The king's attitude to Catherine's dowry was typical of his attitude to money and this was something that the prince of Wales would rebel against rather than copy when he came to power, for by now he witnessed its harsh effects all round him. Everyone with anything to lose was complaining about it. In May 1508 a court lady grumbled to Fuensalida, 'His avarice is unbelievable,' and her opinion was echoed by a Venetian envoy who summed up the king after his death as 'a very great miser but a man of vast ability'.

Henry VII had committed the ungentlemanly act of enforcing the collection of royal dues, which had not been done so thoroughly and successfully for many reigns. But he had little choice. An English king was supposed to pay most of the expenses of government as well as of his palaces out of his own revenues, which were made up of the proceeds of his lands, of feudal dues, of justice and of customs duties. If he failed to accomplish this nearly impossible task, he had to seek parliament's permission for a special tax, a perilous procedure, since nothing spurred the English to revolt more quickly than taxation. The trouble was that in collecting his dues Henry VII relied on officers responsible to no one but himself. Edmund Dudley, president of the council, and Sir Richard Empson, chancellor of the duchy of Lancaster, the best known and most hated of these officers, were believed to be corrupt.

And although this has been called in question by modern historians, and it is possible that they were merely loyal officers doing their job, the belief in their guilt was general and seems to have been shared by young Henry. There were also paid informers, mainly royal officers, but including some laymen too. Prince Henry was used to the sight of these unromantic characters rubbing shoulders with the furs and velvets of nobles and rich merchants in the palace corridors. He knew that they were on their way to give information against some unlucky citizen to 'the council learned in the law', the department largely under the control of Dudley and Empson, which dealt with royal debt-collecting.

Even more objectionable from Prince Henry's point of view was his father's role. If there was a good sum of money to be had, Henry VII was quite prepared to behave like any common usurer, and with many of the important debts to the crown he dealt personally. Outside the tapestried door near the king's own private apartments, not only merchants but gentry and peers waited nervously, bishops as well as their temporal brethren, for the possessions of rich ecclesiastics were all too often at the king's disposal. Small illegalities and tax avoidances were normally hard to trace. For reporting these the king offered the informer half the proceeds and, as a result, reports of misdemeanours increased: a big landowner had turned people out of their houses for the purpose of sheep farming; a butcher had slaughtered an animal inside the walls of London; another citizen had tanned leather or imported silk goods without paying his dues to the king; a group of hatters had fixed prices for hats. All of them could be used to increase the much-needed trickle of coins into the royal coffers.

So much did the more prosperous citizens of London hate the king's financial policies that they decided that God must hate them too. In August, when the sweating sickness again assaulted the city and the court, killing no less than three of Prince Henry's attendants and attacking one of the principal officers of the king's chamber, as well as Princess Mary's 'governess', Londoners saw the divine finger in human affairs. They whispered that this noisome new epidemic was 'a portent, a sign of the harshness of the monarch towards his people, by which almost all were heavily oppressed and under which they sweated'.

The king's feudal rights entitled him to a regular stream of fees from the landed gentry. Many of these were unfortunate enough to be tenants-in-chief (that is, persons who held land directly of the king). Payment was due to the king when an heir entered into his inheritance and when the widow of a tenant-in-chief remarried. On a tenant-in-chief's death, if the heir was under twenty-one he became a royal ward, which meant that the king was entitled during the child's minority to the profits from his lands, and also entitled to sell his marriage to the highest bidder.

Gentry who had been used to avoiding payment on these occasions, were naturally indignant when they found they could no longer do so, and especially when their evasions were punished by heavy fines and confiscations of property. They were quick to spread rumours of extortion. And there were plenty of men round the prince to make sure he heard them too.

Of course, men would be careful how they spoke in front of the king's son – to criticize the king could be accounted treason. They remembered that in 1501 'for speaking words against the king' two men had had their ears cut off. But there were other methods that spoke as loudly as words: a faded doublet, a heavy sigh, a reference to some favourite house that must be sold . . . The prince had in front of his own eyes evidence of his father's apparent meanness, examples of men whose finances and lives were painfully straitened by his financial demands. In the past six years they had threatened most of the men who were nearest the prince in rank and so his most natural friends and companions, men who fought with him at the barricades, and whose red-and-white lances shivered against his in the lists, men who hawked and hunted with him in the royal parks and dined near him on feast days, men who sang with him and laughed with him and grew up with him. It was a lucky peer whose seal and signature did not appear on one of the documents in the king's coffers.

The loyalty due to his own kind would have made the prince feel indignant when he saw how anxious even the most determinedly lively of his companions looked on being summoned to the king or to that ominously titled department of the privy chamber, 'the council learned in the law'. Prince Henry's companion and tutor, the delightful and cultured Lord Mountjoy, still lived under the heavy financial threats that had been imposed when he became governor of the fortress of Hammes in the pale of Calais in 1503.

One of Mountjoy's guarantors, George Neville, Lord Abergavenny, elder brother of Prince Henry's playmate Edward Neville, had had much worse burdens placed on his shoulders. In 1507, for flouting the law against keeping a small army of retainers not engaged in domestic duties, he was fined the enormous sum by contemporary standards of £70,650, that at a time when many other noblemen continued to keep retainers without penalty, and when a great procession of liveried servants was still a necessary badge of high rank. And although the king reduced the sum to £5000 to be paid in instalments of £500 over ten years, the resulting worry and fear, as in Mountjoy's case, was spread far beyond one man. No fewer than twenty-six people had to guarantee to pay up should Abergavenny default in his allegiance to the king.

Henry Percy, earl of Northumberland, too, was still caught up in the king's terrifying network of suspended penalties. Of the £10,000 he had been fined for illegally disposing of the king's ward in marriage, he was still paying off small sums when the king required him to, still not knowing whether or when he might have to pay the crippling whole.

Worst hit of all was the spendthrift young earl of Kent, who had been one of the challengers in the June games of 1507 and who was to become one of the prince's closest boon companions. The £1683 6s. 8d. that he owed the king in 1506 resulted the following year in a 'recovery' being made against him by Edmund Dudley, Sir Richard Empson and others of 'the council learned' of more than 10,000 acres of his lands. From the rents of these the king would repay himself. But not content with this haul, Henry VII decided that after the earl's death all the lands seized by Dudley were to revert to the king and his heirs. The spectre of financial ruin must have taken the merriment from most court festivities, floating frighteningly above the friendly clash of weapons, the tinkling of the hawk bells, the clink of golden cups, the music of minstrels and part song.

Prince Henry disliked anything that interfered with his pastimes. But all his education would make him revolt against his father's alleged meanness. 'Be bountiful, liberal, generous and lavish,' his tutor John Skelton had advised in *Speculum Principis*. Kings in the romances were scatterers of gold and jewels. They did not count every penny like his father, who, until his eyesight became too weak, personally inspected and signed each page of his treasurer's account books. Prince Henry was at an age to think most critically of his father. What made the king's 'avarice' more unforgivable was his reputation for being so rich. All the signs are that Prince Henry did not appreciate the truth, which was that, despite all his ruthless money-gathering, as well as his shrewd buying up of plate and jewels whenever he could acquire them cheaply, the king did little more than cover his onerous expenses. When he died, it has been estimated, he had amassed no more than between £200,000 and £300,000 worth of jewels and plate, the equivalent of 'something like two years' gross yield of the permanent revenues'. He left no cash balance at all. Prince Henry would not realize the king of England's vital need for money until much later in his own life, when, having squandered vast sums, he himself would resolve his resulting problem in radical fashion with Cromwell's help and the wealth of the monasteries. The seventeen-year-old prince was aware, however, that his father's financial policies were making him threateningly unpopular.

It was a dangerous situation and Prince Henry would immediately rectify it when he became king. That time was fast approaching.

CHAPTER 15

Prince in Waiting

'What may you not promise yourself from a prince with
whose extraordinary and almost divine character you
are well acquainted?'   *Lord Mountjoy*

BY the autumn of 1508 it was clear to the hawk-eyed courtiers
that Prince Henry had not long to wait before he inherited the
king's purple, blue and crimson robes of state. After his illness
in the spring of 1507 the king had rallied; in the summer,
riding manfully from deer park to deer park and hunting every
day, he had put on weight. But this year the picture had been
ominously different. From February until the beginning of
May he had been so ill that he had hardly been seen outside his
privy chamber. And although the king made light of his illness
for political reasons, sending a message to Fuensalida that he
only had gout in one foot, a rumour crossed the Channel that
his complaint was fatal. The king of France wrote to Ferdinand
that Henry VII was in the last stage of 'consumption', and the
most serene and most excellent Spanish king, relaying the
information back to England and Fuensalida, instructed him to
'speak kindly to the prince of Wales' and to 'dwell on the
great love which King Ferdinand bears him'. But the irritatingly high-handed Spanish ambassador was rarely now granted
an interview with Henry VII.

In August the king was hunting again, but his body remained thin and his face unhealthily yellow, leading Fuensalida to speculate on the merits of his successor. 'The princess
may well become queen of England,' he wrote to Ferdinand, in
a perceptive report, 'but that prospect offers her the most
unfortunate life that ever woman had. Do you really believe,

211

your Highness, that there is any chance of the prince being better than his father? Pray God that may come true but there are no signs of it.' Fuensalida, who had himself contrived to exchange words with the prince only once, was retailing the gossip of a watching court.

Although Henry VII incredibly continued negotiations for his own marriage with 'Joanna the mad', a more realistic note was struck in the match between his daughter Mary and the archduke Charles. To guarantee its completion Prince Henry, as well as the king, gave a bond for 250,000 crowns. And when the Flemish ambassadors arrived at Greenwich Palace in December for the betrothal the prince was one of the reception committee. But this match with Maximilian's grandson was particularly dear to Henry VII's heart and he would play his kingly role resolutely to the end. He himself presided over the ceremony in the queen's presence chamber at Richmond Palace on 17 December when, before the Flemish embassy and numerous English lords and bishops, his daughter Mary held right hands with Charles's proxy, Lord Bergues, and made the betrothal vows. He rallied his energies to preside over the endless entertainments that followed, the three days of tournament and disguisings, in which pageant floats were decorated with simulated hawthorn leaves, roses and marigolds. And he personally received from the ambassadors a jewel worth 50,000 crowns, called romantically *le riche fleur-de-lis*.

Although the king must have known that he was failing, his Christmas was as merry as ever, with an abbot of misrule and the usual plays and disguisings. But as the excitement of the festivities waned and the cold new year of 1509 closed round the shining palace, Prince Henry must have known too how parlous was his father's health. And he would have been unnatural if with the knowledge there had not come secretly a white-hot flame of expectation. Because soon he would be free. He would be free of the constraint he had suffered ever since he had come to live at court instead of being sent to Ludlow in 1504. He would be free to marry Catherine and to make friends with her father, to ride out from the royal parks alone if he so pleased, and to speak his mind whatever the company.

The approaching demands of kingship could not daunt a youth convinced that he was in every way a superior being and that he had been educated expressly for the task. 'The prince knows little,' Fuensalida had written to Ferdinand in 1508. But Fuensalida was out of date. For Prince Henry had studied all the subjects that leading scholars of the day believed could create the perfect sovereign. Erasmus in his *Institutio Principis Christiani* (The Education of a Christian Prince), written in 1516 for Charles when he had become king of Spain, quoted the great Plato as saying: 'The man rightly instructed becomes almost a divine being.' And in young Henry's case the hopeful dictum seemed to have worked.

Splendidly cultured, admirably pious, he professed the humanist ideals of peace and learning. 'We wish all potentates to content themselves with their territories; we are content with this island of ours.' Such enlightened utterances made by Henry soon after he became king would delight the trusting Lord Mountjoy. And similarly gilded sentiments so misled his tutors in the early months of 1509 that they believed they had indeed created 'almost a divine being', beautiful in character as in appearance, who when he came to power would transform England into a land 'of milk, of honey and of nectar'. Such golden opinions cannot have failed to increase the confidence of their subject.

Indeed for an ambitious, extrovert seventeen-year-old who had never had enough of the limelight the prospect before him was stimulating and exciting. When he became king the very year would be known by his name and dated from his accession by English chroniclers: everyone would refer to him as 'his Grace' and 'our most sovereign lord'. The knowledge of his approaching duties was also fuel for his egotism, as we can see from *The Tree of Commonwealth* – an allegorical treatise on English government and society, written by Edmund Dudley in 1509 and 1510. Although Henry would not read the treatise until after he came to the throne, it describes some of the flattering ideas on monarchy that were current in the very early years of the sixteenth century, and by which he was already affected. As a key to Henry's attitude and future policies, they are worth a brief description.

According to Dudley, the king was not only sovereign lord of the feudal hierarchy, but also the inspiration of the common good. His authority was God-given. The roots of the commonwealth (or general welfare) were the love of God, justice, truth, concord, and international peace, and in all these the king was pre-eminent.

Dudley's treatise foreshadowed some of young Henry's future most revolutionary policies. In the love of God the king must set an example that should, Dudley wrote, 'enforce and encourage the bishops and other of the spirituality to be the very lanterns of light'. As in this way, according to Dudley, the king was the inspiration of the English Church, so was he the inspiration of the English law. Justice too, Dudley wrote, 'must needs come of our sovereign lord himself, for the whole authority there is given to him by God to minister by himself or by his deputies to his subjects . . .' The king's judgement was unassailable. The root of truth, wrote Dudley, 'fastens itself chiefly in the king' whose duty he considered it was 'to punish false men and to advance and promote true men', while concord or unity in the kingdom came as a direct result of the king's justice, his promotion of good men and punishment of bad.

When he composed this famous book it was very much in Dudley's interest to please the king, for Henry VII was dead and Dudley in the Tower in danger of execution. But while Dudley may have burnished, he did not invent. In sixteenth-century England – although he could not make laws or raise taxes without the consent of parliament – the king did indeed reign supreme in many other ways, becoming in Thomas More's critical words, 'a sort of fountain from which a constant shower of benefits or injuries rains down'.

In early 1509 as Henry VII, seeming daily more shrunken in his luxurious robes, drew close to the logs in his wide fireplaces, it is easy to picture how ambitious courtiers fed these flattering ideas on kingship into the heir to the throne.

The king was still his own chief minister, but there were signs that his judgement was failing. In December his special ally, Maximilian, had joined Louis XII, Ferdinand and the pope in an alliance that did not include England, an aggressive alliance against the rich republic of Venice. And as his bodily energy waned so the king's temper became ever more uncontrolled. So angry did the pompous and tactless Fuensalida make him that he could not abide 'to see or to hear' him and gave orders he was not to be allowed to ride through the palace gates. When nevertheless Fuensalida arrived, the king had his servants seize the mule by the bridle and thus forcibly eject the aristocratic ambassador from the courtyard.

Afraid for his soul now that he was in danger of death, Henry VII grew daily more pious. Sometimes he wept in penitence for nearly an hour, and he assured his 'secret servants' that 'if it pleased God to send him life they should see him a new changed man'. But he had not yet made proper provision for the future peace of his kingdom.

The council were worried. Remembering what had happened after Edward IV's death, they were afraid of a contested succession. The king had had Sir William Courtenay and the young earl of Dorset (arrested on some pretext now lost to us) moved to prison in Calais, presumably so that they could not easily communicate with Edmund de la Pole who was still in the Tower; and he had also prudently ordered the manufacture of many new bows and arrows for his armoury. But that was all he had done. In January the council begged him to marry the prince of Wales to someone, any princess he thought most profitable. Because, they pointed out anxiously, 'he is already very manly and the kingdom is in danger with only one heir'. The king promised to consider their request, but all February the council – as well as Prince Henry – waited in vain for his decision. With the rest of the court, the seventeen-year-old prince knew that the councillors were debating among themselves the rival merits of a Hapsburg or a French princess. None of them mentioned Catherine.

Meanwhile the princess of Wales lived ever more wretchedly. By the beginning of March 1509 she had sold or pawned much of her plate, as well as all the furnishings and ornaments she could spare; her apartments looked as though she had been robbed. Even this money vanished in the ocean of her debts. But the king smoothly refused her request for money, reminding her ungallantly that he already provided her daily bread: 'We are not bound to give your servants *food*, or even yourself, but the love we bear to you would not allow us to do otherwise.' The one bright spot in Catherine's dark world was Diego Fernandez, the clever young Spanish friar who had become her confessor by April 1507. It was, however, a dangerous association. For the friar was reputed licentious and had been seen with a party of revellers in the streets of London. Gossip was soon busy with his name and Catherine's: she had sold some of her plate to buy him books, she laughed at his lewd jokes, consulted him on intimate matters of health and allowed herself to be completely dominated by him.

In February 1509 he even persuaded her to disobey the king's orders. Catherine had been told to move with Princess Mary to Richmond, a short ride from where she was staying. On the day appointed for the journey, Mary and her escort waited a whole hour for Catherine to join them. Only then did she send a message: she was not coming. She had been sick the previous night and the friar had said she must not go; if she did it would be a mortal sin. The king was furious. When she arrived at Richmond the next day, accompanied by only six people, she found the private gate normally used by the royal family locked; she was forced to jostle through the common entrance with everyone else. But although the king punished her in this petty way and scolded her for allowing the friar such influence, he did nothing more – which Fuensalida judged a bad sign. For while Catherine was probably too proud of her rank and too determined to marry the prince to have risked an affair, the scandal could be used to smear the reputation of a future queen. It looked as though the king had no intention of marrying her to his son.

Prince Henry's reaction sheds light on his whole future attitude to women; amazingly, he did no more than echo his father's disapproval. He was clearly not in the least jealous. For after his father's death he would allow Catherine to keep her dissolute friar until he was legally convicted of fornication in about 1515. In young Henry's character vanity and romanticism were too strong for jealousy. How could any woman possibly prefer any man to him? And how could he doubt his ideal princess would remain chaste? Already Henry was showing that extraordinary trustfulness with which he would treat all the women he loved – for just as long as he loved them.

His feelings for Catherine, however, he hid carefully in 1509 from the rest of the court. On 6 March ambassadors arrived at Richmond from Maximilian and Margaret of Savoy. King Henry was too ill to grant them an audience. He ordered the prince to receive them and listen to their latest proposal: that the prince should marry the daughter of the duke of Bavaria. So the youth was forced politely and convincingly to discuss the political ramifications of this marriage without giving away the fact that he had set his heart on wedding Catherine. This was a difficult feat of diplomacy even with the aid of skilled councillors; and it suggests yet again that seventeen-year-old Henry was far from being the naïve untutored creature of Fuensalida's hostile opinion.

Although the king would allow almost no one to see him, his failure to emerge from his bedchamber, coupled with the frequent attendance of many grave, black-gowned physicians burdened with huge urine flasks, plasters, herbal potions and other tools of their trade, told the courtiers the truth. Before the end of the month others knew too: the king was growing worse, was being consumed by his illness, so thin he could hardly walk, and when he spoke there were long pauses between his words. He could not recover.

Henry VII himself still had moments of optimism. For 25 March the treasurer of the chamber's accounts list, 'to the king's grace for playing money 40s.'. But by 30 March the king recognized what everyone else knew, and he set his large spidery signature on a last copy of his will. He bequeathed lavish sums to be spent on efforts to save his soul from damnation, that last rebellious threat to his security: 10,000 Masses were to be said within a month of his death; £5000 was to be spent on completing his new chapel in Westminster Abbey. He also provided – as had King Henry V in his will – for the setting up of a committee to investigate any complaints against his administration.

On 16 April he proclaimed a general pardon. And a few days earlier, on 10 April, two separate sums of money, £33 6s. 8d. and £19 18s. 4d., had been extracted from the royal coffers 'for the wages of certain priests singing in divers places for the king's grace'. But the Almighty was not to be bribed or placated; as he scattered sand to dry the ink of his signature on his will, he had three more weeks to live.

In Richmond Palace, Prince Henry waited by the wide, canopied and curtained bed. The man whose authority had made him by contrast a shadow was almost a shadow himself, the sallow face nearly all jutting bone, the body that raised the ermine covers pathetically slight. Kneeling with Archbishop Warham and the bird-like Margaret Beaufort, herself nearing death, Prince Henry knew that he was the strong one now.

But the skeletal hand on the soft cream fur had not quite let go the reins of power. Leading councillors still entered through the tapestry-hung door to consult the king, who until his last breath remained head of state.

Did his Grace have any last wishes about the prince's marriage? one of the council, Warham perhaps – or Fisher or Fox – asked.

Through the mists of his struggle with mortality the king's mind groped for firmness, and his voice came strained between pauses. 'We do not wish,' the king said, 'to make up . . . the prince's mind . . . we wish to . . . leave him . . . free to choose for himself.' At least, that was the story the councillors afterwards told Fuensalida, but the prince's story was different.

'Marry Catherine,' he said, had been his father's last wish.

The councillors may have lied to achieve their own political ends, or the prince may have lied, or indeed the king may have said both things at different moments, as life waned and the instinct of political cunning struggled against the desire to die in charity, the technique of arranging things to his best advantage in this world being quite different from that required in the next.

In the night of Saturday 21 April 1509 – after rumours that the king was dead had been around for some days – Prince Henry finally lost the father who for the past seven years had loved and dominated him, chosen his education, his friends and his pastimes. Now out of all his once large family only Margaret and Mary and his grandmother were left; and Margaret was in an alien country, Mary was a little girl and his grandmother was dying. There was no one left to lean on. When the king drew his last harsh difficult breath, then lay quite still beneath the ermine cover, the crowded stuffy room must have felt very empty to Prince Henry. Surrounded by prayer-murmuring archbishop, bishops, councillors and doctors, he was alone.

But a quiet period of adjustment after a father's death was a luxury no heir to the throne in the early sixteenth century could afford. This was the moment of change, Henry knew, the moment when a Yorkist sprig – Richard de la Pole in France, his brother Edmund in the Tower of London, or perhaps even Henry Courtenay – might inspire a revolt of the magnates. Until the old king was coffined and the new king proclaimed and established on the throne with strong backing, there was danger. Since Henry VI's accession no English king had succeeded without bloodshed. Quick decision and action were needed; as few people as possible must know until the perilous moment was passed. But Prince Henry needed the support of the great ones.

All the daylight hours of Sunday and into the night, while the gates remained open and torches continued to blaze, the cobbled courtyard of Richmond Palace was loud with the sounds of great men arriving with their servants, the hoof-beats, commands and welcomes, subdued laughter and suddenly low grave tones. The officers of state and the lords temporal and spiritual were answering a summons of the council. Until all the great ones were there under the watching eyes of the yeomen of the guard, no one outside the palace should know that the king was dead.

It is probable that Prince Henry had already resolutely decided on the part he would play at this critical time. He cannot have lacked for advice and encouragement, from his humanist tutors and friends who were convinced that he was ready to rule, and also, as Stow's *Annals* suggest, from Margaret Beaufort.

Months later, rumours of the power struggle that took place in the hours succeeding the king's death would emerge. There was a rumour that Buckingham and Northumberland had agreed that the former should be lord protector and the latter 'should rule all from Trent north and have Berwick and the Marches'. Another rumour said that Fox was manoeuvring to put the earls of Surrey and Shrewsbury, Ruthall, Lord Darcy, Mr Marney and Mr Brandon out of the king's favour. Yet another held that Fox would 'bring in and bolster himself to rule all' with Buckingham and Northumberland.

In such an atmosphere, where faction plotted against faction, Prince Henry had little time for thoughts of his father's death. His one-time tutor, John Skelton, advised him to 'rule and not be ruled', and Henry had been subservient for too long to welcome a new master.

As the embalmers busied themselves with the past, anointing the old king's body with spices, Prince Henry was busy with the future. Some time and somehow on that Saturday night and Sunday, this seventeen-year-old youth succeeded in convincing the council that he had no intention of being a puppet, that he was an adult king with his own ideas on policy; and he managed to impose his will on the council, so that when discussions again took place they did so with him in command, Fox, Ruthall and Surrey at his elbow as advisers only. Although he would depend on the skills of his councillors, and although he would not always attend to the boring details of administration, preferring to spend his time hunting, tourneying, flirting and dancing, from that Sunday following his father's death, the final decision would always be his.

The most immediate problem to be dealt with was that of security and safety. The brief imprisonment at this time of Sir Henry Stafford, on some charge that we do not know, was perhaps a warning to his brother, the duke of Buckingham, not to aspire to the throne, nor to make any dangerous move.

But danger to the prince's accession could come from lesser men than the great magnates with royal blood in their veins. It could come from rich citizens who had been offended by the methods Henry VII used to fill his coffers. For fear of an uprising foreign merchants in London hastened to put their goods in store; so Fuensalida reported, and this one fact illustrates the uncertainty of the times. To stop the flood of discontent from turning to revolt, the prince and his councillors planned what would appear to uninformed people to be a complete change in financial policy. And while this was put into operation, the new king should go to the safest place in England.

On Monday morning in the public meeting places of London, trumpet blasts loudly called for the attention of the citizens. Heralds read a proclamation: Henry VII was dead; the new king was his son – Henry VIII. That afternoon Londoners, on the wharfs and water steps of the city, saw the royal barge row quietly and swiftly without music down river to the Tower. It was not yet safe or suitable for Henry to show himself; he would remain 'closely and secretly with his council' until his father was buried.

But if the citizens were disappointed in their desire for a sight of their new ruler, they had other dramatic incidents to watch. On that day and succeeding days light flashed on the halberds and swords of small groups of guards marching with chained men in their midst towards London's prisons. At the market stalls in Cheap, citizens stopped bargaining to gape at the almost incredible sight: they were arresting the informers. Empson and Dudley themselves had been tricked 'by a politic mean' into coming to the Tower; they were now locked in cells. Giovanni Battista Grimaldi of Genoa, known as John Baptist or Grumbold by the Londoners, 'the most cruel and subtlest wretch of them all' had flung himself into sanctuary in Westminster Abbey. Later in the week three informers were set in the pillory, so that Londoners could wreak a personal revenge; the new king knew how to win the hearts of his people. 'The City,' Fuensalida reported, was 'so full of gaiety as if they had all been let out of prison.'

Striding round the precincts of the Tower in the gentle summer sunshine, King Henry VIII might hear voices celebrating his succession in ale-rich song from the streets of his capital, and reflect on this pleasing sign of his popularity, a popularity which he knew would grow with his next announcement.

On 25 April the trumpet call sounded through the streets again: the king proclaimed a general pardon 'much more ample, gracious and beneficial' than his father's – a phrase that smacks of young Henry's own composition. To further delight the citizens, the herald proclaimed that 'all vagabonds and sturdy beggars should avoid the city'. Meanwhile the details of his father's funeral, with all the colourful symbolism that a king's estate required, were being worked out by court officials. Young Henry was engrossed by a happier matter – the question of his own marriage.

Before his accession Henry had listened quietly to his councillors' arguments. Should he marry Catherine he would be contravening the command in Leviticus, 'The man who takes his brother's wife in marriage does a forbidden thing'; against that law Pope Julius's dispensation of 1504 could not prevail, Archbishop Warham had told the prince. And the prince had agreed he would do nothing against his conscience. Through the court a rumour had spread, 'The Prince is not much inclined to the Spanish marriage'; Henry's childhood with an autocratic father had taught him to wrap his meaning in ambiguous statements.

Now the time had come to speak out. Catherine should be his queen; no one else. The matter must be arranged at once. The mature men of the council were shocked and surprised at the force with which their seventeen-year-old monarch suddenly asserted himself.

On 27 April the Spanish ambassador Fuensalida, to whom no important member of the council had been so much as polite for months and who had been forbidden the court since December, was sought out in his own lodging by Thomas Ruthall whom Henry VIII retained as Latin secretary.

King and council, the astonished Fuensalida was told blusteringly, were very annoyed with Ferdinand for not having answered Henry VII's last letter. Such tardiness would not benefit negotiations for Catherine's marriage. The king wished much to serve the princess, and Fuensalida would be well advised to do what was necessary.

Two days later, long before Fuensalida had had time to get a reaction from Ferdinand on this new turn of events, Richard Fox, bishop of Winchester and keeper of the Privy Seal, arrived with Ruthall at his lodging. They demanded precipitate agreement on the financial and political aspects of Catherine's marriage, her dowry and the question of Ferdinand's ratification of Charles's marriage to Mary. Fuensalida was puzzled by the English councillors' sudden desire for haste; had they not spent years carefully raising obstacles to the match? Besides, he was still indignant at the slights he had received. But when, insensitive as ever to changes in other men's moods, he muttered stiffly that he didn't see that anything had changed, Fox's reply was full of rueful reminiscence. 'You must remember now the king is king and not prince,' he said. 'One must speak in a different way in this matter than when he was prince . . . Until now things were discussed with his father and now one must treat with him who is king.' For once Fox's words have the feeling ring of truth. Fox himself, it seems, had been shaken when his young king, hitherto so obedient, had suddenly shouldered him out of the way to seize real power.

Young Henry had asserted his will over his council in more than the matter of his marriage. For marriage to Catherine was no isolated project. For him, already a typical renaissance monarch, it was part of a wider foreign policy, a policy of aggression very different from his father's balancing act. His father had always tried to avoid war. The eighth Henry planned a new alliance with Spain and the Hapsburgs with the specific object of making war upon an expansionist France. As so often in later life, Henry's love for a woman fitted with extraordinary jigsaw neatness into his foreign policy.

Henry's first essay in royal diplomacy was delightfully successful. It enabled him both to eat his cake and have it, an achievement that could not have been bettered by his own father. When Fox and Ruthall rode into the Tower they brought news that Ferdinand was willing to agree to nearly all Henry's terms. The financial deal was extremely good. The Spanish ambassador had agreed to pay all the dowry money in coin, disregarding what Catherine would bring her husband in plate and jewels. Although Fuensalida had sent out of the country the money that had been brought in in February 1508, he had promised to replace it quickly.

The political side of things was good too. Henry was as eager as his father for the proposed marriage of his sister Mary and Charles. Fuensalida promised that he would publicly kiss Mary's hand at court and call her 'Princess', in earnest of his master's goodwill, and this was soon confirmed. The Spanish king instructed Fuensalida to send a message to King Henry 'full of all the good and sweet words' that the ambassador could think of and promising that Ferdinand 'would do for the son what he would not do for the father'.

And while in all this Henry was clearly the gainer, there was still room for him to play the generous lover. Was he not rescuing his princess from penury? Had he not agreed both to marry her and also to give her the lands once owned by his mother, Queen Elizabeth? No longer would she sigh for just one horse to carry her when she was tired. Now she could make her choice from her own rich stables. No longer would she lead a pinched humiliating existence, begging for food and clothes for herself and her few servants. Now she would enjoy apartments only slightly less sumptuous than the king's, with ample money, a large household of her own, the most delicate dishes, the richest garments and an impressive retinue of ladies-in-waiting.

To Windsor, where Catherine was staying, Henry sent a magnanimous message telling of his love and her changed future. Since December Catherine had refused to see Fuensalida, believing that his tactlessness had worsened her relations with the dying king. Now Henry begged her to admit him so that the negotiations could be completed. Surrounded by the luxurious furnishings of his palace in the Tower, its windows open to the fragrant summer smell of the garden and the more pungent aroma of the river, her seventeen-year-old suitor waited confidently for Fox and Ruthall to return with her reply. But this time when they rode into the Tower and requested admittance to the privy chamber, they brought news of a rebuff.

With Fuensalida they had ridden all the way from London to Windsor Castle. But in emotional reaction at this sudden swift new turn of fortune, Catherine had refused to see him. After all these years of insults and suffering and waiting at the mercy of the English king's whim, was she now to be married at a moment's notice? When the ambassador defied her orders and thrust his way into her apartment, she indignantly ordered him out.

CHAPTER 16

Our Sovereign Lord the King

*'The rose both white and rede
In one rose now dothe grow ...
England, now gaddir flowris,
Exclude now all dolowrs.'*

John Skelton

———

WHEN King Henry's chosen bride refused to see the Spanish ambassador, it appeared at first that his present good fortune had received a check. We can imagine the disappointment that Catherine's action caused the seventeen-year-old bridegroom, who firmly believed he was conferring a supreme favour. But Spanish pride soon gave way to ambition. A day or two later Henry heard the desired news: Catherine had relented. She had admitted Fuensalida, with Fox. By the evening of 8 May 1509 the marriage was finally agreed. The wife whom Prince Henry had married *verba de praesenti* nearly six years before was at last to be his in the flesh.

But first ritual and propriety must be observed and the old king buried with a splendour that would reflect that of the monarchy. The processions and final religious services took no less than two days and as usual the new king had no part in them. But he could see from the Tower on the evening of 9 May the glimmer of torches outlining the main streets of London when his father's funeral procession arrived from Richmond Palace. And as it set out on its journey to St Paul's he could see the cathedral spire tall against the mauve dusk and hear the chant of dirges.

That night Henry VII lay in state in St Paul's before the high altar. Not until the following evening was the old king's reign finally tidied away, when the coffin was carried to Westminster Abbey and lowered into the vault beside the dead queen. The household officials cast their white staffs of office into the grave, the vault was closed, the heralds took off their tabards bearing the royal coat of arms, hung them on the rails of the catafalque and cried 'lamentably in French, "The noble King Henry VII is dead." Then they put them on again and cried with a loud voice, " *Vive le noble Roi Henri le VIII.*"'

At last Henry knew he had succeeded peaceably. Incredibly, after the blood-stained pattern of former accessions and despite all the possible rival claims of his many cousins of the royal blood, it seemed there would be no attempt at rebellion. At last he could feel safe. He emerged from the Tower, ordered the black drapes removed from the palaces and, sitting in state, had himself rowed in the royal barge, pennants flying in the sunshine, down to shining riverside Greenwich, which ever afterwards was to be his favourite abode. And here at last privately 'in the queen's closet' on 11 June, after all the years of waiting and uncertainty, he married Catherine. Henry doted on this bride five and a half years older than he, who gave him both womanly love and the maternal affection he had lacked so long. To Ferdinand he wrote flatteringly in Latin: '. . . day by day do her inestimable virtues more and more shine forth, flourish and increase, so that even if we were still free, it is she, nevertheless, that we would choose for our wife before all other.'

At Greenwich Henry's attention was pleasantly divided between making love to Catherine and preparing for his midsummer coronation in which he could indulge to the full both his taste for the limelight and for magnificence.

On 21 June, Henry rode with Catherine from Greenwich over London Bridge, up Gracechurch Street into the Tower where custom decreed he should spend Thursday and Friday nights before the procession through the walled city. Ever since the accession of Richard II this procession had been a preliminary to the coronation, in token of the fact that the goodwill of London was an essential part of the basis of power of any English king.

On Saturday the city was crammed with people, not only Londoners, but country folk as well who had flocked into the capital to see their king 'in the full bloom of his youth and high birth'. They were not disappointed. When the new king rode out of the Tower his huge handsome young figure flashed crimson and gold in the sunshine. He wore a jacket of 'raised gold', the placard embroidered with diamonds, rubies, emeralds and great pearls, surmounted by a robe of crimson velvet furred with ermines and adorned from shoulder to opposite hip with still more jewels, a baldric of enormous rubies. His curled auburn hair hatless according to tradition, he rode a horse brilliantly caparisoned in gold with a deep ermine border. A long way behind him, to show her lesser importance, rode his queen, gowned in white satin and ermine, in a shining white litter supported on the backs of two white palfreys; directly before him rode the heralds in their coat armour; and around him rode the barons of the Cinque Ports, supporting on long silver staves the canopy of state over his head.

The procession, meant to impress the onlookers, could not fail also to impress the young king himself. For it was rich with the symbols of his power and his titles, including those of one-time French possessions. Two gentlemen in gold-embroidered gowns bore the king's own robe of state and crown, their horses 'trapped in burned silver, drawn over with cords of green silk and gold'; two more gentlemen bore about their bodies 'travers' the robes of state of Guienne and Normandy, on their heads the ermine powdered caps of state of the two duchies. The nine children of honour, in blue velvet powdered with gold fleurs-de-lis, rode great coursers in velvet trappings, each embroidered with the title of one of the king's territories – not only England, Cornwall, Wales and Ireland, but also France, Gascony, Guienne, Normandy and Anjou. Henry was far from being the only Englishman who believed he had a right to French lands.

A brief shower of rain fell just as Catherine passed the

inn called the Cardinal's Hat, otherwise the day was perfect. The crowds cheered and doffed their caps with wild enthusiasm, as did the craft guilds standing along Cheap. And to add to this incense of popularity, there was real incense too. As Henry drew near St Paul's, priests in rich copes, holding silver crosses, swung censers of silver as he passed.

That night the royal couple spent in Westminster Palace, preparing for their coronation of the next day with the help of the abbot of Westminster. Although Henry had already been proclaimed king, to 'become king in the fullest sense, he must first be inaugurated into the government by legal and ecclesiastical rites', which had grown up through the centuries and combined both Teutonic and Celtic Christian practices. The most important part of the ceremony at this date was not the crowning, as it is today. The object of the abbot's coming was 'to prepare the consciences of the king and queen for the receiving of the sacred unction', and the pious Henry undoubtedly prepared himself with devotion for what he and everyone else regarded as a deeply spiritual, if not mystical, experience.

From midnight Henry fasted in preparation and, the following morning, rose well before six. He bathed, heard Mass, then in the presence of his lords in his privy chamber, stood patiently while the chamberlain clothed him in garments designed so that certain parts of his body could be anointed. First, a shirt of lawn, then a crimson shirt, then a 'cote' of crimson satin, all with 'openings' fastened with gold and silver laces. On his lower half went a pair of breeches and crimson hose laced to the 'cote' with silk ribbon, and laid on top of everything, was a surcote ornamented with miniver and ermine, and a 'great mantle of crimson satin' lined with miniver, with 'a great lace of silk' with two crimson tassels. The finishing touch on Henry's auburn head was 'a little cap of state' adorned with ermine and gold ribbon.

Thus splendidly if quaintly arrayed, and surrounded by holy relics, chanting choristers, monks, abbots, lords and bishops, he processed to Westminster Abbey, up the aisle and on to the red-carpeted platform in the middle of the church.

Here he rested on a chair furnished with cloth-of-gold cushions, while the queen sat on a similar chair placed slightly below his. It was the start of a ceremony that would be physically exhausting but spiritually unforgettable, and which would add a new dazzling aura to the prince's already brilliant image of himself.

Henry stood on the platform and faced east, west, north and south, while William Warham, archbishop of Canterbury, presented him to the people and desired to know if they would 'receive, obey and take the same most noble prince for their king', a relic of the days when kings had been elected by their people. The congregation of peers, churchmen and commons 'with great reverence, love and desire', answered, 'Yea, yea, yea, so be it. God save King Henry. King Henry. King Henry.'

The prostration before the altar, when Henry and Catherine lay full length on cloth-of-gold cushions, can scarcely have filled Henry with humility, while he could still hear that swelling acceptance of him echoing in his ears.

Henry had then to take the oath. But he was not too over-awed by the occasion to consider critically the words as he spoke them. On the sacrament of the high altar he had to swear to protect the rights of the Church and all Christian peoples, to prevent robbery and all unrighteous deeds to all men, and to exercise justice and mercy in the decision of all cases. He had also to promise to maintain the laws chosen by his people. The first and the last of these promises he would later modify in his own hand so that the rights of the Church, which the king was to guarantee, were qualified by the vital phrase 'not prejudicial to his jurisdiction and dignity royal', and the laws which he was to maintain were qualified by 'chosen with his consent'. Although the modified oath was never in fact used, these alterations suggest that already at the age of seventeen Henry with overweening self-confidence had decided that he alone should be the arbiter of right and justice in the kingdom.

Majestic and solemn, with the moving words and music of a great religious occasion, the ceremony proceeded until it reached its most deeply spiritual moment – the moment of

consecration. It was to confirm Henry in his own conviction
that he had a unique relationship with God. And this was a
belief profoundly shared by his contemporaries, for in this
rite, they believed, a king was purified by the grace of God;
he became the 'Lord's anointed'.

Henry's upper robes removed and the silver fastenings of
his 'cote' and shirts undone, he knelt before the altar. With oil
poured from a gold ampulla, the archbishop of Canterbury
made the sign of the cross 'in the palms of his hands, on his
breast, between his shoulders, and on the blades of his arms'.
Then the archbishop made the sign of the cross on Henry's
head with the specially holy chrism oil. According to medieval
belief the king had now changed, become 'another man',
with 'a new status', God's 'office bearer' in the world. Just how
much he had changed was open to Henry's own interpretation.

Newly arrayed in the priest-like royal vestments, Henry
seated himself in St Edward's chair, where St Edward's crown
was lowered on to his head and he received the ring signifying
that he was wedded to his people, the sceptre signifying peace,
and the ball and crown signifying monarchy. Thence
thirty-eight bishops escorted him, to the strains of *Te Deum
Laudamus* sung by the choir, up the steps to the highest point
of the red-carpeted platform in the centre of the church, and
there they 'elevated' him on to the throne, where he received
the fealty and the homage of the prelates and the lords, beginning with the archbishop of Canterbury himself.

Mere weakness must have added to the impression the
ceremony made on young Henry, who could not break his
fast until after Catherine had also been anointed and crowned
(fortunately a much briefer ceremony), and he had listened
to yet another Mass. Then at last he was able to withdraw, to
consume a hasty meal and exchange his priest-like vestments
for a purple velvet surcoat and a purple velvet mantle, lined
with ermine, with a long train. Suddenly there was a cacophony
of trumpets, organ, drums and church bells to signify in the
Great Chronicle's words that the eighth Henry had been 'glori-
ously crowned to the comfort of all the land'.

Glittering under his purple canopy, huge and extraordinarily confident for his youth, his egotism confirmed and applauded, the new king walked out of the arched doorway of Westminster Abbey on to the red carpet and into one of the most revolutionary reigns of English history.

Select Bibliography

The two standard bibliographies for the period are, of course, *Bibliography of British History, Tudor Period, 1485–1603*, ed. Conyers Read (1959) and *Tudor England, 1485–1603*, ed. Mortimer Levine (1968). Listed below by brief titles and abbreviations where appropriate are the books I have found most useful and those I have referred to in my notes.

ANDRÉ, BERNARD: *Vita Henrici VII* in *Memorials*, see below; *Annales Henrici VII*, ditto.

ANGLO, S.: 'The British History in Early Tudor Propaganda', *Bulletin of the John Rylands Library*, 44 (1961); *Spectacle, Pageantry and Early Tudor Policy* (1969); 'The Court Festivals of Henry VII', *Bulletin of the John Rylands Library*, 43 (1960–61).

ARCHBOLD, W. A. J.: 'Sir William Stanley and Perkin Warbeck', *English Historical Review*, XIV (1899).

ARMSTRONG, C. A. J.: 'An Italian Astrologer at the Court of Henry VII' in *Italian Renaissance Studies, a Tribute to C. M. Ady* (1960).

BACON, SIR FRANCIS: *History of the Reign of Henry VII*, ed. Spedding (1878).

BARBER, R.: *The Knight and Chivalry* (1970).

BAYLEY, J.: *History and Antiquities of the Tower* (1821).

BLACKMORE, HOWARD L.: *Arms and Armour* (1965).

BOWLE, JOHN: *Henry VIII* (1964).

BRODIE, D. M.: 'Edmund Dudley, Minister of Henry VII', *Royal Historical Society*, 4th series, XV (1932).

BROOK, ROY: *The Story of Eltham Palace* (1960).

BRUCE, M. L.: *Anne Boleyn* (1972).

BUCK, GEORGE: *Complete History of England* I (1706).

BUSCH, W.: *England under the Tudors*, trans. A. M. Todd, I (1895).

Cal. Span.: *Calendar of State Papers, Spanish* (1862–   ) and *Supplement to Vols. I & II*, ed. G. A. Bergenroth (1868).

Cal. Ven.: *Calendar of State Papers, Venetian 1202–1509* (1864).

CHALONER, SIR THOMAS THE ELDER: 'In Laudem Henrici Octavi' in *De Rep. Anglorum* (1579).

CHRIMES, S. B.: *Henry VII* (1972); *Lancastrians, Yorkists and Henry VII* (1964); *English Constitutional Ideas in the Fifteenth Century* (1936).

Close Rolls, Calendar of, 1500–1509 (1963).

COLLIER, JEREMY: *Ecclesiastical History* IX (1847).

COOPER, C. H.: *Memoir of Margaret, Countess of Richmond and Derby* (1874).

COOPER, J. P.: 'Henry VII's Last Years Reconsidered', *Historical Journal* II (1959).

CURTIS, S. J.: *History of Education in Great Britain* (1953).

DAWSON, ROBERT: *Memoirs of St George* (1714).

DE LA BERE, IVAN: *The Queen's Orders of Chivalry* (1961).

Documentos Ineditos para la Historia de España XVIII (1952).

DOLMETSCH, MABEL: *Dances of England and France 1450–1600* (1949).

DORAN, JOHN: *The Book of the Princes of Wales* (1860).

DUDLEY, EDMUND: *The Tree of Commonwealth*, ed. D. M. Brodie (1948).

EHSES, STEFAN: *Römische Dokumente zur Geschichte der Ehescheidung Heinrichs VIII 1527–1534* (1893).

ELTON, G. R.: 'Henry VII: Rapacity and Remorse', *Historical Journal* I (1958); 'Henry VII: a Restatement', *Historical Journal* IV (1961); *England under the Tudors* (1955).

ELYOT, SIR T.: *The Governour* (1907).

ERASMUS, D.: *Epistles of*, trans. F. Morgan Nichols (1901); *Institutio Principis Christiani* (1921).

Excerpta Historica, ed. S. Bentley (1831).

FISHER, J.: *The Funeral Sermon of Margaret Countess of Richmond and Derby* (1708).

FLÜGEL, J. C.: 'On the Character and Married Life of Henry VIII' in *Men and their Motives* (1934).

FUENSALIDA, GUTIERRE GOMEZ DE: *Correspondencia de*, ed. Duke of Berwick and Alba (1907).

FURNIVALL, F. J.: *The Babees Book* etc. (1868).

GACHARD, L. P.: *Collection des Voyages des Souverains des Pays Bas* (1874–82).

GAIRDNER, J.: *Henry VII* (1889); *History of the Life and Reign of Richard III*, to which is added *The Story of Perkin Warbeck from Original Documents* (1898).

Great Chronicle of London, ed. A. H. Thomas and I. D. Thornley (1938).

GREEN, MARY EVERETT: *Lives of the Princesses of England* V (1854).

HALL, EDWARD: *Chronicle*, ed. H. Ellis (1809); ed. Charles Whibley (1904).

HALSTED, C. A.: *Life of Margaret Beaufort* (1839).

HAZLITT, W. C.: *Remains of the Early Popular Poetry of England*, II (1864-66).

HELM, P. J.: *England under the Yorkists and Tudors* (1968).

Henry VII, The Will of, ed. T. Astle (1775).

HEXTER, JACK: 'Education of the Aristocracy in the Renaissance' in *Reappraisals in History* (1962).

H.O.: *Collection of Ordinances and Regulations for the Government of the Royal Household*, Society of Antiquaries of London (1790).

KENDALL, P. M.: *Richard III* (1955).

KINGSFORD, C. L.: *Chronicles of London* (1905).

King's Works, History of the, R. Allen Brown, H. M. Colvin and A. J. Taylor (1963).

KIRBY, J. L.: 'Blackheath and the Cornish Rising of 1497', *Greenwich and Lewisham Antiquarian Society*, IV (1936-53).

LANDER, J. R.: 'Bonds, Coercion and Fear: Henry VII and the Peerage' in *Florelegium Historiale: Essays Presented to Wallace K. Ferguson* (1971); *The Wars of the Roses* (1965).

LEGG, L. G. WICKHAM: *English Coronation Records* (1901).

LELAND, J.: *De Rebus Britannicis Collectanea*, IV and V (1744).

Letters of King Henry VIII, ed. M. St Clare Byrne (1936).

L & P HENRY VII, *Letters and Papers of Richard III and Henry VII* (1861-63).

L & P HENRY VIII, *Letters and Papers of the Reign of Henry VIII* (1862-1920).

LYSONS, D. AND S.: *Magna Britannia* I (1806).

MACNALTY, A. S.: *Henry VIII-A Difficult Patient* (1952).

MANCINI, DOMINIC: *De Occupatione Regni Anglie per Ricardum Tercium Libellus*, ed. C. A. J. Armstrong (1969).

Materials for a History of the Reign of Henry VII, ed. William Campbell (1873-77).

MATTINGLY, G.: *Catherine of Aragon* (1961).

Memorials of Henry VII, ed. J. Gairdner (1858).

MORE, THOMAS: *Richard III* (1883); *Utopia* (1916).

MYERS, A. R.: *The Household of Edward IV* (1959).

NELSON, WILLIAM: *John Skelton Laureate*, Columbia University Studies no. 139 (1939).

NICHOLS, F. M.: *The Hall of Lawford Hall* (1891).

NORFOLK: *Household Books of John Duke of Norfolk and Thomas*

Earl of Surrey 1481–1490, ed. J. Payne Collier (1844).

NORRIS, H.: *Costume and Fashion* II & III (i) (1927 & 1938).

NORTHUMBERLAND, EARL OF: *The Regulations and Establishment of the Household* (1827).

PASSINGHAM, W. J.: *A History of the Coronation* (1937).

Patent Rolls, Calendar of, 1494–1509 (1916).

POLLARD, A. F.: *The Reign of Henry VII from Contemporary Sources*, I & III (1913).

POLLET, MAURICE: *John Skelton, Poet of Tudor England* (1971).

Privy Purse Expenses of Elizabeth of York, ed. N. H. Nicolas (1830).

ROTHERY, GUY CADOGAN: *Armorial Insignia of the Princes of Wales* (1911).

Rotuli Parliamentorum (1767–1832).

ROWSE, A. L.: *The Tower of London in the History of the Nation* (1972).

RUHRAH, JOHN: *Pediatrics of the Past* (1925).

RUSSELL, J. GLEDHILL: *The Field of Cloth of Gold* (1969).

RYMER, T.: *Foedera, Conventiones etc.* (1704–35).

SALTER, F. M.: 'Skelton's Speculum Principis', *Speculum, a Journal of Medieval Studies*, IX (1934).

Sarum Missal, ed. John Wickham Legg (1916); trans. A. H. Pearson (1884).

SCARISBRICK, J. J.: *Henry VIII* (1968).

SCOFIELD, CORA: *The Life and Reign of Edward IV* (1923).

SCHRAMM, P. E.: *A History of the English Coronation* (1937).

SIMON, JOAN: *Education and Society in Tudor England* (1966).

SKEEL, C. A. J.: *The Council in the Marches of Wales* (1904).

SKELTON, JOHN: *Complete Poems*, ed. Philip Henderson (1948).

Skelton's Poetical Works, ed. A. Dyce (1843).

SMITH, LACEY BALDWIN: *Henry VIII: The Mask of Royalty* (1971).

STEVENS, J.: *Music and Poetry in the Early Tudor Court* (1961).

STOREY, R. L.: *The Reign of Henry VII* (1968); *The End of the House of Lancaster* (1966).

STOW, JOHN: *Annals* (1601); *The Survey of London* (1912).

STRONG, ROY: *Tudor and Jacobean Portraits* (1969).

STRUTT, JOSEPH: *Sports and Pastimes* (1830).

VERGIL, POLYDORE: *The Anglica Historia*, ed. D. Hay (1950).

WILKINSON, BERTIE: *The Coronation in English History*, Pamphlets 3252 (1953).

WILLIAMS, D.: 'The Family of Henry VII', *History Today*, IV (1954).

WILLIAMS, NEVILLE: *Henry VII* (1973); *Henry VIII and his Court* (1971).

WOLFFE, B. P.: 'The Management of English Royal Estates under the Yorkist Kings', *English Historical Review*, LXXI (1956); 'Henry VII's Land Revenues and Chamber Finance', *English Historical Review*, LXXIX (1964); *The Crown Lands 1461-1536* (1970).

ZURITA: *Anales de la Corona de Aragon* VI (1668-70).

Notes and Sources

PROLOGUE

For Mountjoy's eulogy of the new Henry VIII see Erasmus, *Epistles*, p. 457.

CHAPTER 1

The 'great cradle of estate' is described in Leland IV, pp. 184, 302. For treatment of newborn babies at this time see Ruhrah. For contemporary descriptions of Edward IV see Lander, *The Wars of the Roses*, pp. 224–6. Rowse emphasizes Henry VIII's Plantagenet characteristics in his *The History of the Tower of London*. *The Song of the Lady Bessy* is printed at the end of Gairdner, *Richard III*. For contemporary descriptions of Elizabeth of York see Chrimes, *Henry VII*, p. 302; and for her early history see preface to her *Privy Purse Expenses*. For reported disagreement between Henry VII and Elizabeth see *Cal. Span.* I, p. 154. Margaret Beaufort 'wept marvellously . . .' Fisher, p. 29.

CHAPTER 2

For public rejoicing at Arthur's birth see Leland IV, p. 204. For effusions and political role of the court poets see Anglo, *The British History in Early Tudor Propaganda* and Pollet. Henry's birth is mentioned in André, *Memorials*, p. 58. 'Beholde the soveren sede' is printed in Stevens, p. 355. For royal christening ritual see Leland IV, pp. 180–2, 253, 302 and Hall, ed. Whibley, II, pp. 242, 343. For the baptism see *Sarum Missal*. See Brook for a plan of Eltham Palace and *King's Works* for architectural details. Henry's nurse Anne Luke, later Oxenbrigge or Oxonbrigge, and her two husbands are mentioned in *Patent Rolls*, pp. 11, 46, 345, 422, 488, 489, 581. Elyot, p. 19 describes the ideal wet nurse; see also Ruhrah, pp. 83, 84, 103, 159. Contemporary treatises on baby care are collected in Ruhrah, see pp. 88, 90, 177, 179, 211. 'Our sweet children', Halsted, p. 190. For nursery furnishings and regulations see Leland IV, pp. 183, 184, 301, 302. Eltham was Henry's main childhood abode:

see Erasmus *Epistles* I, pp. 201, 202, *Great Chronicle*, p. 254, L & P Henry VII I, p. 389, Salter, *Speculum Principis*. For popular toys see Strutt, pp. 144, 145. 'Hoses . . . for my lord Harry' etc., see selections from the royal Book of Payments in *Excerpta Historica*, pp. 85–133. For the king's fools see Anglo, *The Court Festivals of Henry VII*.

CHAPTER 3

For Richard, duke of York's robes see *Privy Purse Expenses of Elizabeth of York*, pp. 155, 156. For Edward IV's attempts to protect his sons see H.O. *Regulations for the Government of Prince Edward*. For details on Warbeck see Gairdner, *Richard III*, which includes *The Story of Perkin Warbeck from Original Documents*. 'Plots . . . began to multiply . . .' Vergil, p. 65. For the training in manners of a boy of high rank see Furnivall. *The Great Chronicle*, p. 254, describes Henry's entry into London at the age of three. I am indebted to Dr Roy Strong for advice on the portraits of Henry VIII as a child. For a fourteenth-century description of the ceremony of creation of Knights of the Bath see De la Bere, pp. 100, 101. A description of Henry's creation as duke of York is in L & P Henry VII I, p. 388 *et seq.* For scoring in jousts see Barber, p. 169.

CHAPTER 4

Details of aristocratic nursery diet are taken from Northumberland, p. 73. English water was undrinkable according to *Cal. Span.*, p. 156. Skelton described Henry as the 'Hector of the north', see Salter, *Carmen ad Principem*. The accusations against Stanley are printed in Archbold. Anglo, *The Court Festivals of Henry VII*, which prints a selection of accounts of John Heron, treasurer of the chamber, includes details of the king's Christmas. A lord chamberlain's duties are described in H.O. *Articles Ordained by King Henry VII*, p. 119, and *Liber Niger*, pp. 31, 32. 'If ye knew King Harry . . .' Pollard I, p. 244. Throwing at cocks on Shrove Tuesday was a court as well as a popular pastime according to payments listed in Anglo, *The Court Festivals of Henry VII;* see this source also for bridles and spurs bought for the royal fools. Dawson describes the creation of a Knight of the Garter. For Jaspar, duke of Bedford's bequest to Henry see *Patent Rolls*, p. 303. For Henry's lessons in archery see Strutt, p. 61. 'Hawk bells given at Hatfield . . .' *Excerpta Historica*, p. 123. Alterations to Eltham Palace are described in *King's Works*.

CHAPTER 5

A payment to the king's 'yeomen riding in the country to search for the sickness' is listed in *Excerpta Historica*, p. 94. For Warbeck's reception in Scotland see L & P Henry VII II, pp. 327-9. Kingsford, *Chronicles*, p. 210 describes Warbeck's panic-stricken retreat across the river Tweed. 'All our sweet children', Halsted, p. 190. I have based my belief that Arthur left Eltham for Ludlow in late 1496 or early 1497 on the above phrase and on the following facts: the *Great Chronicle*, pp. 275, 276, describing the duke of York's flight to the Tower before the advancing Cornish rebels, does not mention Arthur, thus suggesting that he was already safely out of the way in May 1497; for Christmas 1497 Henry and Margaret were staying with the king but Arthur was not with them (*Great Chronicle*, p. 286); L & P Henry VIII IV (iii) pp. 2577, 2578 states that Arthur's servants were with him for five or six years before his death; and by 24 January 1498 Eltham is known in the *Patent Rolls* as the duke of York's household. Etiquette for a king's brother is detailed in H.O., *Articles Ordained by King Henry VII*. For the duke of York's household, see *Patent Rolls*, pp. 126, 127. For details of Sheen Palace see *King's Works* I, pp. 998 to 1001. For the duke of York's sojourn there before his flight to the Tower see *Great Chronicle*, pp. 275, 276. For gentlemen sent to London with Henry see Vergil, p. 94, note 6. Audley's reasons for joining the rebellion have been explored by Kirby, see p. 31. Proof of the queen's affection for the king is in *Antiquarian Repertory*, pp. 322, 323. 'In a Glorius Garden Grene' is printed in Stevens, p. 381. For St Edward's charter see Stow, *Survey of London*, pp. 410, 411. The king's opinion of the 'base Cornishmen' is from *Cal. Ven.*, quoted in Pollard I, p. 186. The provisioning in Scotland of Warbeck's ship is minutely described in L & P Henry VII II, appendix B, p. 331. Warbeck's proclamation in Cornwall is printed in Pollard I, p. 150. For Warbeck's confession see Kingsford, *Chronicles*, p. 219, Pollard I, pp. 183-5.

CHAPTER 6

Margaret Beaufort understood little more than church Latin; see Fisher, p. 7, C. H. Cooper, p. 5, *Cal. Span.* I, p. 156. See *Cal. Span.* I, p. 156 also for an example of the way decisions were taken in the royal family. Skelton's eulogy of the new duke of York is printed with *Speculum Principis* by Salter; but Nelson's argument for dating this *Carmen* seems to me more logical than Salter's. For Skelton's embroidered gown see Skelton, ed. Dyce I, p. xiii. Elyot believed that a boy of seven should be taken 'from all company of women' and

given a tutor. For evidence that Skelton was Henry's tutor, see Salter
and Skelton, ed. Dyce, p. xxii. For Edward V's curriculum see H.O.,
Regulations for the Government of Prince Edward, p. 27. John St John
was educated with princes from his first years according to his
epitaph in Bletsoe church, Lysons, p. 59. Giles Dewes was Henry's
French master according to the epistle to Henry VIII prefixed to
Palsgrave's *L'éclaircissement de la Langue Francoyse*, see Skelton, ed.
Dyce I, p. xxiii. For Henry's lute see Anglo, *The Court Festivals of
Henry VII*, p. 33. Mountjoy was modest and serious-minded: see
Nichols, pp. 217, 241. For his history lessons at the king's request
see Nichols, p. 196, footnote 9, p. 216, footnote 373. For Erasmus's
account of his visit to Eltham Palace see *Epistles*, pp. 201, 202.
'Tyburne thou me assynyd', Skelton, ed. Dyce I, p. 125. 'Behynd in
our hose', Skelton, ed. Dyce I, p. 194. *Upon a Dead Man's Head*, see
above p. 18. 'A pitchy torchlight': E. B. Browning quoted in Pollet,
p. 176.

CHAPTER 7

Henry received a lute and won at cards against his father: Anglo,
The Court Festivals of Henry VII, p. 33. Brief histories of Elizabeth
of York's sisters are given in the preface to her *Privy Purse Expenses*.
The ceremony of the void, when spiced cakes and wine were served,
is described in H.O. For the marquis of Dorset's financial penalties
see Lander, *Bonds, Coercion and Fear*, p. 342. 'It is our intention to
keep our subjects low . . .', *Cal. Span.* I, p. 177. Henry VII 'opened his
eyes wide with joy', *Cal. Span.* I, p. 11. 'Bearing in mind what happens
every day . . .' *Cal. Span.* I, p. 7. For Warbeck's escape in 1498 see
Pollard I, pp. 190, 191. 'The king has aged so much . . .' *Cal. Span.* I,
p. 206. 'It is expedient that one man should die . . .' Armstrong.
'After kissing the royal feet . . .' L & P Henry VII I, p. 113.

CHAPTER 8

For purchase of Codnore Castle see *Close Rolls*, no. 160 and *Patent
Rolls*, p. 583. Margaret Beaufort's retainers were promised a post in
Henry's increased household: Pollard I, p. 219. *Speculum Principis*
is Add. MS. 26,787 in the British Library, see Salter; but since Arthur
was not brought up at Eltham, Salter's theory that Skelton was
Arthur's as well as Henry's tutor seems to me untenable. For details
of Richmond Palace see contemporary description of Catherine's
reception in England in *Antiquarian Repertory*, p. 249 *et seq.*; this also
contains the fullest account of the pageants which greeted her in
London, of her wedding to Arthur and the entertainments that

followed; but see also Leland V, p. 356 *et seq.* For Catherine's carts full of possessions see Fuensalida, p. 421, *Cal. Span.* I, p. 259. For the coal merchant in the pillory see Kingsford, *Chronicles*, p. 233. The royal bed-making ritual is described in H.O., *Articles Ordained by King Henry VII*, pp. 121, 122. The lords conducted Arthur to the nuptial bed, L & P Henry VIII IV (iii), pp. 2577, 2580. Henry's dancing was to the king and queen 'right great and singular pleasure', *Antiquarian Repertory*, p. 302. 'Good Lord, preserve the Estrige Fether', Fayrfax MS. printed in Stevens, pp. 380, 381. For Henry's attendance at Margaret's proxy marriage see Leland IV, p. 263.

<h3 style="text-align:center">CHAPTER 9</h3>

Arthur 'began to decay' after he lay with Catherine at Shrovetide according to L & P Henry VIII IV (iii), p. 2580. The parents' grief at Arthur's death is touchingly described in *Antiquarian Repertory*, pp. 322, 323. For Catherine's alleged virginity see *Cal. Span.* I, p. 272. The payment in the royal accounts for the creation of the prince of Wales in 1504 is printed in Anglo, *The Court Festivals of Henry VII*, p. 39. Henry inherited the prince of Wales's 'great and notable possessions', *Rotuli Parliamentorum*, p. 522. 'To our dearest son Henry, prince of Wales . . .', *Rymer Foedera* XIII, p. 11. William Parron's Latin horoscope (Royal MS., 12 B VI in the British Library) is described in Armstrong. For commissions to purveyors to the prince of Wales's household see *Patent Rolls*, pp. 322, 325, 327, 343. For food and drink and number of servants allowed the prince when he visited court see H.O., *Liber Niger*, p. 24. For Skelton's departure from Eltham and Hone's arrival see Nelson, pp. 74, 75, Skelton, ed. Dyce I, p. xxiii. Henry's signature on a charter to the earl of Ormond and on a grant of revenues to the dean and canons of St Stephen's Chapel, *Patent Rolls*, pp. 419, 545. Henry's name on a commission of oyer and terminer, *Patent Rolls*, p. 326. See Nichols, pp. 200, 201 for the origin of Erasmus's essay on matrimony. Brandon and Neville were brought up with Henry, see Neville Williams, p. 204. For John St John's career see Lysons, p. 59. Henry Courtenay joins the royal household, *Privy Purse Expenses of Elizabeth of York*, p. xxvi. A description of the May tournaments (Harley MS. 69) is printed in Strutt, pp. xxix, xxx; see also Hazlitt ii, pp. 109–30, Anglo, *Spectacle, Pageantry and Early Tudor Policy*, pp. 109, 110. For Elizabeth's death see Pollard I, pp. 231, 232, Kingsford, *Chronicles*, p. 258, *Cal. Ven.* no. 833. A translation of Henry's letter to Erasmus mentioning Elizabeth's death is in *Epistles*, pp. 423, 424. For Henry's Oedipus complex see Flügel. Margaret Beaufort's special affection for Henry is shown by her reference to him as 'my lord of York, your fair sweet son' in a letter to Henry VII, Pollard I, no. 150.

CHAPTER 10

For Fleming's report from Calais see Pollard I, p. 240 *et seq*. I have based my conclusion regarding the date when Henry came to live permanently at court on Hernan Duque's report, Pollard I, p. 238: 'The prince of Wales is with the king. Formerly the king did not like to take the prince of Wales with him in order not to interrupt his studies.' This date is also strongly suggested by the fact that after July 1504 there are no further commissions extant to purvey for the household of the prince of Wales. For Henry VII's 'wild men' see *Great Chronicle*, p. 320. Fuensalida, p. 449 describes Henry as living in *una camera*, a chamber, which in the court context can mean more than one room. Henry, like Arthur, received 'dignities proper to a king's sons': L & P Henry VIII IV (iii), p. 2578. For Henry's servants see *Patent Rolls*, pp. 386, 387, 391. For his trumpeters and players see Anglo, *The Court Festivals of Henry VII*, pp. 40, 43, 44. Pollard I, p. 280 quoting from *Cal. Ven.* describes Philip on his visit to England as receiving 'as much honour as if he had been the prince of England'. 'For fear of his life . . .' Fuensalida, p. 449. For financial penalties imposed on the 'great ones' see Lander, *Bonds, Coercion and Fear*. For Mountjoy's elder-brotherly feeling for Henry see *Excerpta Historica*, p. 286.

'My dearest and only desired joy', Pollard I, p. 218. 'I shall be as glad to please you . . .', Halsted, pp. 209, 210. For Henry VII's violet gown see Pollard I, p. 161. Hernan Duque is ordered to propose a marriage between Catherine and Henry, 'the prince of Wales who now is', *Cal. Span.* I, pp. 267, 272. 'She must accept what she can get': *Cal. Span.* I, p. 270. For wording of the betrothal ceremony see Leland IV, pp. 261, 262. Songs of Henry VII's court are gathered in Fayrfax MS. (British Library Add. 5465) printed in Stevens, p. 352 *et seq*. For analysis of contemporary love literature see Barber. Stevens's chapter on 'The Game of Love' is particularly illuminating on this courtly fashion. For Henry VII's presents to Catherine see *Cal. Span.* I, p. 375. For his offer to 'convoke all the physicians in England' see Pollard I, pp. 237, 238. Catherine's instruction to do all she can to preserve the love of the prince of Wales, *Cal. Span.*, p. 406. Fox's deposition that he does not remember Henry VII forbidding his son from showing signs of love to Catherine, L & P Henry VIII IV (iii), p. 2588. 'The prince of Wales is with the king' etc., Pollard I, p. 238. Prince Henry rode in the St George's day procession, *Great Chronicle*, p. 239. For love tokens given to Catherine by Henry see his protest in this chapter and Fox's deposition in L & P Henry VIII IV (iii), p. 2588. For Henry's protest in Latin against betrothal to Catherine see Collier, p. 66 *et seq*. Fox's statement in his deposition that Henry VII all along intended his son to marry Catherine seems a piece of special pleading. The papal brief giving Henry authority over his wife is printed in Ehses, p. xliii. The brief is addressed to 'the noble prince Arthur of Wales', obviously a mistake. For a typically romantic reading list of a contemporary nobleman see Norfolk, *Household Books*, p. xxvii.

CHAPTER 12

In October 1507 De Puebla wrote of Prince Henry: 'He is already taller than his father, and his limbs are of a gigantic size': Pollard I, pp. 298, 299, *Cal. Span.* I, p. 439. The prince referred to Catherine as 'my wife' in his letter to Philip, Add. MS. 21, 404, British Library, L & P Henry VII I, p. 285. For Catherine's growing shabbiness see Pollard I, p. 287. 'My son and I are free' etc., Fuensalida, pp. 415, 458, *Cal. Span.* I, p. 413. Henry's instructions regarding the queen of Naples: *Cal. Span.* I, p. 360. 'I have in my days promoted many a man unadvisedly . . .', Fisher, p. 41. For Ferdinand's declaration of affection for Catherine see *Cal. Span.* I, p. 404. Ferdinand's distrust of Henry VII is shown by his withdrawal of the second half of her dowry even after it had arrived in England in 1508, *Cal. Span. Supplement*, p. 29. Catherine had to borrow money to pay for food, *Cal. Span.* I, p. 350. 'I keep the prince with me because I wish to improve him', Pollard I, p. 238. Eight hundred merchants 'all lost and ruined', *Cal. Span.* I, p. 367. Catherine loses her household, Pollard I, p. 260. Her cook is captured and enslaved, *Cal. Span.* I, p. 382. She has to sell some of her dowry bracelets to buy just one new black velvet dress, Pollard I, p. 287.

CHAPTER 13

There are two contemporary accounts of Philip's forced arrival in England and reception at court. Both anonymous, the fuller account in Gachard is probably by a Flemish member of Philip's suite; the other account in *Memorials* is thought to be by an English herald. My description of the great wind is from the *Greyfriars Chronicle*, Pollard I, p. 262. '. . . with great pomp passing the narrow seas', *Memorials*, p. 282. Details of the king's dress when he met

Philip are from the *Paston Letters*, Pollard I, p. 263. 'I am a plain sailor . . .' *Memorials*, p. 288. For Margaret Beaufort's hostility to the French see Fisher, pp. 38, 39. For the prince's double-edged compliment to the French envoy see Gachard, p. 426. Prince Henry's letter in French to Philip is Add. MS. 21, 404 in the British Library, L & P Henry VII, I, pp. 285, 286. For Henry's letter to Erasmus see *Letters of King Henry VIII* and Erasmus, *Epistles*. Henry seen walking in a gallery with his father, *Great Chronicle*, p. 331. Henry VII's mystery illness in 1507, *Cal. Span.* I, p. 408.

CHAPTER 14

For the poem describing the May and June games at Greenwich in 1507 see Hazlitt, pp. 109–30. Henry a competitor in tournaments, Fuensalida, pp. 418, 422, 454, André, *Annales*, p. 124. For Catherine's assessment of her husband's libido see *Cal. Span. Supplement* p. 122. For Margaret Beaufort's visit to court in April 1508 see Fuensalida, p. 422. Works Margaret Beaufort had published in her last years: see C. H. Cooper, pp. 96, 108, 109. Henry VII's description of Catherine as 'full of virtues and good qualities', Fuensalida, p. 417. If Joanna were mad, the king declared, he would not marry her for three kingdoms, Fuensalida, p. 461. He was prevented by his council from inviting Joanna to stay on at court, *Cal. Span.* I, p. 440. Ferdinand made Catherine his ambassador in matrimonial negotiations, *Cal. Span.* I, p. 414. Henry VII sends her £200, *Cal. Span.* I, p. 432. 'There is no finer youth . . .' Pollard I, p. 299. For Prince Henry's hostility to France see Neville Williams, p. 26, Pollard I, p. 330. For Catherine's confidence that she would be able to handle the prince see Fuensalida, p. 484. 'That God hath joined such a pair . . .' Fuensalida, p. 418. Fuensalida, p. 449 describes the king's murderous tirade against his son, Prince Henry's cowed manner and enforced seclusion. Catherine, not invited to watch the tournament with the king (Fuensalida, p. 454), was also left out of the royal boating party, Fuensalida, p. 468. Her lack of a mount, Fuensalida, p. 476. For court gossip on alternative matches for the prince see Fuensalida, pp. 423, 468. Henry VII insists that the whole dowry is to be paid in coin, *Cal. Span.* I, p. 461. The prince is sent out of the room, Fuensalida, p. 468. 'His avarice is unbelievable', Fuensalida, p. 449. For illegalities and tax avoidances for which fines were due to the king see Elton, *Rapacity and Remorse*. Sweating sickness killed three of Prince Henry's attendants, Fuensalida, p. 476. This new epidemic a portent, Vergil, p. 143. '. . . terrifying system of suspended penalties', Lander, *Bonds, Coercion and Fear*, p. 335. For the king's attitude to retaining see Storey, *The Reign of Henry VII*, pp. 154–6. 'Something like two years' gross yield of the permanent revenues', Wolffe, quoted in Chrimes, *Henry VII*, p. 218.

CHAPTER 15

For the king's illnesses see André, *Annales*, p. 108, *Cal. Span.* I, p. 460, Fuensalida, pp. 456, 457, 472. See Fuensalida, p. 484 for the ambassador's prophecy that the prince would turn out to be no better than his father. For Mary's marriage festivities see *Cal. Span.* I, pp. 447, 448, L & P Henry VII I, p. 373, Green. For Christmas and New Year festivities see Anglo, *The Court Festivals of Henry VII*. 'The prince knows little', Fuensalida, p. 484. The king can abide neither 'to see or to hear' Fuensalida, Pollard I, p. 317. 'If it pleased God to send him life they should see him a new changed man', Elton, *Rapacity and Remorse*, p. 35. 'The kingdom is in danger with only one heir', *Cal. Span. Supplement*, p. 24. New bows and arrows made, Fuensalida, p. 495. The princess's apartments look as though she has been robbed, Fuensalida, p. 516. For her relations with her confessor see Pollard I, pp. 321–9, *Cal. Span. Supplement*, pp. 13–46. The prince does no more than echo the king's displeasure, *Cal. Span. Supplement*, p. 31. Proposal that the prince marry the daughter of the duke of Bavaria, *Cal. Span. Supplement*, p. 23. Henry VII so thin that he could hardly walk, Fuensalida, p. 512. On the significance of Henry VII's general pardon see Elton and J. P. Cooper in *Historical Journal*, I, II, IV. For differing accounts of the dying king's words to his son on the subject of Catherine see *Letters of Henry VIII*, pp. 8, 9, 10, Fuensalida, p. 517. The king's death is kept secret, Fuensalida, p. 516, Zurita, p. 193. For rumours of the power struggle inside the council see J. P. Cooper, p. 123. For Henry VIII's imposition of his will see Fuensalida, p. 520. 'Closely and secretly with his council', *Great Chronicle*, p. 336. The prince agrees that he will do nothing against his conscience, Fuensalida, p. 516. For the new king's marriage negotiations with Catherine see Fuensalida p. 518 *et seq.* 'You must remember that now the king is king and not prince', Fuensalida, p. 520. Ferdinand's message 'full of . . . good and sweet words', Fuensalida, p. 526. Catherine orders the ambassador from her chamber, Fuensalida, p. 522.

CHAPTER 16

For Henry VII's funeral obsequies see Leland IV, p. 303 *et seq.*, Pollard I, p. 330. '. . . in the queen's closet', L & P Henry VIII IV (iii), p. 2578. For the new king's letter to Ferdinand see *Letters of Henry*

VIII, p. 11. The fullest chronicle account of the coronation is in Hall, but see also *Great Chronicle*, p. 339 *et seq.* For the detailed ritual of the coronation see Legg, particularly p. 219 *et seq.* For the oath as revised by Henry see Legg, pp. 240, 241. The quotation 'to become king in the fullest sense . . .' is from Schramm, chapter 1.

Index

Index

INDEX